THE COMEDIES OF LADY GREGORY, BEING THE FIRST VOLUME OF THE COLLECTED PLAYS

edited and with a foreword by
Ann Saddlemyer

COLIN SMYTHE
GERRARDS CROSS
1979

Copyright © 1971 The Lady Gregory Estate
Foreword Copyright © 1971 Colin Smythe Ltd.

First published in one volume on 1 March 1971
by Colin Smythe Ltd, Gerrards Cross, Buckinghamshire
as the fifth volume of the Coole Edition
ISBN 0–900675–29–2

First published in paperback format in 1979

British Library Cataloguing in Publication Data

Gregory, Isabella Augusta, *Lady*
   The collected plays
   1: The comedies of Lady Gregory – Coole ed.
   I. Title   II. Saddlemyer, Ann
   822′.9′12   PR4728.G5A19

   ISBN 0–86140–016–X

Printed in Great Britain

FOREWORD

"It's a queer world, sergeant, and it's little any mother knows when she sees her child creeping on the floor what might happen to it before it has gone through its life, or who will be who in the end."

"That's a queer thought now, and a true thought. Wait now till I think it out."

(*The Rising of the Moon*)

Playwriting came as a surprise to Lady Gregory. It all began so simply, and for her, like one of her own Cloon townsfolk, "the talk" soon became all. "Things seemed to grow possible as we talked," was how she described the meeting with William Butler Yeats which gave rise to the Irish Literary Theatre and laid the foundations of the Abbey Theatre. So too with her own playwriting career: "I began by writing bits of dialogue, when wanted. Mr. Yeats used to dictate parts of *Diarmuid and Grania* to me, and I would suggest a sentence here and there." Sentences were soon joined by ideas, plots, construction and suggestions for stage-dressing. Finally, in 1903, she witnessed the production of her first play, *Twenty-Five*. She was fifty years old and was to provide the Abbey Theatre with comedies, tragedies, translations, adaptations, plays of history, wonder and the supernatural for the next twenty-five years.

It was probably inevitable that she began with comedy, although Lady Gregory herself claimed to prefer tragedy and the history play. She apologizes in one of her notes, "I had been forced to write comedy because it was wanted for our theatre, to put on at the end of verse plays." Elsewhere, again self-deprecatingly, she explains that comedies were needed to give the audience a rest from the poetry of her colleagues: "the listeners, and this especially when they are lovers of verse, have to give so close an attention to the lines . . . that ear and mind crave ease and unbending." Yeats offers evidence from a different sphere, perhaps more acceptable to those who came to respect the perseverance and judgment of the self-styled "charwoman of the Abbey":

"I have sometimes told one close friend that her only fault is a

v

habit of harsh judgment with those who have not her sympathy, and she has written comedies where the wickedest people seem but bold children. She does not know why she has created that world where no one is ever judged, a high celebration of indulgence, but to me it seems that her ideal of beauty is the compensating dream of a nature wearied out by over-much judgment."[1]

Whatever the reason, comedy was to serve as not only the base of the Abbey Theatre, but of her own dramatic development. In this volume of nineteen plays, six of them never before published, can be traced the themes and framework of all her plays. The raggedy ballad-singer of *The Rising of the Moon* makes way for the messengers of history in *Kincora*, *The White Cockade*, *Dervorgilla* and of the supernatural in *The Travelling Man*, returning finally to the political commentary of *The Wrens* and *The Old Woman Remembers*. The private fantasies of the townsfolk of Cloon deepen to encompass the wonderful world of *The Dragon* and *The Jester* or darken to the sombre possibilities of *The Full Moon*, *Aristotle's Bellows*, *Shanwalla* and *The Image*. When she turned to translation and adaptation, there too her choice of Molière, Goldoni and Cervantes reflects her preoccupation with personal idiosyncracy and cracked idealists.

At the heart of her comic world lies the county and village of Cloon. Lying on the border between County Clare and County Galway, on the main line from Ennis to Loughrea, it is her own village of Gort, and it is nowhere. It is Ireland, and it is everywhere. Here anything, and nothing, can happen and does; life is earnest, but not real; everyone breathlessly belongs to, actively participates in, eagerly contributes to the fable, but nobody believes in it or in anybody else. Here, the dramatist celebrates her country and her countrymen, delighting in "our incorrigible genius for myth-making, the faculty that makes our traditional history a perpetual joy, because it is, like the Sidhe, an eternal Shapechanger." The hard-pressed editors of *Coats* mourn for the easy wonders of the past, when "there used always to be something happening such as famines, or the invention of printing. The whole world has got very slack." What is certain in Cloon time is the craving for talk. "Did she see him?" asks Taig the chimney sweep. "She did, I suppose, or the thing was near him. She never was tired talking of him."

They may not take each other seriously, the townsfolk of Cloon, but their creator does. Her characters might in fact be traced back to the Elizabethan concept of humours, for it is no accident that in her notes Lady Gregory invokes the spirit of Ben Jonson as frequently as that of Molière. She relies too upon Hobbes' definition of comedy, that which gives rise to the "sudden Glory, the Passion which maketh those Grimaces called Laughter." Elsewhere she insists that her work differs from farce, "comedy with character left out"; for here, "Character comes in, and why it is so I cannot explain, but as soon as one creates a character, he begins to put out little feet of his own and take his own way." Once created, he takes possession of plot and idea, "turning it to be as simple as a folk-tale, where the innocent of the world confound the wisdom of the wise." "It's hard know what might happen," admits the inquisitive Porter of *The Wrens*, "from when we get up in the morning to when we get to bed at night, or half that time."

Setting and structure too remain simple and sharply outlined, and here again the comedies indicate most clearly her working method. "I usually first see a play as a picture," she explains in her important notes to *Damer's Gold*. Her comments on *The Wrens* add significantly, "Sometimes in making a plan for a play I set the scene in some other country that I may be sure the emotion displayed is not bounded by any neighbourhood but is a universal one." Cloon is believable because it is not real; her stories are comedies of human nature rather than philosophical tale-spinning. Because of her ability to stand back and observe characters and form with a critical almost impersonal eye, her plays tend on the whole to be classical in form and interlocking in structure. The ruthlessness with which she excised all suggestion of clogging sentiment or romantic fiction from her first comedy through four versions over a period of twenty-four years illustrates this constant struggle towards clarification of action, motive, setting and character. *A Losing Game* (1902) has an ambiguous situation and wooden characters; the mood is pathetic, the idea patriotic and sentimental; the Fay brothers were also worried that the play "might incite to emigration". *Twenty Five* (1903) simplifies setting, characterization and motive, but remains soft at the centre and the card game is unrealistic. (Of the London performance in May 1903 Yeats reported, "The game of cards is still the weak place, but with all defects the little play has a real charm. If we could amend the cards it would be a strong play too."²) *The Jackdaw* (1907), safely confined to the streets of Cloon, transfers the card game to a possibility only, rejected by the suspicious characters themselves; but still the play borders on sentiment, grudging though Michael Cooney might be as benefactor. Finally *On the Racecourse* (1916–1926) eliminates romance and fantasy by completely reversing the original motivation and swiftly introducing two recognition scenes. The original sentiment is banished to an unpublished play and the Grimace called Laughter has become satisfactorily wry.

Similarly, alterations incorporated here in the text from her own copy of *The Bogie Men* indicate the playwright's dissatisfaction with the published work. Originally Taig forces Darby to leave the coach-shed while the two sweeps effect their transformation; she has simplified construction and production by keeping both characters onstage throughout. She also strengthens the dialogue by eliminating much of the talk between the two characters when they are at cross-purposes. Doubtless these alterations would have been further tested in performance before the creator was completely satisfied, but once again we can observe her determination to toughen pattern and eliminate any weakness or slowing-down of the action. And by weaving the ballad more securely into the fabric of the little play by giving both cousins a stanza as they don their disguises, she has undelined the contrapuntal mirror-image effect observable in such plays as *Coats*, *The Workhouse Ward*, and *The Jester*.

Comedy of human nature inevitably leads to commentary on human involvement, and for a nationalist like Lady Gregory this expression is bound to be a political one. No wonder, then, that under the dreams of the myth-makers there frequently lies the more sombre note of conflicting loyalties. The Magistrate of *Spreading the News* reflects all too readily the inability (or unwillingness) of the "over-government" to listen with sympathy and understand with knowledge Ireland's plight. To the Irishman who must serve both master and country the problem becomes acute, as in *The Rising of the Moon*; in a note to the players Lady Gregory explains the Policeman's actions as not a change of mind but the release and temporary ascendancy of "a deeper instinct, his Irish heart and memory of youth that had been moved unconsciously to himself." Closely related is a second characteristic, the Irishman's delight in a quarrel, whether harmlessly self-perpetuating as in *The Workhouse Ward* and the weaker *Coats*, or symbolic of the inner turmoil of Ireland, as in *The Wrens* and her folk-history plays.

But intense though her own love of country and admiration for its image-makers is, as reflected in the other volumes of Lady Gregory's plays, here the brilliant sunshine of Cloon dispels most shadows; and the creator, like her creatures, can delight in the story for the sake of the story itself. "All that I am craving is the talk," whimpers Michael Miskell from his bed in Cloon Workhouse. "There to be no one at all to say out to whatever thought might be rising in my innate mind! To be lying here and no conversible person in it would be the abomination of misery!" Even where the first idea is tragic, as in *Spreading the News*, the echo of laughter soon chases the plot and its people down the path of nonsense where death itself is but a rumour. As Hyacinth Halvey discovers to his discomfort, in Lady Gregory's world, unlike Synge's, the Playboy can exist only in the minds of the gullible, daft myth-makers themselves. In this world the oath, like the curse, carries greater awe than the threat of more conventional slings and arrows, the greatest penalty of all is to be deprived of "The Talk". So Red Hanrahan, borrowed for this purpose from Yeats's neighbouring Sligo (although even there "the wild old men in flannel" speak in Kiltartan[3]), suffers the double curse of self-imposed dumbness and cannot be released from his oath until rumour confounds itself.

Although uneven in quality and repetitive in form, the plays discovered among Lady Gregory's papers and here published for the first time prove yet again her admission that "desire for experiment is like fire in the blood" and are testimony to her claim that she gave up play-writing in 1927 "rather from pride than modesty". We can assume that these five typescripts may represent only a few of the plays she completed but refrained from releasing for production or publication. Although only two can be tentatively dated, all of them appear to have been written during the last fifteen years of her life, and all show the characteristics of that later period in the strong dependence on ballad and musical accompaniment to plot. *Michelin* can safely be dated alongside *On the Racecourse*, for not only does the ragged beggar bear a close resemblance to the disreputable protagonists of the Galway fairground, but the reunited young lovers capture the romance so rigidly excised from *Twenty-Five*. In turn, *The Meadow Gate* sings of mistaken love and the boon of companionship, while *The Dispensary* (originally titled *The Doctor* and dated July 1929) successfully employs mistaken identity and cross-purposes towards a romantic ending. *The Lighted Window*, which can also be dated July 1929, might be read with *The Old Woman Remembers* as a final tribute towards the history of those image-makers who belong "in the book of the people". And the longest of these unpublished plays, *The Shoelace*, both in contrapuntal structure and reversal of roles successfully blends the fantasy of the wonder plays with the underlying serious challenge of *The Jester*. There is no more significant comment on the differences in form, subject-matter and purpose between Lady Gregory's plays and those of her two fellow directors of the Abbey Theatre, than this characteristic version of the "cracked fool" ballad-singer who chooses the wandering life of the Tramp in the glens to the echoing trumpets on the King's threshold.

One of Lady Gregory first collaborations was with Douglas Hyde, founder of the Gaelic League and later Ireland's first President, for whom she wrote the scenario for *The Poorhouse*; later, using the same scenario but completely re-writing the dialogue, she made it her own in *The Workhouse Ward*. Ten years later still her scenario received the final tribute of parody (printed by her own publishers, The Talbot Press) in the anonymous Sinn Fein allegory, *The Worked-out Ward*. The metamorphosis of cantankerous paupers Michael Miskell and Mike McInerney into barely disguised Nationalists John Dillon (M.P. for County Mayo and renowned for the violence of his language in the House) and Stephen Gwynn (M.P. for Galway and well-known political historian and poet) is one which she herself might well have agreed with, for the resounding defeat of the Home Rule party in 1918 must have seemed to many partially the result of leaders caring more for their own political histories than for the future welfare of shabby Kathleen Ni Houlihan. It is hardly accidental that Lady Gregory's most savage indictment of her countrymen occurs in the bitter tragedy *The Deliverer*, where the Hebrew rejection of Moses is obviously an analogue for the Irish hounding of Parnell. Once again the wry grimace of comedy admits no weak sentiment at the centre.

ANN SADDLEMYER

[1] W. B. Yeats, *Mythologies* (London: Macmillan, 1959), p. 326.
[2] *The Letters of W. B. Yeats*, ed. Allan Wade (New York: Macmillan, 1955), p. 400.
[3] See Yeats's note of acknowledgement to Lady Gregory's collaboration in *Early Poems and Stories* (London: Macmillan, 1925), p. 528.

THE PLAYS OF LADY GREGORY
HISTORY OF FIRST PRODUCTIONS BY THE ABBEY
THEATRE COMPANY AND PUBLICATION DATES

Colman and Guaire [1901]. Not produced. Published under title
My First Play (London: Elkin Mathews and Marrot, 1930).

A Losing Game. Not produced. Published only in *The Gael* (New
York), December 1902.

Twenty-Five [*A Losing Game* revised]. Produced 14 March
1903. Never published.

The Poorhouse (with Douglas Hyde). Produced 3 April 1907. Published in *Samhain*, September 1903; with *Spreading the News*
and *The Rising of the Moon* as Vol. IX of Abbey Theatre Series
(First Series) (Dublin: Maunsel, 1906).

The Rising of the Moon. Produced 9 March 1907. Published in
Samhain, December 1904; with *Spreading the News* and *The
Poorhouse* as Vol. IX of Abbey Theatre Series (First Series)
(Dublin: Maunsel, 1906); and included in *Seven Short Plays*
(Dublin: Maunsel, 1909).

Spreading the News. Produced 27 December 1904. Published in
Samhain, November 1905; with *The Rising of the Moon* and
The Poorhouse as Vol. IX of Abbey Theatre Series (First Series)
(Dublin: Maunsel, 1906); and included in *Seven Short Plays*
(Dublin: Maunsel, 1909).

Kincora. First version produced 25 March 1905; revised version
11 February 1909. Published as Vol. II of Abbey Theatre Series
(First Series) (Dublin: The Abbey Theatre, 1905); revised form
in *Irish Folk-History Plays First Series* (New York and London:
Putnam, 1912).

The White Cockade. Produced 9 December 1905. Published as
Vol. VIII of Abbey Theatre Series (First Series) (Dublin:

Maunsel, 1906); included in *Irish Folk-History Plays Second Series* (New York and London: Putnam, 1912).

Hyacinth Halvey. Produced 19 February 1906. Published in *Samhain*, December 1906; and included in *Seven Short Plays* (Dublin: Maunsel, 1909).

The Doctor in Spite of Himself (from Molière). Produced 16 April 1906. Published in *The Kiltartan Molière* (Dublin: Maunsel, 1910).

The Gaol Gate. Produced 20 October 1906. Published in *Seven Short Plays* (Dublin: Maunsel, 1909).

The Canavans. Produced 8 December 1906; revised version produced 31 October 1907. Published in *Irish Folk-History Plays Second Series* (New York and London: Putnam, 1912).

The Jackdaw. Produced 23 February 1907. Published in *Seven Short Plays* (Dublin: Maunsel, 1909).

Dervorgilla. Produced 31 October 1907. Published in *Samhain*, November 1908; included in *Irish Folk-History Plays First Series* (New York and London: Putnam, 1912).

The Unicorn from the Stars (with W. B. Yeats) [a re-working of *Where There is Nothing* written by Yeats in 1902 with the help of Lady Gregory and Douglas Hyde]. Produced 21 November 1907. Published in *The Unicorn from the Stars and Other Plays* (New York: Macmillan, 1908) and included in the Third Volume of *The Collected Works of William Butler Yeats* (Stratford-on-Avon: Shakespeare Head Press, 1908).

Teja (from Sudermann). Produced 19 March 1908. Never published.
The Rogueries of Scapin (from Molière). Produced 4 April 1908. Published in *The Kiltartan Molière* (Dublin: Maunsel, 1910).

The Workhouse Ward [*The Poorhouse* revised]. Produced 20 April 1908. Published in *Seven Short Plays* (Dublin: Maunsel, 1909).

The Travelling Man. Produced 2 March 1910. Published in *Seven Short Plays* (Dublin: Maunsel, 1909).

The Miser (from Molière). Produced 21 January 1909. Published in *The Kiltartan Molière* (Dublin: Maunsel, 1910).

The Image. Produced 11 November 1909. Published as Vol. I of Abbey Theatre Series (Second Series) (Dublin: Maunsel, 1910).

Mirandolina (from Goldoni). Produced 24 February 1910. Published separately (London and New York: Putnam, 1924).

The Full Moon. Produced 10 November 1910. Published by the Author at the Abbey Theatre, 1911; included in *New Comedies* (New York and London: Putnam, 1913).

Coats. Produced 1 December 1910. Published in *New Comedies* (New York and London: Putnam, 1913).

The Deliverer. Produced 12 January 1911. Published in *Irish Folk-History Plays Second Series* (New York and London: Putnam, 1912).

Grania. Not produced. Published in *Irish Folk-History Plays First Series* (New York and London: Putnam, 1912).

McDonough's Wife. Produced 11 January 1912. Published in *New Comedies* (New York and London: Putnam, 1913).

The Bogie Men. Produced 4 July 1912 at the Court Theatre, London. Published in *New Comedies* (New York and London: Putnam, 1913). Later revised.

Damer's Gold. Produced 21 November 1912. Published in *New Comedies* (New York and London: Putnam 1913).

The Wrens. Produced 1 June 1914 at the Court Theatre, London. Published in *The Image and Other Plays* (London: Putnam, 1922).

Shanwalla. Produced 8 April 1915. Published in *The Image and Other Plays* (London: Putnam, 1922). Later revised.

The Golden Apple. Produced 6 January 1920. Published separately (London: John Murray, 1916).

The Dragon. Produced 21 April 1919. Published separately (Dublin: Talbot Press, 1920); included in *Three Wonder Plays* (London: Putnam, 1923).

Hanrahan's Oath. Produced 29 January 1918. Published in *The Image and Other Plays* (London: Putnam, 1922).

The Jester. Not produced professionally. Published in *Three Wonder Plays* (London: Putnam, 1923).

Aristotle's Bellows. Produced 17 March 1921. Published in *Three Wonder Plays* (London: Putnam, 1923).

The Old Woman Remembers. Produced 31 December 1923. Published in *The Irish Statesman,* 22 March 1924; included in *A Little Anthology of Modern Irish Verse,* selected by Lennox Robinson (Dublin: Cuala Press, 1928).

The Story Brought by Brigit. Produced 15 April 1924. Published separately (London and New York: Putnam, 1924).

On the Racecourse [a re-writing of *Twenty-Five*]. Not produced. Published separately (London and New York: Putnam, 1926).

The Would-Be Gentleman (from Molière). Produced 4 January 1926. Published in *Three Last Plays* (London and New York: Putnam, 1928).

Sancho's Master. Produced 14 March 1927. Published in *Three Last Plays* (London and New York: Putnam, 1928).

Dave. Produced 9 May 1927. Published in *Three Last Plays* (London and New York: Putnam, 1928).

PLAYS UNPUBLISHED AND UNPRODUCED

Michelin
The Meadow Gate
The Dispensary
The Shoelace
The Lighted Window
Heads or Harps (with W. B. Yeats)

CONTENTS

xvi

CONTENTS

Appendices

DEDICATIONS OF THE PLAYS
IN THIS VOLUME

Seven Short Plays, which contains five comedies, is dedicated to W. B. Yeats:

> To you, W. B. Yeats, good praiser, wholesome dispraiser, heavy-handed judge, open-handed helper of us all, I offer a play of my plays for every night of the week, because you like them, and because you have taught me my trade.

Abbey Theatre
May 1, 1909.

New Irish Comedies is dedicated to:

The Rt. Hon. W. F. Bailey,
Counsellor, Peacemaker, Friend.

Abbey Theatre, 1913.

TWENTY-FIVE

TWENTY FIVE

PERSONS

MICHAEL FORD. *A middle-aged Farmer.*
KATE FORD. *His young wife.*
BRIDGET FORD. *His sister.*
CHRISTIE HENDERSON.
MARY BRENNAN. *A neighbour.*
A FIDDLER.

SCENE. MICHAEL FORD's kitchen.
Fireplace L.I.E. Stool in front of fireplace.
A table centre with chairs right & left of it.
A chest down stage right.
A dresser at back of stage.
Bottle of whiskey & glasses on dresser; also pack of cards.

MICHAEL FORD *discovered down stage right, rummaging at chest.* KATE *seated on stool at fire: She leans her head on her hand.*

MICHAEL. All the clothes will fit in this chest and a share of the blankets. The rest can go in a bundle. There's some small things here, no good to keep or to sell, you could give them among the neighbours. There's something here wrapped up in a handkerchief . . . (KATE *raises her head*) . . . a little book it is. What is it I wonder.

KATE (*rising*). It's nothing. (*Extends her hand.*) Give it here to me.

MICHAEL (*holding up candle*). Wait till I see. Songs that are in it. "The Harp of Tara" it is called. There is some name written in it. . .

KATE (*comes to centre*). Give it here to me.

MICHAEL. Wait till I see . . . . . Christie Henderson. I don't know that name. May be it was some friend you had among the boys in Kilcolgan.

KATE. You are always thinking I have friends among the boys, Michael, and it's not right for you to think it. If you have any fault to find with me, say it out.

MICHAEL. Well, I don't say that I have, but when there is a

3

young wife in the house, Jack the Journeyman is apt to come slipping round the corner.

KATE (*taking book*). It's time for you to go and bring the fiddler in for the spree. The youngsters will be coming in half an hour or so. And you have your sister to call in for, and you might as well ask Mary Brennan to come along with her.

MICHAEL. I will, and John Brennan. (*Speaking as he goes up.*) I dare say a good many of the neighbours will gather in after a while to see the last of us in this house. (*He goes out.*)

KATE (*crossing and banging down lid of chest*). Jealous he is! He's jealous, I think, of the birds on the tree if he thinks it's Kilcolgan they come from. He should have more sense than what he has. And if he is jealous, it isn't of Christie Henderson he need be jealous, he that thought more of his songs and his sprees than he did of me, going off to America the way he did. (*A knock at door.*) Who is that? I didn't think the neighbours would be here yet awhile. (*Opens door.* CHRISTIE HENDERSON *enters. A pause. He takes her hand.*) Christie Henderson!

CHRISTIE. It is a great surprise to you to see me Katy?

KATE. I never thought you would come back from America.

CHRISTIE (*lets go her hands*). Didn't I say! I would come back to you Kate. But you didn't wait for me.

KATE. How did you know where to find me Christie?

CHRISTIE. Two days ago I landed and last night I got to Kilcolgan and I went up to the house, thinking to surprise you.

KATE. You found no one in it (*speaking as she crosses to fire.*) I left it a year ago.

CHRISTIE (*speaking as he crosses towards fire at back*). The neighbours told me that. The herd is dead they said and the family scattered and Kate is married to a man of the Fords in Kilbecanty.

KATE. I am married indeed.

CHRISTIE. You are married indeed. Tell me. Kate, do you like him?

KATE. I must like him. Amn't I married to him?

CHRISTIE. Does he treat you well?

KATE. He does indeed. He is kind enough most times. He takes a little drop now and again when he's in trouble, but there's many do that.

CHRISTIE. O Katie, Katie, I thought we would have had the one house between us and you coaxing my child on your knee.

KATE. Well, what could I do? I had to get a house over my head. You went away and left me and if you had stopped itself you

were more for wild talk than for work and it's much if you could have got together the priest's fee. (*Sits right of table.*) I never had any word from you. You weren't long putting me out of your head.
CHRISTIE. Don't be angry with me Kate. Look here what I earned for you, fifty pounds I have here in gold and notes. If I didn't write I was never any great hand at writing and may be the thoughts I had of you were enough to go round the world of themselves. But it's no matter. (*He rises and goes up to dresser.*) It's a good house you got and a grand dresser you got, and I dare say you are better pleased with it than if you had come along with me.
KATE. Indeed it's little luck I've had with me, and little good I did for myself. If the house is good, that's no good to me, for I won't be in it long.
CHRISTIE (*comes behind her chair on her left*). How is that?
KATE. There have great misfortunes come on Michael Ford since I married him a year ago and we are to auction the holding to-morrow and to go then to Manchester. He has a brother there will find work for him.
CHRISTIE. That is bad. What brought him to that?
KATE. Bad seasons and debts he had on him, and the will of God. We cannot wrestle with our bad luck any longer, we must give in.
CHRISTIE (*puts hand on her shoulder*). Manchester is no good place for you to go to and you used to country ways.
KATE. It will be death to me to be there and it will be death to Michael too.
CHRISTIE. Look here Kate, would fifty pounds keep the place for you?
KATE. It would Christie but I can't take it and you know that well enough.
CHRISTIE. It is for you I brought it. Look, there's my return ticket back. That's all I want. My place is kept for me when I go back. Take it now and welcome.
KATE. I can do no such thing. I can't take your money.
CHRISTIE. It is yours it is. There take it. I would never have worked without the thought of you.
KATE (*rises*). I tell you I can't take it. If I would take it itself, Michael wouldn't let me.
(*Crosses to chest.*)
CHRISTIE. Sure you could say you found it in a field under a bush or that some uncle you had in America sent it to you. I'll say I brought it from him.

KATE. I have no uncle in America. It's no use I couldn't take it Christie.

CHRISTIE. You will take it. (*Takes up money.*) I have my mind made up. I'll leave it in the corner of the cowshed outside. You can let on to find it in the morning.

(*Goes towards door.*)

KATE (*rushes up to door and puts her back against it.*) You will not leave it there or anywhere. (*A noise heard.*) There now you can't go out. I hear Michael coming. O Christie don't tell him I knew you before, he might be questioning me.

CHRISTIE. Never fear I'll not tell him, but I'll get my way yet. (*Puts bag in his pocket.*) If you don't take it one way you will have to take it another way. (*Enter* MICHAEL FORD, BRIDGET FORD, MARY BRENNAN *and* FIDDLER.)

MICHAEL. Here's Bridget with me and Mary Brennan.

CHRISTIE (*to* MICHAEL). Can you tell me the road to Gort? I think I missed it turning up the road a while ago.

MICHAEL. You did indeed. You must go down to the high road again and turn to the left. You are a stranger here I suppose.

CHRISTIE. I landed at Queenstown yesterday. I was never in this part before.

MICHAEL (*pouring whiskey into glasses*). Well sit down now till you rest yourself. There's a few of the neighbours coming in to spend the evening with us.

(CHRISTIE *sits on stool at fire.* MICHAEL *hands whiskey.*)

MARY. Indeed Michael I'm sorry to think what brings us here, to say good-bye to you before you quit the house.

MICHAEL. Well we'd best not be thinking about that, but to try and forget it for this night.

(*Offers whiskey to* CHRISTIE.)

CHRISTIE (*rises*). I don't take any drink, thank you all the same, but I wish health and prosperity to the woman of the house without it. (*Sits. The others drink.*) It's a long time since I sat beside a turf fire before.

MICHAEL. What was it brought you to County Galway?

CHRISTIE. Looking for a treasure I had a dream about.

MICHAEL. And did you find it?

CHRISTIE. I did not. Some other man went there before me and brought it away. I dreamed about it often enough; but whatever happened I didn't dream right. I suppose it was a morning dream and they go by contraries.

6

MARY. They do so and if you will tell a morning dream to the trees fasting they will all wither.

CHRISTIE. Faith it's well I didn't meet many trees on the road yesterday; they'd be withered now the same as Raftery's bush. Woman of the house, do you ever have good dreams?

KATE. I don't think much about dreams. It's best not to mind them but to be working in the daytime.

CHRISTIE. That's true indeed. It's a pity the master didn't teach me that and I a little chap going to school.

MICHAEL. Well stop the evening with us and welcome. We'll be having a dance by and bye when the youngsters come. (*He lays a pack of cards on the table.*)

CHRISTIE (*rising and coming to table*). That's what will suit me better than dancing. I didn't play a game of cards this long while.

MICHAEL. I won't play to-night. I have no mind to lose anything I have.

CHRISTIE. May be you might win. It's nothing to me if I lose. I'm a rich man.

MICHAEL. Let someone else play with you. I haven't the money.

MARY. Here Michael Ford play a good game and it will put courage in you. (*Puts down money.*) Here now I'll give you the loan of this half crown.

MICHAEL. I might lose it.

MARY. If you do itself, I can take it back in laying hens at the sale to-morrow.

CHRISTIE. There now. I have nothing but gold, but I'll put down gold against your half crown.

BRIDGET. You are a rich man indeed. May be you found the treasure after all.

CHRISTIE. I am rich indeed. Wouldn't you call a man rich when gold and bank notes are no more to him than tin tacks, withered leave and wisps of straw. Here, come on. I'll deal.

(MICHAEL *sits right of table.*)

FIDDLER (*comes over to table: takes up a sovereign, bites it*). That's good gold anyway, wherever it came from.

KATE (*to* MICHAEL). Don't play with him. It's a queer thing to be playing like that for gold.

MARY. Play on man, play on.

CHRISTIE. I've turned up the ace. That's five to me and I rob. Now I bet you five to one I'll beat you.

MICHAEL. Well, I'll take you. Come, play on that (*puts down card*) and that. (*Puts down another.*) Here's the ace of diamonds to you. (*Puts down.*) Come now. (*Puts down.*) Here again. (*Puts down.*) The game's mine.

FIDDLER. That was bad play and he having the ace all the time.

KATE. Michael, don't you see he's not playing right? You ought not to be playing with him.

CHRISTIE. It's a pity women to be in the house and cards going on. What do they know about them?

MICHAEL. Don't be bothering me Kate. Leave me alone can't you. (KATE *beckons over* BRIDGET.)

BRIDGET. What is it Kate?

KATE. I don't like Michael to be playing cards. Could you find some excuse to stop him?

BRIDGET. Why would you want to stop him? It takes his mind off his trouble and he can lose no more than that half a crown.

KATE. It's not afraid of him losing I am but I don't want him to be winning . . .

BRIDGET. You don't want him to be winning! It's a queer wife you are and he in such want as he is of all he can gather.

MICHAEL. Twenty-five, that's mine.

MARY (*coming to* KATE). Do you hear that, Mrs. Ford. It's Michael has won that game too. Isn't that good luck he has . . . They are doubling the stakes now.

KATE. Can't you stop him? I don't like him to be winning money that way. There will be no luck on it.

MARY. Well I never saw there was more luck on one shilling I'd make more than on another, wherever it came from.

BRIDGET. You may thank God, Kate Ford, for this night, that might put enough in your pocket to cover the journey.

KATE. Oh can't you believe me when I say he mustn't win that money? I tell you I have a reason for it . . . Can't you take my word for it and can't you help me? Can't you say you want the cards for a game for yourself or some other thing?

BRIDGET. Leave them alone.

KATE. I tell you he is winning too much. Look it's notes they have on the table now. I must stop them.

BRIDGET. I will not let you stop them. Stop her Mary.

MARY. Stop quiet now Mrs. Ford. We'll leave no gap for you to pass through.

KATE. I have no mind for joking or playing. Let me go I say.

BRIDGET (*taking her by the shoulder*). Look here now, Kate. I don't know what you are at, but whatever you are at, it is no good you will do your husband by it. If he has a chance that it was may be God sent in his way, to save the roof that is over his head and the house he brought you to, you'd best not interfere, for if you do it's a thing he will never forgive you and I will never forgive you and that you will be sorry for yourself and you wandering here and there.

KATE. O Bridget don't be tormenting me. You don't know the sore heart I have. It may be best to tell you the truth. Before I came here, when I was in Kilcolgan.

MARY. What was it happened in Kilcolgan? Did you lose money playing cards? Tell it out now.

KATE. There was nothing happened. It's nonsense I'm talking. I want you to stop this game because the table will be wanted by and bye. We should get it cleared.

MARY. There is plenty of time for that. What are you at at all? Can you think of no better excuse than that Mrs. Ford?

KATE. And there are many things Michael should be seeing to. He didn't sort out the things in the shed yet or divide the garden into lots.

MARY (*bursting out laughing*). Divide the garden into lots: It's well he do that in the dark night.

BRIDGET. Kate Ford it's my opinion that you have lost your wits.

KATE. Michael! Stop playing till I speak to you.

(*She frees herself from the others and comes to the right of centre.*)

MICHAEL. Wait a minute, wait a minute . . . Nine of clubs, he's beaten on that. The Butt's in. . . . That's mine (*He stands up holding out money in his hands to* KATE.) Look Kate at what is there. Fifty pounds that I have won by fair play, nothing more and nothing less.

FIDDLER. Fifty pounds! There never was such a game played in this parish. Faith Michael Ford you won't quit Kilbecanty this time.

CHRISTIE. Well I must learn to play a better game before I come this way again. I'm no match for the people of Kilbecanty.

KATE. Michael give back that money.

BRIDGET. Don't be quarrelling with your luck I tell you.

KATE (*to* CHRISTIE). I know well it wasn't real play; it's only humbugging you were. Take back your money.

CHRISTIE. There are some things no man can take back and they once gone from him.

KATE. You will take this back any way.

9

BRIDGET. Be easy now Kate. Who knows who was it sent that luck into the house.

KATE. Michael give back that money. It's not rightly won. If you won't do it of yourself I can make you do it with what I am going to say. Before you came in to-night. . . .

CHRISTIE (*standing up hurriedly and looking at the woman*). Wouldn't anyone say I was her old sweetheart come back and she taking my side against her own man. (KATE *shrinks back and goes up right, her face in her hands.*)

MARY. Well it must be a grand thing to be a rich man.

CHRISTIE. It's grand indeed. It's a grand thing to be able to take up your money in your hand and to think no more of it when it slips away from you than you would of a trout that would slip back into the stream. I told you in the beginning I was a rich man.

BRIDGET (*who has picked up ticket from floor*). Here's a return ticket to America. Third class it is. (*To* CHRISTIE) Is it you it belongs to?

MARY. Not at all. It wasn't in the steerage he came. I tell you, sovereigns are as plenty with him as holes in a riddle.

CHRISTIE (*looking at ticket*). That ticket . . . suppose it dropped from the bag . . . Who owns it? I think it belongs to some poor man was in the ship with me. Coming home he was to look for his wife.

MARY. And what happened him? Did he die?

CHRISTIE. He died or some one died . . . or something happened . . . Give it here to me. I want it for a labouring man I know that has to quit Ireland to-morrow.

(*Puts ticket in hatband and hat on head and crosses to* MICHAEL *and shakes hands.*)

Well I must be going now. This was a grand night we had.

MICHAEL (*feebly*). May be you'll come back some other time to take your revenge.

CHRISTIE. Who knows? I might get my revenge yet. But I don't think I'll be passing this way again. Isn't it near time for the dance to begin? Woman of the house will you take a turn with me before I go?

KATE. I won't dance to-night.

CHRISTIE. You wouldn't refuse the greatest stranger in the house. Give me a dance now and I'll be thinking of you some time when I'm dancing with some high up lady having golden shoes, in a white marble court by the sea. Here Fiddler give us a reel. (FIDDLER *strikes up.* CHRISTIE *takes* KATE'S *hand. Dance for a minute. Stops. Kisses her and flings over to the door. Turns round and waves his hat.)*

CHRISTIE. Good-bye neighbours, that was a grand evening we had.

Curtain.

SPREADING THE NEWS

SPREADING THE NEWS

PERSONS
  BARTLEY FALLON.
  MRS. FALLON.
  JACK SMITH.
  SHAWN EARLY.
  TIM CASEY.
  JAMES RYAN.
  MRS. TARPEY.
  MRS. TULLY.
  A Policeman (JO MULDOON).
  A REMOVABLE MAGISTRATE.

SCENE. *The outskirts of a Fair. An Apple Stall.* MRS. TARPEY *sitting at it.* MAGISTRATE *and* POLICEMAN *enter.*

MAGISTRATE. So that is the Fair Green. Cattle and sheep and mud. No system. What a repulsive sight!

POLICEMAN. That is so, indeed.

MAGISTRATE. I suppose there is a good deal of disorder in this place?

POLICEMAN. There is.

MAGISTRATE. Common assault?

POLICEMAN. It's common enough.

MAGISTRATE. Agrarian crime, no doubt?

POLICEMAN. That is so.

MAGISTRATE. Boycotting? Maiming of cattle? Firing into houses?

POLICEMAN. There was one time, and there might be again.

MAGISTRATE. That is bad. Does it go any farther than that?

POLICEMAN. Far enough, indeed.

MAGISTRATE. Homicide, then! This district has been shamefully neglected! I will change all that. When I was in the Andaman Islands, my system never failed. Yes, yes, I will change all that. What has that woman on her stall?

POLICEMAN. Apples mostly—and sweets.

MAGISTRATE. Just see if there are any unlicensed goods underneath—spirits or the like. We had evasions of the salt tax in the Andaman Islands.

POLICEMAN (*sniffing cautiously and upsetting a heap of apples*). I see no spirits here—or salt.

MAGISTRATE (*to* MRS. TARPEY). Do you know this town well, my good woman?

MRS. TARPEY (*holding out some apples*). A penny the half-dozen, your honour.

POLICEMAN (*shouting*). The gentleman is asking do you know the town! He's the new magistrate!

MRS. TARPEY (*rising and ducking*). Do I know the town? I do, to be sure.

MAGISTRATE (*shouting*). What is its chief business?

MRS. TARPEY. Business, is it? What business would the people here have but to be minding one another's business?

MAGISTRATE. I mean what trade have they?

MRS. TARPEY. Not a trade. No trade at all but to be talking.

MAGISTRATE. I shall learn nothing here.

(JAMES RYAN *comes in, pipe in mouth. Seeing* MAGISTRATE *he retreats quickly, taking pipe from mouth.*)

MAGISTRATE. The smoke from that man's pipe had a greenish look; he may be growing unlicensed tobacco at home. I wish I had brought my telescope to this district. Come to the post-office, I will telegraph for it. I found it very useful in the Andaman Islands.

(MAGISTRATE *and* POLICEMAN *go out left.*)

MRS. TARPEY. Bad luck to Jo Muldoon, knocking my apples this way and that way. (*Begins arranging them.*) Showing off he was to the new magistrate.

(*Enter* BARTLEY FALLON *and* MRS. FALLON.)

BARTLEY. Indeed it's a poor country and a scarce country to be living in. But I'm thinking if I went to America it's long ago the day I'd be dead!

MRS. FALLON. So you might, indeed.

(*She puts her basket on a barrel and begins putting parcels in it, taking them from under her cloak.*)

BARTLEY. And it's a great expense for a poor man to be buried in America.

MRS. FALLON. Never fear, Bartley Fallon, but I'll give you a good burying the day you'll die.

BARTLEY. Maybe it's yourself will be buried in the graveyard of Cloonmara before me, Mary Fallon, and I myself that will be dying unbeknownst some night, and no one a-near me. And the cat itself

16

may be gone straying through the country, and the mice squealing over the quilt.

MRS. FALLON. Leave off talking of dying. It might be twenty years you'll be living yet.

BARTLEY (*with a deep sigh*). I'm thinking if I'll be living at the end of twenty years, it's a very old man I'll be then!

MRS. TARPEY (*turns and sees them*). Good morrow, Bartley Fallon; good morrow, Mrs. Fallon. Well, Bartley, you'll find no cause for complaining to-day; they are all saying it was a good fair.

BARTLEY (*raising his voice*). It was not a good fair, Mrs. Tarpey. It was a scattered sort of a fair. If we didn't expect more, we got less. That's the way with me always; whatever I have to sell goes down and whatever I have to buy goes up. If there's ever any misfortune coming to this world, it's on myself it pitches, like a flock of crows on seed potatoes.

MRS. FALLON. Leave off talking of misfortunes, and listen to Jack Smith that is coming the way, and he singing.

(*Voice of* JACK SMITH *heard singing:*)

> I thought, my first love,
> There'd be but one house between you and me,
> And I thought I would find
> Yourself coaxing my child on your knee.
> Over the tide
> I would leap with the leap of a swan,
> Till I came to the side
> Of the wife of the Red-haired man!

(JACK SMITH *comes in; he is a red-haired man, and is carrying a hayfork.*)

MRS. TARPEY. That should be a good song if I had my hearing.

MRS. FALLON (*shouting*). It's "The Red-haired Man's Wife."

MRS. TARPEY. I know it well. That's the song that has a skin on it!

(*She turns her back to them and goes on arranging her apples.*)

MRS. FALLON. Where's herself, Jack Smith?

JACK SMITH. She was delayed with her washing; bleaching the clothes on the hedge she is, and she daren't leave them, with all the tinkers that do be passing to the fair. It isn't to the fair I came myself, but up to the Five Acre Meadow I'm going, where I have a contract for the hay. We'll get a share of it into tramps to-day. (*He lays down hayfork and lights his pipe.*)

BARTLEY. You will not get it into tramps to-day. The rain will be down on it by evening, and on myself too. It's seldom I ever started on a journey but the rain would come down on me before I'd find any place of shelter.

JACK SMITH. If it didn't itself, Bartley, it is my belief you would carry a leaky pail on your head in place of a hat, the way you'd not be without some cause of complaining.

(*A voice heard,* "Go on, now, go on out o' that. Go on I say.")

JACK SMITH. Look at that young mare of Pat Ryan's that is backing into Shaughnessy's bullocks with the dint of the crowd! Don't be daunted, Pat, I'll give you a hand with her.

(*He goes out, leaving his hayfork.*)

MRS. FALLON. It's time for ourselves to be going home. I have all I bought put in the basket. Look at there, Jack Smith's hayfork he left after him! He'll be wanting it. (*Calls.*) Jack Smith! Jack Smith!—He's gone through the crowd—hurry after him, Bartley, he'll be wanting it.

BARTLEY. I'll do that. This is no safe place to be leaving it. (*He takes up fork awkwardly and upsets the basket.*) Look at that now! If there is any basket in the fair upset, it must be our own basket!

(*He goes out to right.*)

MRS. FALLON. Get out of that! It is your own fault, it is. Talk of misfortunes and misfortunes will come. Glory be! Look at my new egg-cups rolling in every part—and my two pound of sugar with the paper broke——

MRS. TARPEY (*turning from stall*). God help us, Mrs. Fallon, what happened your basket?

MRS. FALLON. It's himself that knocked it down, bad manners to him. (*Putting things up.*) My grand sugar that's destroyed, and he'll not drink his tea without it. I had best go back to the shop for more, much good may it do him!

(*Enter* TIM CASEY.)

TIM CASEY. Where is Bartley Fallon, Mrs. Fallon? I want a word with him before he'll leave the fair. I was afraid he might have gone home by this, for he's a temperate man.

MRS. FALLON. I wish he did go home! It'd be best for me if he went home straight from the fair green, or if he never came with me at all? Where is he, is it? He's gone up the road (*jerks elbow*) following Jack Smith with a hayfork.

(*She goes out to left.*)

TIM CASEY. Following Jack Smith with a hayfork! Did ever any one hear the like of that. (*Shouts.*) Did you hear that news, Mrs. Tarpey?

MRS. TARPEY. I heard no news at all.

TIM CASEY. Some dispute I suppose it was that rose between Jack Smith and Bartley Fallon, and it seems Jack made off, and Bartley is following him with a hayfork!

MRS. TARPEY. Is he now? Well, that was quick work! It's not ten minutes since the two of them were here, Bartley going home and Jack going to the Five Acre Meadow; and I had my apples to settle up, that Jo Muldoon of the police had scattered, and when I looked round again Jack Smith was gone, and Bartley Fallon was gone, and Mrs. Fallon's basket upset, and all in it strewed upon the ground—the tea here—the two pound of sugar there—the egg-cups there—Look, now, what a great hardship the deafness puts upon me, that I didn't hear the commincement of the fight! Wait till I tell James Ryan that I see below; he is a neighbour of Bartley's, it would be a pity if he wouldn't hear the news!

(*She goes out. Enter* SHAWN EARLY *and* MRS. TULLY.)

TIM CASEY. Listen, Shawn Early! Listen, Mrs. Tully, to the news! Jack Smith and Bartley Fallon had a falling out, and Jack knocked Mrs. Fallon's basket into the road, and Bartley made an attack on him with a hayfork, and away with Jack, and Bartley after him. Look at the sugar here yet on the road!

SHAWN EARLY. Do you tell me so? Well, that's a queer thing, and Bartley Fallon so quiet a man!

MRS. TULLY. I wouldn't wonder at all. I would never think well of a man that would have that sort of a mouldering look. It's likely he has overtaken Jack by this.

(*Enter* JAMES RYAN *and* MRS. TARPEY.)

JAMES RYAN. That is great news Mrs. Tarpey was telling me! I suppose that's what brought the police and the magistrate up this way. I was wondering to see them in it a while ago.

SHAWN EARLY. The police after them? Bartley Fallon must have injured Jack so. They wouldn't meddle in a fight that was only for show!

MRS. TULLY. Why wouldn't he injure him? There was many a man killed with no more of a weapon than a hayfork.

JAMES RYAN. Wait till I run north as far as Kelly's bar to spread the news! (*He goes out.*)

TIM CASEY. I'll go tell Jack Smith's first cousin that is standing there south of the church after selling his lambs. (*Goes out.*)

MRS. TULLY. I'll go telling a few of the neighbours I see beyond to the west. (*Goes out.*)

19

SHAWN EARLY. I'll give word of it beyond at the east of the green.

(*Is going out when* MRS. TARPEY *seizes hold of him.*)

MRS. TARPEY. Stop a minute, Shawn Early, and tell me did you see red Jack Smith's wife, Kitty Keary, in any place?

SHAWN EARLY. I did. At her own house she was, drying clothes on the hedge as I passed.

MRS. TARPEY. What did you say she was doing?

SHAWN EARLY (*breaking away*). Laying out a sheet on the hedge. (*He goes.*)

MRS. TARPEY. Laying out a sheet for the dead! The Lord have mercy on us! Jack Smith dead, and his wife laying out a sheet for his burying! (*Calls out.*) Why didn't you tell me that before, Shawn Early? Isn't the deafness the great hardship? Half the world might be dead without me knowing of it or getting word of it at all! (*She sits down and rocks herself.*) O my poor Jack Smith! To be going to his work so nice and so hearty, and to be left stretched on the ground in the full light of the day!

(*Enter* TIM CASEY.)

TIM CASEY. What is it, Mrs. Tarpey? What happened since?

MRS. TARPEY. O my poor Jack Smith!

TIM CASEY. Did Bartley overtake him?

MRS. TARPEY. O the poor man!

TIM CASEY. Is it killed he is?

MRS. TARPEY. Stretched in the Five Acre Meadow!

TIM CASEY. The Lord have mercy on us! Is that a fact?

MRS. TARPEY. Without the rites of the Church or a ha'porth!

TIM CASEY. Who was telling you?

MRS. TARPEY. And the wife laying out a sheet for his corpse. (*Sits up and wipes her eyes.*) I suppose they'll wake him the same as another?

(*Enter* MRS. TULLY, SHAWN EARLY, *and* JAMES RYAN.)

MRS. TULLY. There is great talk about this work in every quarter of the fair.

MRS. TARPEY. Ochone! cold and dead. And myself maybe the last he was speaking to!

JAMES RYAN. The Lord save us! Is it dead he is?

TIM CASEY. Dead surely, and the wife getting provision for the wake.

SHAWN EARLY. Well, now, hadn't Bartley Fallon great venom in him?

MRS. TULLY. You may be sure he had some cause. Why would

he have made an end of him if he had not? (*To* MRS. TARPEY, *raising her voice.*) What was it rose the dispute at all, Mrs. Tarpey?

MRS. TARPEY. Not a one of me knows. The last I saw of them, Jack Smith was standing there, and Bartley Fallon was standing there, quiet and easy, and he listening to "The Red-haired Man's Wife."

MRS. TULLY. Do you hear that, Tim Casey? Do you hear that, Shawn Early and James Ryan? Bartley Fallon was here this morning listening to red Jack Smith's wife, Kitty Keary that was! Listening to her and whispering with her! It was she started the fight so!

SHAWN EARLY. She must have followed him from her own house. It is likely some person roused him.

TIM CASEY. I never knew, before, Bartley Fallon was great with Jack Smith's wife.

MRS. TULLY. How would you know it? Sure it's not in the streets they would be calling it. If Mrs. Fallon didn't know of it, and if I that have the next house to them didn't know of it, and if Jack Smith himself didn't know of it, it is not likely you would know of it, Tim Casey.

SHAWN EARLY. Let Bartley Fallon take charge of her from this out so, and let him provide for her. It is little pity she will get from any person in this parish.

TIM CASEY. How can he take charge of her? Sure he has a wife of his own. Sure you don't think he'd turn souper and marry her in a Protestant church?

JAMES RYAN. It would be easy for him to marry her if he brought her to America.

SHAWN EARLY. With or without Kitty Keary, believe me it is for America he's making at this minute. I saw the new magistrate and Jo Muldoon of the police going into the post-office as I came up—there was hurry on them—you may be sure it was to telegraph they went, the way he'll be stopped in the docks at Queenstown!

MRS. TULLY. It's likely Kitty Keary is gone with him, and not minding a sheet or a wake at all. The poor man, to be deserted by his own wife, and the breath hardly gone out yet from his body that is lying bloody in the field!

(*Enter* MRS. FALLON.)

MRS. FALLON. What is it the whole of the town is talking about? And what is it you yourselves are talking about? Is it about my man Bartley Fallon you are talking? Is it lies about him you are telling, saying that he went killing Jack Smith? My grief that ever he came into this place at all!

JAMES RYAN. Be easy now, Mrs. Fallon. Sure there is no one at all in the whole fair but is sorry for you!

MRS. FALLON. Sorry for me, is it? Why would any one be sorry for me? Let you be sorry for yourselves, and that there may be shame on you for ever and at the day of judgment, for the words you are saying and the lies you are telling to take away the character of my poor man, and to take the good name off of him, and to drive him to destruction! That is what you are doing!

SHAWN EARLY. Take comfort now, Mrs. Fallon. The police are not so smart as they think. Sure he might give them the slip yet, the same as Lynchehaun.

MRS. TULLY. If they do get him, and if they do put a rope around his neck, there is no one can say he does not deserve it!

MRS. FALLON. Is that what you are saying, Bridget Tully, and is that what you think? I tell you it's too much talk you have, making yourself out to be such a great one, and to be running down every respectable person! A rope, is it? It isn't much of a rope was needed to tie up your own furniture the day you came into Martin Tully's house, and you never bringing as much as a blanket, or a penny, or a suit of clothes with you and I myself bringing seventy pounds and two feather beds. And now you are stiffer than a woman would have a hundred pounds! It is too much talk the whole of you have. A rope is it? I tell you the whole of this town is full of liars and schemers that would hang you up for half a glass of whiskey. (*Turning to go.*) People they are you wouldn't believe as much as daylight from without you'd get up to have a look at it yourself. Killing Jack Smith indeed! Where are you at all, Bartley, till I bring you out of this? My nice quiet little man! My decent comrade! He that is as kind and as harmless as an innocent beast of the field! He'll be doing no harm at all if he'll shed the blood of some of you after this day's work! That much would be no harm at all. (*Calls out*) Bartley! Bartley Fallon! Where are you? (*Going out.*) Did any one see Bartley Fallon?

(*All turn to look after her.*)

JAMES RYAN. It is hard for her to believe any such a thing, God help her!

(*Enter* BARTLEY FALLON *from right, carrying hayfork.*)

BARTLEY. It is what I often said to myself, if there is ever any misfortune coming to this world it is on myself it is sure to come!

(*All turn round and face him.*)

BARTLEY. To be going about with this fork and to find no one to take it, and no place to leave it down, and I wanting to be gone out of this—Is that you, Shawn Early? (*Holds out fork.*) It's well I met you. You have no call to be leaving the fair for a while the way I have, and how can I go till I'm rid of this fork? Will you take it and keep it until such time as Jack Smith——

SHAWN EARLY (*backing*). I will not take it, Bartley Fallon, I'm very thankful to you!

BARTLEY (*turning to apple stall*). Look at it now, Mrs. Tarpey, it was here I got it; let me thrust it in under the stall. It will lie there safe enough, and no one will take notice of it until such time as Jack Smith——

MRS. TARPEY. Take your fork out of that! Is it to put trouble on me and to destroy me you want? putting it there for the police to be rooting it out maybe. (*Thrusts him back.*)

BARTLEY. That is a very unneighbourly thing for you to do, Mrs. Tarpey. Hadn't I enough care on me with that fork before this, running up and down with it like the swinging of a clock, and afeard to lay it down in any place! I wish I never touched it or meddled with it at all!

JAMES RYAN. It is a pity, indeed, you ever did.

BARTLEY. Will you yourself take it, James Ryan? You were always a neighbourly man.

James Ryan (*backing*). There is many a thing I would do for you, Bartley Fallon, but I won't do that!

SHAWN EARLY. I tell you there is no man will give you any help or any encouragement for this day's work. If it was something agrarian now—

Bartley. If no one at all will take it, maybe it's best to give it up to the police.

TIM CASEY. There'd be a welcome for it with them surely! (*Laughter.*)

MRS. TULLY. And it is to the police Kitty Keary herself will be brought.

MRS. TARPEY (*rocking to and fro*). I wonder now who will take the expense of the wake for poor Jack Smith?

BARTLEY. The wake for Jack Smith!

TIM CASEY. Why wouldn't he get a wake as well as another? Would you begrudge him that much?

BARTLEY. Red Jack Smith dead! Who was telling you?

SHAWN EARLY. The whole town knows of it by this.

BARTLEY. Do they say what way did he die?

23

JAMES RYAN. You don't know that yourself, I suppose, Bartley Fallon? You don't know he was followed and that he was laid dead with the stab of a hayfork?

BARTLEY. The stab of a hayfork!

SHAWN EARLY. You don't know, I suppose, that the body was found in the Five Acre Meadow?

BARTLEY. The Five Acre Meadow!

TIM CASEY. It is likely you don't know that the police are after the man that did it?

BARTLEY. The man that did it!

MRS. TULLY. You don't know, maybe, that he was made away with for the sake of Kitty Keary, his wife?

BARTLEY. Kitty Keary, his wife!

(*Sits down bewildered.*)

MRS. TULLY. And what have you to say now, Bartley Fallon?

BARTLEY (*crossing himself*). I to bring that fork here, and to find that news before me! It is much if I can ever stir from this place at all, or reach as far as the road!

TIM CASEY. Look, boys, at the new magistrate, and Jo Muldoon along with him! It's best for us to quit this.

SHAWN EARLY. That is so. It is best not to be mixed in this business at all.

JAMES RYAN. Bad as he is, I wouldn't like to be an informer against any man.

(*All hurry away except Mrs. Tarpey, who remains behind her stall. Enter magistrate and policeman.*)

MAGISTRATE. I knew the district was in a bad state, but I did not expect to be confronted with a murder at the first fair I came to.

POLICEMAN. I am sure you did not, indeed.

MAGISTRATE. It was well I had not gone home. I caught a few words here and there that roused my suspicions.

POLICEMAN. So they would, too.

MAGISTRATE. You heard the same story from everyone you asked?

POLICEMAN. The same story—or if it was not altogether the same, anyway it was no less than the first story.

MAGISTRATE. What is that man doing? He is sitting alone with a hayfork. He has a guilty look. The murder was done with a hayfork!

POLICEMAN (*in a whisper*). That's the very man they say did the act; Bartley Fallon himself!

MAGISTRATE. He must have found escape difficult—he is trying

24

to brazen it out. A convict in the Andaman Islands tried the same game, but he could not escape my system! Stand aside—Don't go far—have the handcuffs ready. (*He walks up to Bartley, folds his arms, and stands before him.*) Here, my man, do you know anything of John Smith?

BARTLEY. Of John Smith! Who is he, now?

POLICEMAN. Jack Smith, sir—Red Jack Smith!

MAGISTRATE (*coming a step nearer and tapping him on the shoulder*). Where is Jack Smith?

BARTLEY (*with a deep sigh, and shaking his head slowly*). Where is he, indeed?

MAGISTRATE. What have you to tell?

BARTLEY. It is where he was this morning, standing in this spot, singing his share of songs—no, but lighting his pipe—scraping a match on the sole of his shoes——

MAGISTRATE. I ask you, for the third time, where is he?

BARTLEY. I wouldn't like to say that. It is a great mystery, and it is hard to say of any man, did he earn hatred or love.

MAGISTRATE. Tell me all you know.

BARTLEY. All that I know— Well, there are the three estates; there is Limbo, and there is Purgatory, and there is——

MAGISTRATE. Nonsense! This is trifling! Get to the point.

BARTLEY. Maybe you don't hold with the clergy so? That is the teaching of the clergy. Maybe you hold with the old people. It is what they do be saying, that the shadow goes wandering, and the soul is tired, and the body is taking a rest—The shadow! (*Starts up.*) I was nearly sure I saw Jack Smith not ten minutes ago at the corner of the forge, and I lost him again— Was it his ghost I saw, do you think?

MAGISTRATE (*to policeman*). Conscience-struck! He will confess all now!

BARTLEY. His ghost to come before me! It is likely it was on account of the fork! I to have it and he to have no way to defend himself the time he met with his death!

MAGISTRATE (*to policeman*). I must note down his words. (*Takes out notebook.*) (*To Bartley.*) I warn you that your words are being noted.

BARTLEY. If I had ha' run faster in the beginning, this terror would not be on me at the latter end! Maybe he will cast it up against me at the day of judgment— I wouldn't wonder at all at that.

MAGISTRATE (*writing*). At the day of judgment——

BARTLEY. It was soon for his ghost to appear to me—is it coming after me always by day it will be, and stripping the clothes off in the night time?— I wouldn't wonder at all at that, being as I am an unfortunate man!

MAGISTRATE (*sternly*). Tell me this truly. What was the motive of this crime?

BARTLEY. The motive, is it?

MAGISTRATE. Yes; the motive; the cause.

BARTLEY. I'd sooner not say that.

MAGISTRATE. You had better tell me truly. Was it money?

BARTLEY. Not at all! What did poor Jack Smith ever have in his pockets unless it might be his hands that would be in them?

MAGISTRATE. Any dispute about land?

BARTLEY (*indignantly*). Not at all! He never was a grabber or grabbed from any one!

MAGISTRATE. You will find it better for you if you tell me at once.

BARTLEY. I tell you I wouldn't for the whole world wish to say what it was—it is a thing I would not like to be talking about.

MAGISTRATE. There is no use in hiding it. It will be discovered in the end.

BARTLEY. Well, I suppose it will, seeing that mostly everybody knows it before. Whisper here now. I will tell no lie; where would be the use? (*Puts his hand to his mouth, and Magistrate stoops.*) Don't be putting the blame on the parish, for such a thing was never done in the parish before—it was done for the sake of Kitty Keary, Jack Smith's wife.

MAGISTRATE (*to policeman*). Put on the handcuffs. We have been saved some trouble. I knew he would confess if taken in the right way.

(*Policeman puts on handcuffs.*)

BARTLEY. Handcuffs now! Glory be! I always said, if there was ever any misfortune coming to this place it was on myself it would fall. I to be in handcuffs! There's no wonder at all in that.

(*Enter Mrs. Fallon, followed by the rest. She is looking back at them as she speaks.*)

MRS. FALLON. Telling lies the whole of the people of this town are; telling lies, telling lies as fast as a dog will trot! Speaking against my poor respectable man! Saying he made an end of Jack Smith! My decent comrade! There is no better man and no kinder man in the whole of the five parishes! It's little annoyance he ever gave to any one! (*Turns and sees him.*) What in the earthly world do I see before me? Bartley Fallon in charge of the police! Handcuffs on him! O Bartley, what did you do at all at all?

BARTLEY. O Mary, there has a great misfortune come upon me! It is what I always said, that if there is ever any misfortune——

MRS. FALLON. What did he do at all, or is it bewitched I am?

MAGISTRATE. This man has been arrested on a charge of murder.

MRS. FALLON. Whose charge is that? Don't believe them! They are all liars in this place! Give me back my man!

MAGISTRATE. It is natural you should take his part, but you have no cause of complaint against your neighbours. He has been arrested for the murder of John Smith, on his own confession.

MRS. FALLON. The saints of heaven protect us! And what did he want killing Jack Smith?

MAGISTRATE. It is best you should know all. He did it on account of a love affair with the murdered man's wife.

MRS. FALLON (*sitting down*). With Jack Smith's wife! With Kitty Keary!—Ochone, the traitor!

THE CROWD. A great shame, indeed. He is a traitor indeed.

MRS. TULLY. To America he was bringing her, Mrs. Fallon.

BARTLEY. What are you saying, Mary? I tell you——

MRS. FALLON. Don't say a word! I won't listen to any word you'll say! (*Stops her ears.*) O, isn't he the treacherous villain? Ohone go deo!

BARTLEY. Be quiet till I speak! Listen to what I say!

MRS. FALLON. Sitting beside me on the ass car coming to the town, so quiet and so respectable, and treachery like that in his heart!

BARTLEY. Is it your wits you have lost or is it I myself that have lost my wits?

MRS. FALLON. And it's hard I earned you, slaving—and you grumbling, and sighing, and coughing, and discontented, and the priest wore out anointing you, with all the times you threatened to die!

BARTLEY. Let you be quiet till I tell you!

MRS. FALLON. You to bring such a disgrace into the parish. A thing that was never heard of before!

BARTLEY. Will you shut your mouth and hear me speaking?

MRS. FALLON. And if it was for any sort of a fine handsome woman, but for a little fistful of a woman like Kitty Keary, that's not four feet high hardly, and not three teeth in her head unless she got new ones! May God reward you, Bartley Fallon, for the

27

black treachery in your heart and the wickedness in your mind, and
the red blood of poor Jack Smith that is wet upon your hand!
(*Voice of Jack Smith heard singing.*)

> The sea shall be dry,
> The earth under mourning and ban!
> Then loud shall he cry
> For the wife of the red-haired man!

BARTLEY. It's Jack Smith's voice—I never knew a ghost to sing
before—. It is after myself and the fork he is coming! (*Goes back.
Enter Jack Smith.*) Let one of you give him the fork and I will be
clear of him now and for eternity!

MRS. TARPEY. The Lord have mercy on us! Red Jack Smith!
The man that was going to be waked!

JAMES RYAN. Is it back from the grave you are come?

SHAWN EARLY. Is it alive you are, or is it dead you are?

TIM CASEY. Is it yourself at all that's in it?

MRS. TULLY. Is it letting on you were to be dead?

MRS. FALLON. Dead or alive, let you stop Kitty Keary, your
wife, from bringing my man away with her to America!

JACK SMITH. It is what I think, the wits are gone astray on the
whole of you. What would my wife want bringing Bartley Fallon
to America?

MRS. FALLON. To leave yourself, and to get quit of you she
wants, Jack Smith, and to bring him away from myself. That's
what the two of them had settled together.

JACK SMITH. I'll break the head of any man that says that! Who
is it says it? (*To Tim Casey.*) Was it you said it? (*To Shawn Early.*)
Was it you?

ALL TOGETHER (*backing and shaking their heads*). It wasn't I
said it!

JACK SMITH. Tell me the name of any man that said it!

ALL TOGETHER (*pointing to Bartley*). It was *him* that said it!

JACK SMITH. Let me at him till I break his head!

(*Bartley backs in terror. Neighbours hold Jack Smith back.*)

JACK SMITH (*trying to free himself*). Let me at him! Isn't he the
pleasant sort of a scarecrow for any woman to be crossing the ocean
with! It's back from the docks of New York he'd be turned (*trying
to rush at him again*), with a lie in his mouth and treachery in his
heart, and another man's wife by his side, and he passing her off as
his own! Let me at him can't you.

(*Makes another rush, but is held back.*)

MAGISTRATE (*pointing to Jack Smith*). Policeman, put the hand-cuffs on this man. I see it all now. A case of false impersonation, a conspiracy to defeat the ends of justice. There was a case in the Andaman Islands, a murderer of the Mopsa tribe, a religious enthusiast——

POLICEMAN. So he might be, too.

MAGISTRATE. We must take both these men to the scene of the murder. We must confront them with the body of the real Jack Smith.

JACK SMITH. I'll break the head of any man that will find my dead body!

MAGISTRATE. I'll call more help from the barracks. (*Blows Policeman's whistle.*)

BARTLEY. It is what I am thinking, if myself and Jack Smith are put together in the one cell for the night, the handcuffs will be taken off him, and his hands will be free, and murder will be done that time surely!

MAGISTRATE. Come on! (*They turn to the right.*)

Curtain.

The earliest printings of this play left the last word to Mrs. Tarpey. The two of them in charge now, and a great troop of people going by from the fair. Come up here the whole of you! It would be a pity you to be passing, and I not to be spreading the news!

HYACINTH HALVEY

HYACINTH HALVEY

PERSONS:
HYACINTH HALVEY
JAMES QUIRKE, *a butcher*
FARDY FARRELL, *a telegraph boy*
SERGEANT CARDEN
MRS. DELANE, *Postmistress at Cloon*
MISS JOYCE, *the Priest's House-keeper*

SCENE: *Outside the Post Office at the little town of Cloon. MRS. DELANE at Post Office door. MR. QUIRKE sitting on a chair at butcher's door. A dead sheep hanging beside it, and a thrush in a cage above. FARDY FARRELL playing on mouth organ. Train whistle heard.*

MRS. DELANE. There is the four o'clock train, Mr. Quirke.

MR. QUIRKE. Is it now, Mrs. Delane, and I not long after rising? It makes a man drowsy to be doing the half of his work in the night time. Going about the country, looking for little stags of sheep, striving to knock a few shillings together. That contract for the soldiers gives me a great deal to attend to.

MRS. DELANE. I suppose so. It's hard enough on myself to be down ready for the mail car in the morning, sorting letters in the half dark. It's often I haven't time to look who are the letters from —or the cards.

MR. QUIRKE. It would be a pity you not to know any little news might be knocking about. If you did not have information of what is going on who should have it? Was it you, ma'am, was telling me that the new Sub-Sanitary Inspector would be arriving to-day?

MRS. DELANE. To-day it is he is coming, and it's likely he was in that train. There was a card about him to Sergeant Carden this morning.

MR. QUIRKE. A young chap from Carrow they were saying he was.

MRS. DELANE. So he is, one Hyacinth Halvey; and indeed if all that is said of him is true, or if a quarter of it is true, he will be a credit to this town.

33

MR. QUIRKE. Is that so?

MRS. DELANE. Testimonials he has by the score. To Father Gregan they were sent. Registered they were coming and going. Would you believe me telling you that they weighed up to three pounds?

MR. QUIRKE. There must be great bulk in them indeed.

MRS. DELANE. It is no wonder he to get the job. He must have a great character so many persons to write for him as what there did.

FARDY. It would be a great thing to have a character like that.

MRS. DELANE. Indeed I am thinking it will be long before you will get the like of it, Fardy Farrell.

FARDY. If I had the like of that character it is not here carrying messages I would be. It's in Noonan's Hotel I would be, driving cars.

MR. QUIRKE. Here is the priest's housekeeper coming.

MRS. DELANE. So she is; and there is the Sergeant a little while after her.

(*Enter Miss Joyce.*)

MRS. DELANE. Good-evening to you, Miss Joyce. What way is his Reverence to-day? Did he get any ease from the cough?

MISS JOYCE. He did not indeed, Mrs. Delane. He has it sticking to him yet. Smothering he is in the night time. The most thing he comes short in is the voice.

MRS. DELANE. I am sorry, now, to hear that. He should mind himself well.

MISS JOYCE. It's easy to say let him mind himself. What do you say to him going to the meeting to-night? (*Sergeant comes in.*) It's for his Reverence's *Freeman* I am come, Mrs. Delane.

MRS. DELANE. Here it is ready. I was just throwing an eye on it to see was there any news. Good-evening, Sergeant.

SERGEANT (*holding up a placard*). I brought this notice, Mrs. Delane, the announcement of the meeting to be held to-night in the Courthouse. You might put it up here convenient to the window. I hope you are coming to it yourself?

MRS. DELANE. I will come, and welcome. I would do more than that for you, Sergeant.

SERGEANT. And you, Mr. Quirke.

MR. QUIRKE. I'll come, to be sure. I forget what's this the meeting is about.

SERGEANT. The Department of Agriculture is sending round a lecturer in furtherance of the moral development of the rural

34

classes. (*Reads.*) "A lecture will be given this evening in Cloon Courthouse, illustrated by magic lantern slides—" Those will not be in it; I am informed they were all broken in the first journey, the railway company taking them to be eggs. The subject of the lecture is "The Building of Character."

MRS. DELANE. Very nice, indeed. I knew a girl lost her character, and she washed her feet in a blessed well after, and it dried up on the minute.

SERGEANT. The arrangements have all been left to me, the Archdeacon being away. He knows I have a good intellect for things of the sort. But the loss of those slides puts a man out. The thing people will not see it is not likely it is the thing they will believe. I saw what they call tableaux—standing pictures, you know—one time in Dundrum——

MRS. DELANE. Miss Joyce was saying Father Gregan is supporting you.

SERGEANT. I am accepting his assistance. No bigotry about me when there is a question of the welfare of any fellow-creatures. Orange and green will stand together to-night. I myself and the station-master on the one side; your parish priest in the chair.

MISS JOYCE. If his Reverence would mind me he would not quit the house to-night. He is no more fit to go speak at a meeting than (*pointing to the one hanging outside Quirke's door*) that sheep.

SERGEANT. I am willing to take the responsibility. He will have no speaking to do at all, unless it might be to bid them give the lecturer a hearing. The loss of those slides now is a great annoyance to me—and no time for anything. The lecturer will be coming by the next train.

MISS JOYCE. Who is this coming up the street, Mrs. Delane?

MRS. DELANE. I wouldn't doubt it to be the new Sub-Sanitary Inspector. Was I telling you of the weight of the testimonials he got, Miss Joyce?

MISS JOYCE. Sure I heard the curate reading them to his Reverence. He must be a wonder for principles.

MRS. DELANE. Indeed it is what I was saying to myself, he must be a very saintly young man.

(*Enter Hyacinth Halvey. He carries a small bag and a large brown paper parcel. He stops and nods bashfully.*)

HYACINTH. Good-evening to you. I was bid to come to the post office——

SERGEANT. I suppose you are Hyacinth Halvey? I had a letter about you from the Resident Magistrate.

HYACINTH. I heard he was writing. It was my mother got a friend he deals with to ask him.

SERGEANT. He gives you a very high character.

HYACINTH. It is very kind of him indeed, and he not knowing me at all. But indeed all the neighbours were very friendly. Anything any one could do to help me they did it.

MRS. DELANE. I'll engage it is the testimonials you have in your parcel? I know the wrapping paper, but they grew in bulk since I handled them.

HYACINTH. Indeed I was getting them to the last. There was not one refused me. It is what my mother was saying, a good character is no burden.

FARDY. I would believe that indeed.

SERGEANT. Let us have a look at the testimonials. (*Hyacinth Halvey opens parcel, and a large number of envelopes fall out.*)

SERGEANT (*opening and reading one by one*). "He possesses the fire of the Gael, the strength of the Norman, the vigour of the Dane, the stolidity of the Saxon"——

HYACINTH. It was the Chairman of the Poor Law Guardians wrote that.

SERGEANT. "A magnificent example to old and young"——

HYACINTH. That was the Secretary of the De Wet Hurling Club——

SERGEANT. "A shining example of the value conferred by an eminently careful and high class education"——

HYACINTH. That was the National Schoolmaster.

SERGEANT. "Devoted to the highest ideals of his Mother-land to such an extent as is compatible with a hitherto non-parliamentary career"——

HYACINTH. That was the Member for Carrow.

SERGEANT. "A splendid exponent of the purity of the race"——

HYACINTH. The Editor of the *Carrow Champion.*

SERGEANT. "Admirably adapted for the efficient discharge of all possible duties that may in future be laid upon him"——

HYACINTH. The new Station-master.

SERGEANT. "A champion of every cause that can legitimately benefit his fellow-creatures"—— Why, look here, my man, you are the very one to come to our assistance to-night.

HYACINTH. I would be glad to do that. What way can I do it?

SERGEANT. You are a newcomer—your example would carry

36

weight—you must stand up as a living proof of the beneficial effect of a high character, moral fibre, temperance—there is something about it here I am sure—(*Looks.*) I am sure I saw "unparalleled temperance" in some place——

HYACINTH. It was my mother's cousin wrote that—I am no drinker, but I haven't the pledge taken——

SERGEANT. You might take it for the purpose.

MR. QUIRKE (*eagerly*). Here is an anti-treating button. I was made a present of it by one of my customers—I'll give it to you (*sticks it in Hyacinth's coat*) and welcome.

SERGEANT. That is it. You can wear the button on the platform —or a bit of blue ribbon—hundreds will follow your example—I know the boys from the Workhouse will——

HYACINTH. I am in no way wishful to be an example——

SERGEANT. I will read extracts from the testimonials. "There he is," I will say, "an example of one in early life who by his own unaided efforts and his high character has obtained a profitable situation"—(*Slaps his side.*) I know what I'll do. I'll engage a few corner-boys from Noonan's bar, just as they are, greasy and sodden, to stand in a group—there will be the contrast—The sight will deter others from a similar fate—That's the way to do a tableau —I knew I could turn out a success.

HYACINTH. I wouldn't like to be a contrast——

SERGEANT (*puts testimonials in his pocket*). I will go now and engage those lads—sixpence each, and well worth it—Nothing like an example for the rural classes.

(*Goes off, Hyacinth feebly trying to detain him.*)

MRS. DELANE. A very nice man indeed. A little high up in himself, may be. I'm not one that blames the police. Sure they have their own bread to earn like every other one. And indeed it is often they will let a thing pass.

MR. QUIRKE (*gloomily*). Sometimes they will, and more times they will not.

MISS JOYCE. And where will you be finding a lodging, Mr. Halvey?

HYACINTH. I was going to ask that myself, ma'am. I don't know the town.

MISS JOYCE. I know of a good lodging, but it is only a very good man would be taken into it.

MRS. DELANE. Sure there could be no objection there to Mr. Halvey. There is no appearance on him but what is good, and the Sergeant after taking him up the way he is doing.

37

MISS JOYCE. You will be near to the Sergeant in the lodging I speak of. The house is convenient to the barracks.

HYACINTH (*doubtfully*). To the barracks?

MISS JOYCE. Alongside of it and the barrack yard behind. And that's not all. It is opposite to the priest's house.

HYACINTH. Opposite, is it?

MISS JOYCE. A very respectable place, indeed, and a very clean room you will get. I know it well. The curate can see into it from his window.

HYACINTH. Can he now?

FARDY. There was a good many, I am thinking, went into that lodging and left it after.

MISS JOYCE (*sharply*). It is a lodging you will never be let into or let stop in, Fardy. If they did go they were a good riddance.

FARDY. John Hart, the plumber, left it——

MISS JOYCE. If he did it was because he dared not pass the police coming in, as he used, with a rabbit he was after snaring in his hand.

FARDY. The schoolmaster himself left it.

MISS JOYCE. He needn't have left it if he hadn't taken to card-playing. What way could you say your prayers, and shadows shuffling and dealing before you on the blind?

HYACINTH. I think maybe I'd best look around a bit before I'll settle in a lodging——

MISS JOYCE. Not at all. *You* won't be wanting to pull down the blind.

MRS. DELANE. It is not likely *you* will be snaring rabbits.

MISS JOYCE. Or bringing in a bottle and taking an odd glass the way James Kelly did.

MRS. DELANE. Or writing threatening notices, and the police taking a view of you from the rear.

MISS JOYCE. Or going to roadside dances, or running after good-for-nothing young girls——

HYACINTH. I give you my word I'm not so harmless as you think.

MRS. DELANE. Would you be putting a lie on these, Mr. Halvey? (*Touching testimonials.*) I know well the way *you* will be spending the evenings, writing letters to your relations——

MISS JOYCE. Learning O'Growney's exercises——

MRS. DELANE. Sticking post cards in an album for the convent bazaar.

MISS JOYCE. Reading the *Catholic Young Man*——

38

MRS. DELANE. Playing the melodies on a melodeon——

MISS JOYCE. Looking at the pictures in the *Lives of the Saints*. I'll hurry on and engage the room for you.

HYACINTH. Wait. Wait a minute——

MISS JOYCE. No trouble at all. I told you it was just opposite. (*Goes.*)

MR. QUIRKE. I suppose I must go upstairs and ready myself for the meeting. If it wasn't for the contract I have for the soldiers' barracks and the Sergeant's good word, I wouldn't go anear it (*Goes into shop.*)

MRS. DELANE. I should be making myself ready too. I must be in good time to see you being made an example of, Mr. Halvey. It is I myself was the first to say it; you will be a credit to the town. (*Goes.*)

HYACINTH (*in a tone of agony*). I wish I had never seen Cloon.

FARDY. What is on you?

HYACINTH. I wish I had never left Carrow. I wish I had been drowned the first day I thought of it, and I'd be better off.

FARDY. What is it ails you?

HYACINTH. I wouldn't for the best pound ever I had be in this place to-day.

FARDY. I don't know what you are talking about.

HYACINTH. To have left Carrow, if it was a poor place, where I had my comrades, and an odd spree, and a game of cards—and a coursing match coming on, and I promised a new greyhound from the city of Cork. I'll die in this place, the way I am. I'll be too much closed in.

FARDY. Sure it mightn't be as bad as what you think.

HYACINTH. Will you tell me, I ask you, what way can I undo it?

FARDY. What is it you are wanting to undo?

HYACINTH. Will you tell me what way can I get rid of my character?

FARDY. To get rid of it, is it?

HYACINTH. That is what I said. Aren't you after hearing the great character they are after putting on me?

FARDY. That is a good thing to have.

HYACINTH. It is not. It's the worst in the world. If I hadn't it, I wouldn't be like a prize mangold at a show with every person praising me.

FARDY. If I had it, I wouldn't be like a head in a barrel, with every person making hits at me.

39

HYACINTH. If I hadn't it, I wouldn't be shoved into a room with all the clergy watching me and the police in the back yard.

FARDY. If I had it, I wouldn't be but a message-carrier now, and a clapper scaring birds in the summer time.

HYACINTH. If I hadn't it, I wouldn't be wearing this button and brought up for an example at the meeting.

FARDY (*whistles*). Maybe you're not, so, what those papers make you out to be?

HYACINTH. How would I be what they make me out to be? Was there ever any person of that sort since the world was a world, unless it might be Saint Antony of Padua looking down from the chapel wall? If it is like that I was, isn't it in Mount Melleray I would be, or with the Friars at Esker? Why would I be living in the world at all, or doing the world's work?

FARDY (*taking up parcel*). Who would think, now, there would be so much lies in a small place like Carrow?

HYACINTH. It was my mother's cousin did it. He said I was not reared for labouring—he gave me a new suit and bid me never to come back again. I daren't go back to face him—the neighbours knew my mother had a long family—bad luck to them the day they gave me these. (*Tears letters and scatters them.*) I'm done with testimonials. They won't be here to bear witness against me.

FARDY. The Sergeant thought them to be great. Sure he has the samples of them in his pocket. There's not one in the town but will know before morning that you are the next thing to an earthly saint.

HYACINTH (*stamping*). I'll stop their mouths. I'll show them I can be a terror for badness. I'll do some injury. I'll commit some crime. The first thing I'll do I'll go and get drunk. If I never did it before I'll do it now. I'll get drunk—then I'll make an assault—I tell you I'd think as little of taking a life as of blowing out a candle.

FARDY. If you get drunk you are done for. Sure that will be held up after as an excuse for any breaking of the law.

HYACINTH. I will break the law. Drunk or sober I'll break it. I'll do something that will have no excuse. What would you say is the worst crime that any man can do?

FARDY. I don't know. I heard the Sergeant saying one time it was to obstruct the police in the discharge of their duty——

HYACINTH. That won't do. It's a patriot I would be then, worse than before, with my picture in the weeklies. It's a red crime I must commit that will make all respectable people quit minding me. What can I do? Search your mind now.

40

FARDY. It's what I heard the old people saying there could be no worse crime than to steal a sheep——

HYACINTH. I'll steal a sheep—or a cow—or a horse—if that will leave me the way I was before.

FARDY. It's maybe in gaol it will leave you.

HYACINTH. I don't care—I'll confess—I'll tell why I did it—I give you my word I would as soon be picking oakum or breaking stones as to be perched in the daylight the same as that bird, and all the town chirruping to me or bidding me chirrup——

FARDY. There is reason in that, now.

HYACINTH. Help me, will you?

FARDY. Well, if it is to steal a sheep you want, you haven't far to go.

HYACINTH (*looking round wildly*). Where is it? I see no sheep.

FARDY. Look around you.

HYACINTH. I see no living thing but that thrush——

FARDY. Did I say it was living? What is that hanging on Quirke's rack?

HYACINTH. It's (*fingers it*) a sheep, sure enough——

FARDY. Well, what ails you that you can't bring it away?

HYACINTH. It's a dead one——

FARDY. What matter if it is?

HYACINTH. If it was living I could drive it before me——

FARDY. You could. Is it to your own lodging you would drive it? Sure everyone would take it to be a pet you brought from Carrow?

HYACINTH. I suppose they might.

FARDY. Miss Joyce sending in for news of it and it bleating behind the bed.

HYACINTH (*distracted*). Stop! stop!

MRS. DELANE (*from upper window*). Fardy! Are you there, Fardy Farrell?

FARDY. I am, ma'am.

MRS. DELANE (*from window*). Look and tell me is that the telegraph I hear ticking?

FARDY (*looking in at door*). It is, ma'am.

MRS. DELANE. Then botheration to it, and I not dressed or undressed. Wouldn't you say, now, it's to annoy me it is calling me down. I'm coming! I'm coming! (*Disappears.*)

FARDY. Hurry on, now! hurry! She'll be coming out on you. If you are going to do it, do it, and if you are not, let it alone.

HYACINTH. I'll do it! I'll do it!

41

FARDY (*lifting the sheep on his back*). I'll give you a hand with it.

HYACINTH (*goes a step or two and turns round*). You told me no place where I could hide it.

FARDY. You needn't go far. There is the church beyond at the side of the Square. Go round to the ditch behind the wall—there's nettles in it.

HYACINTH. That'll do.

FARDY. She's coming out—run! run!

HYACINTH (*runs a step or two*). It's slipping!

FARDY. Hoist it up! I'll give it a hoist! (*Halvey runs out.*)

MRS. DELANE (*calling out*). What are you doing Fardy Farrell? Is it idling you are?

FARDY. Waiting I am, ma'am, for the message——

MRS. DELANE. Never mind the message yet. Who said it was ready? (*Going to door.*) Go ask for the loan of—no, but ask news of—Here, now go bring that bag of Mr. Halvey's to the lodging Miss Joyce has taken——

FARDY. I will, ma'am. (*Takes bag and goes out.*)

MRS. DELANE (*coming out with a telegram in her hand*). Nobody here? (*Looks round and calls cautiously.*) Mr. Quirke! Mr. Quirke! James Quirke!

MR. QUIRKE (*looking out of his upper window with soap-suddy face*). What is it, Mrs. Delane?

MRS. DELANE (*beckoning*). Come down here till I tell you.

MR. QUIRKE. I cannot do that. I'm not fully shaved.

MRS. DELANE. You'd come if you knew the news I have.

MR. QUIRKE. Tell it to me now. I'm not so supple as I was.

MRS. DELANE. Whisper now, have you an enemy in any place?

MR. QUIRKE. It's likely I may have. A man in business——

MRS. DELANE. I was thinking you had one.

MR. QUIRKE. Why would you think that at this time more than any other time?

MRS. DELANE. If you could know what is in this envelope you would know that, James Quirke.

MR. QUIRKE. Is that so? And what, now, is there in it?

MRS. DELANE. Who do you think now is it addressed to?

MR. QUIRKE. How would I know that, and I not seeing it?

MRS. DELANE. That is true. Well, it is a message from Dublin Castle to the Sergeant of Police!

MR. QUIRKE. To Sergeant Carden, is it?

MRS. DELANE. It is. And it concerns yourself.

MR. QUIRKE. Myself, is it? What accusation can they be bringing against me? I'm a peaceable man.

MRS. DELANE. Wait till you hear.

MR. QUIRKE. Maybe they think I was in that moonlighting case——

MRS. DELANE. That is not it——

MR. QUIRKE. I was not in it—I was but in the neighbouring field —cutting up a dead cow, that those never had a hand in——

MRS. DELANE. You're out of it——

MR. QUIRKE. They had their faces blackened. There is no man can say I recognized them.

MRS. DELANE. That's not what they're saying——

MR. QUIRKE. I'll swear I did not hear their voices or know them if I did hear them.

MRS. DELANE. I tell you it has nothing to do with that. It might be better for you if it had.

MR. QUIRKE. What is it, so?

MRS. DELANE. It is an order to the Sergeant bidding him immediately to seize all suspicious meat in your house. There is an officer coming down. There are complaints from the Shannon Fort Barracks.

MR. QUIRKE. I'll engage it was that pork.

MRS. DELANE. What ailed it for them to find fault?

MR. QUIRKE. People are so hard to please nowadays, and I recommended them to salt it.

MRS. DELANE. They had a right to have minded your advice.

MR. QUIRKE. There was nothing on that pig at all but that it went mad on poor O'Grady that owned it.

MRS. DELANE. So I heard, and went killing all before it.

MR. QUIRKE. Sure it's only in the brain madness can be. I heard the doctor saying that.

MRS. DELANE. He should know.

MR. QUIRKE. I give you my word I cut the head off it. I went to the loss of it, throwing it to the eels in the river. If they had salted the meat, as I advised them, what harm would it have done to any person on earth?

MRS. DELANE. I hope no harm will come on poor Mrs. Quirke and the family.

MR. QUIRKE. Maybe it wasn't that but some other thing——

MRS. DELANE. Here is Fardy. I must send the message to the Sergeant. Well, Mr. Quirke, I'm glad I had the time to give you a warning.

43

MR. QUIRKE. I'm obliged to you, indeed. You were always very neighbourly, Mrs. Delane. Don't be too quick now sending the message. There is just one article I would like to put away out of the house before the Sergeant will come. (*Enter Fardy.*)

MRS. DELANE. Here now, Fardy—that's not the way you're going to the barracks. Anyone would think you were scaring birds yet. Put on your uniform (*Fardy goes into office.*) You have this message to bring to the Sergeant of Police. Get your cap now, it's under the counter.

(*Fardy reappears, and she gives him telegram.*)

FARDY. I'll bring it to the station. It's there he was going.

MRS. DELANE. You will not, but to the barracks. It can wait for him there.

(*Fardy goes off. Mr. Quirke has appeared at door.*)

MR. QUIRKE. It was indeed a very neighbourly act, Mrs. Delane, and I'm obliged to you. There is just *one* article to put out of the way. The Sergeant may look about him then and welcome. It's well I cleared the premises on yesterday. A consignment to Birmingham I sent. The Lord be praised isn't England a terrible country with all it consumes?

MRS. DELANE. Indeed you always treat the neighbours very decent, Mr. Quirke, not asking them to buy from you.

MR. QUIRKE. Just one article. (*Turns to rack.*) That sheep I brought in last night. It was for a charity indeed I bought it from the widow woman at Kiltartan Cross. Where would the poor make a profit out of their dead meat without me? Where now is it? Well, now, I could have swore that that sheep was hanging there on the rack when I went in——

MRS. DELANE. You must have put it in some other place.

MR. QUIRKE (*going in and searching and coming out*). I did not; there is no other place for me to put it. Is it gone blind I am, or is it not in it, it is?

MRS. DELANE. It's not there now anyway.

MR. QUIRKE. Didn't you take notice of it there yourself this morning?

MRS. DELANE. I have it in my mind that I did; but it's not there now.

MR. QUIRKE. There was no one here could bring it away?

MRS. DELANE. Is it me myself you suspect of taking it, James Quirke?

MR. QUIRKE. Where is it at all? It is certain it was not of itself it walked away. It was dead, and very dead, the time I bought it.

44

MRS. DELANE. I have a pleasant neighbour indeed that accuses me that I took his sheep. I wonder, indeed, you to say a thing like that! I to steal your sheep or your rack or anything that belongs to you or to your trade! Thank you, James Quirke. I am much obliged to you indeed.

MR. QUIRKE. Ah, be quiet woman; be quiet——

MRS. DELANE. And let me tell you, James Quirke, that I would sooner starve and see everyone belonging to me starve than to eat the size of a thimble of any joint that ever was on your rack or that ever will be on it, whatever the soldiers may eat that have no other thing to get, or the English that devour all sorts, or the poor ravenous people that's down by the sea! (*She turns to go into shop.*)

MR. QUIRKE (*stopping her*). Don't be talking foolishness, woman. Who said you took my meat? Give heed to me now. There must some other message have come. The Sergeant must have got some other message.

MRS. DELANE (*sulkily*). If there is any way for a message to come that is quicker than to come by the wires, tell me what it is and I'll be obliged to you.

MR. QUIRKE. The Sergeant was up here making an excuse he was sticking up that notice. What was he doing here, I ask you?

MRS. DELANE. How would I know what brought him?

MR. QUIRKE. It is what he did; he made as if to go away—he turned back again and I shaving—he brought away the sheep—he will have it for evidence against me——

MRS. DELANE (*interested*). That might be so.

MR. QUIRKE. I would sooner it to have been any other beast nearly ever I had upon the rack.

MRS. DELANE. Is that so?

MR. QUIRKE. I bade the Widow Early to kill it a fortnight ago—but she would not, she was that covetous!

MRS. DELANE. What was on it?

MR. QUIRKE. How would I know what was on it? Whatever was on it, it was the will of God put it upon it—wasted it was, and shivering and refusing its share.

MRS. DELANE. The poor thing.

MR. QUIRKE. Gone all to nothing—wore away like a flock of thread. It did not weigh as much as a lamb of two months.

MRS. DELANE. It is likely the Inspector will bring it to Dublin?

MR. QUIRKE. The ribs of it streaky with the dint of patent medicines——

MRS. DELANE. I wonder is it to the Petty Sessions you'll be brought or is it to the Assizes?

MR. QUIRKE. I'll speak up to them. I'll make my defence. What can the Army expect at fippence a pound?

MRS. DELANE. It is likely there will be no bail allowed?

MR. QUIRKE. Would they be wanting me to give them good quality meat out of my own pocket? Is it to encourage them to fight the poor Indians and Africans they would have me? It's the Anti-Enlisting Societies should pay the fine for me.

MRS. DELANE. It's not a fine will be put on you, I'm afraid. It's five years in gaol you will be apt to be getting. Well, I'll try and be a good neighbour to poor Mrs. Quirke.

(MR. QUIRKE, *who has been stamping up and down, sits down and weeps.* HALVEY *comes in and stands on one side.*)

MR. QUIRKE. Hadn't I heart-scalding enough before, striving to rear five weak children?

MRS. DELANE. I suppose they will be sent to the Industrial Schools?

MR. QUIRKE. My poor wife——

MRS. DELANE. I'm afraid the workhouse——

MR. QUIRKE. And she out in an ass-car at this minute helping me to follow my trade.

MRS. DELANE. I hope they will not arrest her along with you.

MR. QUIRKE. I'll give myself up to justice. I'll plead guilty! I'll be recommended to mercy!

MRS. DELANE. It might be best for you.

MR. QUIRKE. Who would think so great a misfortune could come upon a family through the bringing away of one sheep!

HYACINTH (*coming forward*). Let you make yourself easy.

MR. QUIRKE. Easy! It's easy to say let you make yourself easy.

HYACINTH. I can tell you where it is.

MR. QUIRKE. Where what is?

HYACINTH. The sheep you are fretting after.

MR. QUIRKE. What do you know about it?

HYACINTH. I know everything about it.

MR. QUIRKE. I suppose the Sergeant told you?

HYACINTH. He told me nothing.

MR. QUIRKE. I suppose the whole town knows it, so?

HYACINTH. No one knows it, as yet.

MR. QUIRKE. And the Sergeant didn't see it?

HYACINTH. No one saw it or brought it away but myself.

MR. QUIRKE. Where did you put it at all?

HYACINTH. In the ditch behind the church wall. In among the nettles it is. Look at the way they have me stung. (*Holds out hands.*)

MR. QUIRKE. In the ditch! The best hiding place in the town.

HYACINTH. I never thought it would bring such great trouble upon you. You can't say anyway I did not tell you.

MR. QUIRKE. You yourself that brought it away and that hid it! I suppose it was coming in the train you got information about the message to the police.

HYACINTH. What now do you say to me?

MR. QUIRKE. Say! I say I am as glad to hear what you said as if it was the Lord telling me I'd be in heaven this minute.

HYACINTH. What are you going to do to me?

MR. QUIRKE. Do, is it? (*Grasps his hand.*) Any earthly thing you would wish me to do. I will do it.

HYACINTH. I suppose you will tell——

MR. QUIRKE. Tell! It's I that will tell when all is quiet. It is I will give you the good name through the town!

HYACINTH. I don't well understand.

MR. QUIRKE (*embracing him*). The man that preserved me!

HYACINTH. That preserved you?

MR. QUIRKE. That kept me from ruin!

HYACINTH. From ruin?

MR. QUIRKE. That saved me from disgrace!

HYACINTH (*to* MRS. DELANE). What is he saying at all?

MR. QUIRKE. From the Inspector!

HYACINTH. What is he talking about?

MR. QUIRKE. From the magistrates!

HYACINTH. He is making some mistake.

MR. QUIRKE. From the Winter Assizes!

HYACINTH. Is he out of his wits?

MR. QUIRKE. Five years in gaol!

HYACINTH. Hasn't he the queer talk?

MR. QUIRKE. The loss of the contract!

HYACINTH. Are my own wits gone astray?

MR. QUIRKE. What way can I repay you?

HYACINTH (*shouting*). I tell you I took the sheep——

MR. QUIRKE. You did, God reward you!

HYACINTH. I stole away with it——

MR. QUIRKE. The blessing of the poor on you!

HYACINTH. I put it out of sight——

MR. QUIRKE. The blessing of my five children——

HYACINTH. I may as well say nothing——

MRS. DELANE. Let you be quiet now, Quirke. Here's the Sergeant coming to search the shop——

(SERGEANT *comes in:* QUIRKE *leaves go of* HALVEY, *who arranges his hat, etc.*)

SERGEANT. The Department to blazes!

MRS. DELANE. What is it is putting you out?

SERGEANT. To go to the train to meet the lecturer, and there to get a message through the guard that he was unavoidably detained in the South, holding an inquest on the remains of a drake.

MRS. DELANE. The lecturer, is it?

SERGEANT. To be sure. What else would I be talking of? The lecturer has failed me, and where am I to go looking for a person that I would think fitting to take his place?

MRS. DELANE. And that's all? And you didn't get any message but the one?

SERGEANT. Is that all? I am surprised at you, Mrs. Delane. Isn't it enough to upset a man, within three quarters of an hour of the time of the meeting? Where, I would ask you, am I to find a man that has education enough and wit enough and character enough to put up speaking on the platform on the minute?

MR. QUIRKE (*jumps up*). It is I myself will tell you that.

SERGEANT. You!

MR. QUIRKE (*slapping* HALVEY *on the back*). Look at here, Sergeant. There is not one word was said in all those papers about this young man before you but it is true. And there could be no good thing said of him that would be too good for him.

SERGEANT. It might not be a bad idea.

MR. QUIRKE. Whatever the paper said about him, Sergeant, I can say more again. It has come to my knowledge—by chance—that since he came to this town that young man has saved a whole family from destruction.

SERGEANT. That is much to his credit—helping the rural classes——

MR. QUIRKE. A family and a long family, big and little, like sods of turf—and they depending on a—on one that might be on his way to dark trouble at this minute if it was not for his assistance. Believe me, he is the most sensible man, and the wittiest, and the kindest, and the best helper of the poor that ever stood before you in this square. Is not that so, Mrs. Delane?

MRS. DELANE. It is true indeed. Where he gets his wisdom and his wit and his information from I don't know, unless it might be that he is gifted from above.

SERGEANT. Well, Mrs. Delane, I think we have settled that question. Mr. Halvey, you will be the speaker at the meeting. The lecturer sent these notes—you can lengthen them into a speech. You can call to the people of Cloon to stand out, to begin the building of their character. I saw a lecturer do it one time at Dundrum. "Come up here," he said, "Dare to be a Daniel," he said——

HYACINTH. I can't—I won't——

SERGEANT (*looking at papers and thrusting them into his hand*). You will find it quite easy. I will conduct you to the platform— these papers before you and a glass of water—That's settled. (*Turns to go.*) Follow me on to the Courthouse in half an hour— I must go to the barracks first—I heard there was a telegram—— (*Calls back as he goes*) Don't be late, Mrs. Delane. Mind, Quirke, you promised to come.

MRS. DELANE. Well, it's time for me to make an end of settling myself—and indeed, Mr. Quirke, you'd best do the same.

MR. QUIRKE (*rubbing his cheek*). I suppose so. I had best keep on good terms with him for the present. (*Turns.*) Well, now, I had a great escape this day.

(*Both go in as* FARDY *reappears whistling.*)

HYACINTH (*sitting down*). I don't know in the world what has come upon the world that the half of the people of it should be cracked!

FARDY. Weren't you found out yet?

HYACINTH. Found out, is it? I don't know what you mean by being found out.

FARDY. Didn't he miss the sheep?

HYACINTH. He did, and I told him it was I took it—and what happened I declare to goodness I don't know—— Will you look at these? (*Holds out notes.*)

FARDY. Papers! Are they more testimonials?

HYACINTH. They are what is worse. (*Gives a hoarse laugh.*) Will you come and see me on the platform—these in my hand—and I speaking—giving out advice. (FARDY *whistles.*) Why didn't you tell me, the time you advised me to steal a sheep, that in this town it would qualify a man to go preaching, and the priest in the chair looking on.

FARDY. The time I took a few apples that had fallen off a stall, they did not ask me to hold a meeting. They welted me well.

HYACINTH (*looking round*). I would take apples if I could see them. I wish I had broke my neck before I left Carrow and I'd be

49

better off! I wish I had got six months the time I was caught setting snares—I wish I had robbed a church.

FARDY. Would a Protestant church do?

HYACINTH. I suppose it wouldn't be so great a sin.

FARDY. It's likely the Sergeant would think worse of it—Anyway, if you want to rob one, it's the Protestant church is the handiest.

HYACINTH (*getting up*). Show me what way to do it?

FARDY (*pointing*). I was going around it a few minutes ago, to see might there be e'er a dog scenting the sheep, and I noticed the window being out.

HYACINTH. Out, out and out?

FARDY. It was, where they are putting coloured glass in it for the distiller——

HYACINTH. What good does that do me?

FARDY. Every good. You could go in by that window if you had some person to give you a hoist. Whatever riches there is to get in it then, you'll get them.

HYACINTH. I don't want riches. I'll give you all I will find if you come and hoist me.

FARDY. Here is Miss Joyce coming to bring you to your lodging. Sure I brought your bag to it, the time you were away with the sheep——

HYACINTH. Run! Run!

(*They go off. Enter* MISS JOYCE.)

MISS JOYCE. Are you here, Mrs. Delane? Where, can you tell me, is Mr. Halvey?

MRS. DELANE (*coming out dressed*). It's likely he is gone on to the Courthouse. Did you hear he is to be in the chair and to make an address to the meeting?

MISS JOYCE. He is getting on fast. His Reverence says he will be a good help in the parish. Who would think, now, there would be such a godly young man in a little place like Carrow!

(*Enter* SERGEANT *in a hurry, with telegram.*)

SERGEANT. What time did this telegram arrive, Mrs. Delane?

MRS. DELANE. I couldn't be rightly sure, Sergeant. But sure it's marked on it, unless the clock I have is gone wrong.

SERGEANT. It is marked on it. And I have the time I got it marked on my own watch.

MRS. DELANE. Well, now, I wonder none of the police would have followed you with it from the barracks—and they with so little to do——

SERGEANT (*looking in at Quirke's shop*). Well, I am sorry to do what I have to do, but duty is duty.

(*He ransacks shop.* MRS. DELANE *looks on.* MR. QUIRKE *puts his head out of window.*)

MR. QUIRKE. What is that going on inside? (*No answer.*) Is there any one inside, I ask. (*No answer.*) It must be that dog of Tannian's —wait till I get at him.

MRS. DELANE. It is Sergeant Carden, Mr. Quirke. He would seem to be looking for something——

(MR. QUIRKE *appears in shop.* SERGEANT *comes out, makes another dive, taking up sacks, etc.*)

MR. QUIRKE. I'm greatly afraid I am just out of meat, Sergeant —and I'm sorry now to disoblige you, and you not being in the habit of dealing with me——

SERGEANT. I should think not, indeed.

MR. QUIRKE. Looking for a tender little bit of lamb, I suppose you are, for Mrs. Carden and the youngsters?

SERGEANT. I am not.

MR. QUIRKE. If I had it now, I'd be proud to offer it to you, and make no charge. I'll be killing a good kid to-morrow. Mrs. Carden might fancy a bit of it——

SERGEANT. I have had orders to search your establishment for unwholesome meat, and I am come here to do it.

MR. QUIRKE (*sitting down with a smile*). Is that so? Well, isn't it a wonder the schemers does be in the world.

SERGEANT. It is not the first time there have been complaints.

MR. QUIRKE. I suppose not. Well, it is on their own head it will fall at the last!

SERGEANT. I have found nothing so far.

MR. QUIRKE. I suppose not, indeed. What is there you could find, and it not in it?

SERGEANT. Have you no meat at all upon the premises?

MR. QUIRKE. I have, indeed, a nice barrel of bacon.

SERGEANT. What way did it die?

MR. QUIRKE. It would be hard for me to say that. American it is. How would I know what way they do be killing the pigs out there? Machinery, I suppose, they have—steam hammers——

SERGEANT. Is there nothing else here at all?

MR. QUIRKE. I give you my word, there is no meat living or dead in this place, but yourself and myself and that bird above in the cage.

SERGEANT. Well, I must tell the Inspector I could find nothing. But mind yourself for the future.

MR. QUIRKE. Thank you, Sergeant. I will do that. (*Enter* FARDY. *He stops short.*)

SERGEANT. It was you delayed that message to me, I suppose? You'd best mend your ways or I'll have something to say to you. (*Seizes and shakes him.*)

FARDY. That's the way everyone does be faulting me. (*Whimpers.*)

> (*The* SERGEANT *gives him another shake. A half-crown falls out of his pocket.*)

MISS JOYCE (*picking it up*). A half-a-crown! Where, now, did you get that much, Fardy?

FARDY. Where did I get it, is it!

MISS JOYCE. I'll engage it was in no honest way you got it.

FARDY. I picked it up in the street——

MISS JOYCE. If you did, why didn't you bring it to the Sergeant or to his Reverence?

MRS. DELANE. And some poor person, may be, being at the loss of it.

MISS JOYCE. I'd best bring it to his Reverence. Come with me, Fardy, till he will question you about it.

FARDY. It was not altogether in the street I found it——

MISS JOYCE. There, now! I knew you got it in no good way! Tell me, now.

FARDY. It was playing pitch and toss I won it——

MISS JOYCE. And who would play for half-crowns with the like of you, Fardy Farrell? Who was it, now?

FARDY. It was—a stranger——

MISS JOYCE. Do you hear that? A stranger! Did you see e'er a stranger in this town, Mrs. Delane, or Sergeant Carden, or Mr. Quirke?

MR. QUIRKE. Not a one.

SERGEANT. There was no stranger here.

MRS. DELANE. There could not be one here without me knowing it.

FARDY. I tell you there was.

MISS JOYCE. Come on, then, and tell who was he to his Reverence.

SERGEANT (*taking other arm*). Or to the bench.

FARDY. I did get it, I tell you, from a stranger.

SERGEANT. Where is he, so?

FARDY. He's in some place—not far away.

SERGEANT. Bring me to him.

FARDY. He'll be coming here.

SERGEANT. Tell me the truth and it will be better for you.

FARDY (*weeping*). Let me go and I will.

SERGEANT (*letting go*). Now—who did you get it from?

FARDY. From that young chap came to-day, Mr. Halvey.

ALL. Mr. Halvey!

MR. QUIRKE (*indignantly*). What are you saying, you young ruffian you? Hyacinth Halvey to be playing pitch and toss with the like of you!

FARDY. I didn't say that.

MISS JOYCE. You did say it. You said it now.

MR. QUIRKE. Hyacinth Halvey! The best man that ever came into this town!

MISS JOYCE. It's my belief the half-crown is a bad one. May be it's to pass it off it was given to him. There were tinkers in the town at the time of the fair. Give it here to me. (*Bites it.*) No, indeed, it's sound enough. Here, Sergeant, it's best for you take it.

(*Gives it to* SERGEANT, *who examines it.*)

SERGEANT. Can it be? Can it be what I think it to be?

MR. QUIRKE. What is it? What do you take it to be?

SERGEANT. It is, it is. I know it. I know this half-crown——

MR. QUIRKE. That is a queer thing, now.

SERGEANT. I know it well. I have been handling it in the church for the last twelvemonth——

MR. QUIRKE. Is that so?

SERGEANT. It is the nest-egg half-crown we hand round in the collection plate every Sunday morning. I know it by the dint on the Queen's temples and the crooked scratch under her nose.

MR. QUIRKE (*examining it*). So there is, too.

SERGEANT. This is a bad business. It has been stolen from the church.

ALL. O! O! O!

SERGEANT (*seizing* FARDY). You have robbed the church!

FARDY (*terrified*). I tell you I never did!

SERGEANT. I have the proof of it.

FARDY. Say what you like! I never put a foot in it!

SERGEANT. How did you get this, so?

MISS JOYCE. I suppose from the *stranger*?

MRS. DELANE. I suppose it was Hyacinth Halvey gave it to you, now.

FARDY. It was so.

SERGEANT. I suppose it was he robbed the church?

FARDY (*sobs*). You will not believe me if I say it.

MR. QUIRKE. O! the young vagabond! Let me get at him!

MRS. DELANE. Here he is himself now!

(HYACINTH *comes in.* FARDY *releases himself and creeps behind him.*)

MRS. DELANE. It is time you to come, Mr. Halvey, and shut the mouth of this young schemer.

MISS JOYCE. I would like you to hear what he says of you, Mr. Halvey. Pitch and toss, he says.

MR. QUIRKE. Robbery, he says.

MRS. DELANE. Robbery of a church.

SERGEANT. He has had a bad name long enough. Let him go to a reformatory now.

FARDY (*clinging to* HYACINTH). Save me, save me! I'm a poor boy trying to knock out a way of living; I'll be destroyed if I go to a reformatory. (*Kneels and clings to* HYACINTH'S *knees.*)

HYACINTH. I'll save you easy enough.

FARDY. Don't let me be gaoled!

HYACINTH. I am going to tell them.

FARDY. I'm a poor orphan——

HYACINTH. Will you let me speak?

FARDY. I'll get no more chance in the world——

HYACINTH. Sure I'm trying to free you——

FARDY. It will be tasked to me always.

HYACINTH. Be quiet, can't you.

FARDY. Don't you desert me!

HYACINTH. Will you be silent?

FARDY. Take it on yourself.

HYACINTH. I will if you'll let me.

FARDY. Tell them you did it.

HYACINTH. I am going to do that.

FARDY. Tell them it was you got in at the window.

HYACINTH. I will! I will!

FARDY. Say it was you robbed the box.

HYACINTH. I'll say it! I'll say it!

FARDY. It being open!

HYACINTH. Let me tell, let me tell.

FARDY. Of all that was in it.

HYACINTH. I'll tell them that.

FARDY. And gave it to me.

HYACINTH (*putting hand on his mouth and dragging him up*).
Will you stop and let me speak?

SERGEANT. We can't be wasting time. Give him here to me.

HYACINTH. I can't do that. He must be let alone.

SERGEANT (*seizing him*). He'll be let alone in the lock-up.

HYACINTH. He must not be brought there.

SERGEANT. I'll let no man get him off.

HYACINTH. I will get him off.

SERGEANT. You will not!

HYACINTH. I will.

SERGEANT. Do you think to buy him off?

HYACINTH. I will buy him off with my own confession.

SERGEANT. And what will that be?

HYACINTH. It was I robbed the church.

SERGEANT. That is likely indeed!

HYACINTH. Let him go, and take me. I tell you I did it.

SERGEANT. It would take witnesses to prove that.

HYACINTH (*pointing to* FARDY). He will be witness.

FARDY. O! Mr. Halvey, I would not wish to do that. Get me off
and I will say nothing.

HYACINTH. Sure you must. You will be put on oath in the court.

FARDY. I will not! I will not! All the world knows I don't understand the nature of an oath!

MR. QUIRKE (*coming forward*). Is it blind ye all are?

MRS. DELANE. What are you talking about?

MR. QUIRKE. Is it fools ye all are?

MISS JOYCE. Speak for yourself.

MR. QUIRKE. Is it idiots ye all are?

SERGEANT. Mind who you're talking to.

MR. QUIRKE (*seizing* HYACINTH'S *hands*). Can't you see? Can't
you hear? Where are your wits? Was ever such a thing seen in
this town?

MRS. DELANE. Say out what you have to say.

MR. QUIRKE. A walking saint he is!

MRS. DELANE. Maybe so.

MR. QUIRKE. The preserver of the poor! Talk of the holy
martyrs! They are nothing at all to what he is! Will you look at
him! To save that poor boy he is going! To take the blame on
himself he is going! To say he himself did the robbery he is going!
Before the magistrate he is going! To gaol he is going! Taking the
blame on his own head! Putting the sin on his own shoulders!
Letting on to have done a robbery! Telling a lie—that it may be

forgiven him—to his own injury! Doing all that I tell you to save the character of a miserable slack lad, that rose in poverty.

(*Murmur of admiration from* ALL.)

MR. QUIRKE. Now, what do you say?

SERGEANT (*pressing his hand*). Mr. Halvey, you have given us all a lesson. To please you, I will make no information against the boy. (*Shakes him and helps him up.*) I will put back the half-crown in the poor-box next Sunday. (*To* FARDY) What have you to say to your benefactor?

FARDY. I'm obliged to you, Mr. Halvey. You behaved very decent indeed. I'll never let a word be said against you if I live to be a hundred years.

SERGEANT (*wiping eyes with a blue handkerchief*). I will tell it at the meeting. It will be a great encouragement to them to build up their character. I'll tell it to the priest and he taking the chair——

HYACINTH. O stop, will you——

MR. QUIRKE. The chair. It's in the chair he himself should be. It's in a chair we will put him now. It's to chair him through the streets we will. Sure he'll be an example and a blessing to the whole of the town. (*Seizes* HALVEY *and seats him in chair.*) Now, Sergeant, give a hand. Here, Fardy.

(*They all lift the chair with* HALVEY *in it, wildly protesting.*)

MR. QUIRKE. Come along now to the Courthouse. Three cheers for Hyacinth Halvey! Hip! hip! hoora!

(*Cheers heard in the distance as the curtain drops.*)

Curtain.

THE RISING OF THE MOON

THE RISING OF THE MOON

PERSONS
    SERGEANT.
    POLICEMAN X.
    POLICEMAN B.
    A RAGGED MAN.

SCENE. *Side of a quay in a seaport town. Some posts and chains.*
A large barrel. Enter three policemen. Moonlight.
    (SERGEANT, *who is older than the others, crosses the stage to*
        right and looks down steps The others put down a pastepot
        and unroll a bundle of placards.)

POLICEMAN B. I think this would be a good place to put up a
notice. (*He points to barrel.*)
    POLICEMAN X. Better ask him. (*Calls to* SERGEANT) Will this be
a good place for a placard?
    (*No answer.*)
    POLICEMAN B. Will we put up a notice here on the barrel?
    (*No answer.*)
    SERGEANT. There's a flight of steps here that leads to the water.
This is a place that should be minded well. If he got down here, his
friends might have a boat to meet him; they might send it in here
from outside.
    POLICEMAN B. Would the barrel be a good place to put a notice
up?
    SERGEANT. It might; you can put it there.
    (*They paste the notice up.*)
    SERGEANT (*reading it*). Dark hair—dark eyes, smooth face,
height five feet five—there's not much to take hold of in that—It's
a pity I had no chance of seeing him before he broke out of gaol.
They say he's a wonder, that it's he makes all the plans for the
whole organization. There isn't another man in Ireland would have
broken gaol the way he did. He must have some friends among the
gaolers.
    POLICEMAN B. A hundred pounds is little enough for the

59

Government to offer for him. You may be sure any man in the force that takes him will get promotion.

SERGEANT. I'll mind this place myself. I wouldn't wonder at all if he came this way. He might come slipping along there (*points to side of quay*), and his friends might be waiting for him there (*points down steps*), and once he got away it's little chance we'd have of finding him; it's maybe under a load of kelp he'd be in a fishing boat, and not one to help a married man that wants it to the reward.

POLICEMAN X. And if we get him itself, nothing but abuse on our heads for it from the people, and maybe from our own relations.

SERGEANT. Well, we have to do our duty in the force. Haven't we the whole country depending on us to keep law and order? It's those that are down would be up and those that are up would be down, if it wasn't for us. Well, hurry on, you have plenty of other places to placard yet, and come back here then to me. You can take the lantern. Don't be too long now. It's very lonesome here with nothing but the moon.

POLICEMAN B. It's a pity we can't stop with you. The Government should have brought more police into the town, with *him* in gaol, and at assize time too. Well, good luck to your watch.

(*They go out.*)

SERGEANT (*walks up and down once or twice and looks at placard*). A hundred pounds and promotion sure. There must be a great deal of spending in a hundred pounds. It's a pity some honest man not to be better of that.

(A RAGGED MAN *appears at left and tries to slip past.* SERGEANT *suddenly turns.*)

SERGEANT. Where are you going?

MAN. I'm a poor ballad-singer, your honour. I thought to sell some of these (*holds out bundle of ballads*) to the sailors.

(*He goes on.*)

SERGEANT. Stop! Didn't I tell you to stop? You can't go on there.

MAN. Oh, very well. It's a hard thing to be poor. All the world's against the poor!

SERGEANT. Who are you?

MAN. You'd be as wise as myself if I told you, but I don't mind. I'm one Jimmy Walsh, a ballad-singer.

SERGEANT. Jimmy Walsh? I don't know that name.

MAN. Ah, sure, they know it well enough in Ennis. Were you ever in Ennis, sergeant?

SERGEANT. What brought you here?

MAN. Sure, it's to the assizes I came, thinking I might make a few shillings here or there. It's in the one train with the judges I came.

SERGEANT. Well, if you came so far, you may as well go farther, for you'll walk out of this.

MAN. I will, I will; I'll just go on where I was going.

(*Goes towards steps.*)

SERGEANT. Come back from those steps; no one has leave to pass down them to-night.

MAN. I'll just sit on the top of the steps till I see will some sailor buy a ballad off me that would give me my supper. They do be late going back to the ship. It's often I saw them in Cork carried down the quay in a hand-cart.

SERGEANT. Move on, I tell you. I won't have any one lingering about the quay to-night.

MAN. Well, I'll go. It's the poor have the hard life! Maybe yourself might like one, sergeant. Here's a good sheet now. (*Turns one over.*) "Content and a pipe"—that's not much. "The Peeler and the goat"—you wouldn't like that. "Johnny Hart"—that's a lovely song.

SERGEANT. Move on.

MAN. Ah, wait till you hear it. (*Sings:*)

There was a rich farmer's daughter lived near the town of Ross;
She courted a Highland soldier, his name was Johnny Hart;
Says the mother to her daughter, "I'll go distracted mad
If you marry that Highland soldier dressed up in Highland plaid."

SERGEANT. Stop that noise.

(MAN *wraps up his ballads and shuffles towards the steps.*)

SERGEANT. Where are you going?

MAN. Sure you told me to be going, and I am going.

SERGEANT. Don't be a fool. I didn't tell you to go that way; I told you to go back to the town.

MAN. Back to the town, is it?

SERGEANT (*taking him by the shoulder and shoving him before him*). Here, I'll show you the way. Be off with you. What are you stopping for?

MAN (*who has been keeping his eye on the notice, points to it*). I think I know what you're waiting for, sergeant.

SERGEANT. What's that to you?

MAN. And I know well the man you're waiting for—I know him well—I'll be going.

(*He shuffles on.*)

SERGEANT. You know him? Come back here. What sort is he?

MAN. Come back is it, sergeant? Do you want to have me killed?

SERGEANT. Why do you say that?

MAN. Never mind. I'm going. I wouldn't be in your shoes if the reward was ten times as much. (*Goes on off stage to left.*) Not if it was ten times as much.

SERGEANT (*rushing after him*). Come back here, come back. (*Drags him back.*) What sort is he? Where did you see him?

MAN. I saw him in my own place, in the County Clare. I tell you you wouldn't like to be looking at him. You'd be afraid to be in the one place with him. There isn't a weapon he doesn't know the use of, and as to strength, his muscles are as hard as that board (*slaps barrel*).

SERGEANT. Is he as bad as that?

MAN. He is then.

SERGEANT. Do you tell me so?

MAN. There was a poor man in our place, a sergeant from Bally-vaughan.—It was with a lump of stone he did it.

SERGEANT. I never heard of that.

MAN. And you wouldn't, sergeant. It's not everything that happens gets into the papers. And there was a policeman in plain clothes, too . . . It is in Limerick he was. . . . It was after the time of the attack on the police barrack at Kilmallock. . . . Moonlight . . . just like this . . . waterside. . . . Nothing was known for certain.

SERGEANT. Do you say so? It's a terrible county to belong to.

MAN. That's so, indeed! You might be standing there, looking out that way, thinking you saw him coming up this side of the quay (*points*), and he might be coming up this other side (*points*), and he'd be on you before you knew where you were.

SERGEANT. It's a whole troop of police they ought to put here to stop a man like that.

MAN. But if you'd like me to stop with you, I could be looking down this side. I could be sitting up here on this barrel.

SERGEANT. And you know him well, too?

MAN. I'd know him a mile off, sergeant.

SERGEANT. But you wouldn't want to share the reward?

MAN. Is it a poor man like me, that has to be going the roads and singing in fairs, to have the name on him that he took a reward? But you don't want me. I'll be safer in the town.

SERGEANT. Well, you can stop.

MAN (*getting up on barrel*). All right, sergeant. I wonder, now, you're not tired out, sergeant, walking up and down the way you are.

SERGEANT. If I'm tired I'm used to it.

MAN. You might have hard work before you to-night yet. Take it easy while you can. There's plenty of room up here on the barrel, and you see farther when you're higher up.

SERGEANT. Maybe so. (*Gets up beside him on barrel, facing right. They sit back to back, looking different ways.*) You made me feel a bit queer with the way you talked.

MAN. Give me a match, sergeant (*he gives it and man lights pipe*); take a draw yourself? It'll quiet you. Wait now till I give you a light, but you needn't turn round. Don't take your eye off the quay for the life of you.

SERGEANT. Never fear, I won't. (*Lights pipe. They both smoke.*) Indeed it's a hard thing to be in the force, out at night and no thanks for it, for all the danger we're in. And it's little we get but abuse from the people, and no choice but to obey our orders, and never asked when a man is sent into danger, if you are a married man with a family.

MAN (*sings*)—

As through the hills I walked to view the hills and shamrock plain,
I stood awhile where nature smiles to view the rocks and streams,
On a matron fair I fixed my eyes beneath a fertile vale,
And she sang her song it was on the wrong of poor old Granuaile.

SERGEANT. Stop that; that's no song to be singing in these times.

MAN. Ah, sergeant, I was only singing to keep my heart up. It sinks when I think of him. To think of us two sitting here, and he creeping up the quay, maybe, to get to us.

SERGEANT. Are you keeping a good lookout?

MAN. I am; and for no reward too. Amn't I the foolish man? But when I saw a man in trouble, I never could help trying to get him out of it. What's that? Did something hit me?

(*Rubs his heart.*)

SERGEANT (*patting him on the shoulder*). You will get your reward in heaven.

MAN. I know that, I know that, sergeant, but life is precious.

SERGEANT. Well, you can sing if it gives you more courage.

MAN (*sings*)—

> Her head was bare, her hands and feet with iron bands were
> bound,
> Her pensive strain and plaintive wail mingles with the evening
> gale,
> And the song she sang with mournful air, I am old Granuaile.
> Her lips so sweet that monarchs kissed . . .

SERGEANT. That's not it. . . . "Her gown she wore was stained
with gore." . . . That's it—you missed that.

MAN. You're right, sergeant, so it is; I missed it. (*Repeats line.*)
But to think of a man like you knowing a song like that.

SERGEANT. There's many a thing a man might know and might
not have any wish for.

MAN. Now, I daresay, sergeant, in your youth, you used to be
sitting up on a wall, the way you are sitting up on this barrel now,
and the other lads beside you, and you singing "Granuaile"? . . .

SERGEANT. I did then.

MAN. And the "Shan Van Vocht"? . . .

SERGEANT. I did then.

MAN. And the "Green on the Cape?"

SERGEANT. That was one of them.

MAN. And maybe the man you are watching for to-night used
to be sitting on the wall, when he was young, and singing those
same songs. . . . It's a queer world. . . .

SERGEANT. Whisht! . . . I think I see something coming. . . . It's
only a dog.

MAN. And isn't it a queer world? . . . Maybe it's one of the boys
you used to be singing with that time you will be arresting to-day
or to-morrow, and sending into the dock. . . .

SERGEANT. That's true indeed.

MAN. And maybe one night, after you had been singing, if the
other boys had told you some plan they had, some plan to free the
country, you might have joined with them . . . and maybe it is you
might be in trouble now.

SERGEANT. Well, who knows but I might? I had a great spirit in
those days.

MAN. It's a queer world, sergeant, and it's little any mother
knows when she sees her child creeping on the floor what might
happen to it before it has gone through its life, or who will be who
in the end.

SERGEANT. That's a queer thought now, and a true thought. Wait now till I think it out. . . . If it wasn't for the sense I have, and for my wife and family, and for me joining the force the time I did, it might be myself now would be after breaking gaol and hiding in the dark, and it might be him that's hiding in the dark and that got out of gaol would be sitting up here where I am on this barrel. . . . And it might be myself would be creeping up trying to make my escape from himself, and it might be himself would be keeping the law, and myself would be breaking it, and myself would be trying to put a bullet in his head, or to take up a lump of stone the way you said he did . . . no, that myself did. . . . Oh! (*Gasps. After a pause*) What's that? (*Grasps man's arm.*)

MAN (*jumps off barrel and listens, looking out over water*). It's nothing, sergeant.

SERGEANT. I thought it might be a boat. I had a notion there might be friends of his coming about the quays with a boat.

MAN. Sergeant, I am thinking it was with the people you were, and not with the law you were, when you were a young man.

SERGEANT. Well, if I was foolish then, that time's gone.

MAN. Maybe, sergeant, it comes into your head sometimes, in spite of your belt and your tunic, that it might have been as well for you to have followed Granuaile.

SERGEANT. It's no business of yours what I think.

MAN. Maybe, sergeant, you'll be on the side of the country yet.

SERGEANT (*gets off barrel*). Don't talk to me like that. I have my duties and I know them. (*Looks round.*) That was a boat; I hear the oars.

(*Goes to the steps and looks down.*)

MAN (*sings*)—

> O, then, tell me, Shawn O'Farrell,
> Where the gathering is to be.
> In the old spot by the river
> Right well known to you and me!

SERGEANT. Stop that! Stop that, I tell you!

MAN (*sings louder*)—

> One word more, for signal token,
> Whistle up the marching tune,
> With your pike upon your shoulder,
> At the Rising of the Moon.

SERGEANT. If you don't stop that, I'll arrest you.

(*A whistle from below answers, repeating the air.*)

65

SERGEANT. That's a signal. (*Stands between him and steps.*) You must not pass this way. . . . Step farther back. . . . Who are you? You are no ballad-singer.

MAN. You needn't ask who I am; that placard will tell you. (*Points to placard.*)

SERGEANT. You are the man I am looking for.

MAN (*takes off hat and wig.* SERGEANT *seizes them*). I am. There's a hundred pounds on my head. There is a friend of mine below in a boat. He knows a safe place to bring me to.

SERGEANT (*looking still at hat and wig*). It's a pity! It's a pity. You deceived me. You deceived me well.

MAN. I am a friend of Granuaile. There is a hundred pounds on my head.

SERGEANT. It's a pity, it's a pity!

MAN. Will you let me pass, or must I make you let me?

SERGEANT. I am in the force. I will not let you pass.

MAN. I thought to do it with my tongue. (*Puts hand in breast.*) What is that?

(*Voice of* POLICEMAN X *outside*). Here, this is where we left him.

SERGEANT. It's my comrades coming.

MAN. You won't betray me . . . the friend of Granuaile. (*Slips behind barrel.*)

(*Voice of* POLICEMAN B). That was the last of the placards.

POLICEMAN X. (*as they come in*). If he makes his escape it won't be unknown he'll make it.

(SERGEANT *puts hat and wig behind his back.*)

POLICEMAN B. Did any one come this way?

SERGEANT (*after a pause*). No one.

POLICEMAN B. No one at all?

SERGEANT. No one at all.

POLICEMAN B. We had no orders to go back to the station; we can stop along with you.

SERGEANT. I don't want you. There is nothing for you to do here.

POLICEMAN B. You bade us to come back here and keep watch with you.

SERGEANT. I'd sooner be alone. Would any man come this way and you making all that talk? It is better the place to be quiet.

POLICEMAN B. Well, we'll leave you the lantern anyhow.

(*Hands it to him.*)

SERGEANT. I don't want it. Bring it with you.

66

POLICEMAN B. You might want it. There are clouds coming up and you have the darkness of the night before you yet. I'll leave it over here on the barrel. (*Goes to barrel.*)

SERGEANT. Bring it with you I tell you. No more talk.

POLICEMAN B. Well, I thought it might be a comfort to you. I often think when I have it in my hand and can be flashing it about into every dark corner (*doing so*) that it's the same as being beside the fire at home, and the bits of bogwood blazing up now and again.

(*Flashes it about, now on the barrel, now on* SERGEANT.)

SERGEANT (*furious*). Be off the two of you, yourselves and your lantern!

(*They go out.* MAN *comes from behind barrel. He and* SERGEANT *stand looking at one another.*)

SERGEANT. What are you waiting for?

MAN. For my hat, of course, and my wig. You wouldn't wish me to get my death of cold?

(SERGEANT *gives them.*)

MAN (*going towards steps*). Well, good-night, comrade, and thank you. You did me a good turn to-night, and I'm obliged to you. Maybe I'll be able to do as much for you when the small rise up and the big fall down . . . when we all change places at the Rising (*waves his hand and disappears*) of the Moon.

SERGEANT (*turning his back to audience and reading placard*). A hundred pounds reward! A hundred pounds! (*Turns towards audience.*) I wonder, now, am I as great a fool as I think I am?

Curtain.

THE JACKDAW

THE JACKDAW

PERSONS
    JOSEPH NESTOR. *An army pensioner.*
    MICHAEL COONEY. *A farmer.*
    MRS. BRODERICK. *A small shopkeeper.*
    TOMMY NALLY. *A pauper.*
    SIBBY FAHY. *An orange seller.*
    TIMOTHY WARD. *A process server.*

SCENE. *Interior of a small general shop at Cloon.* MRS. BRODERICK *sitting down.* TOMMY NALLY *sitting eating an orange* SIBBY *has given him.* SIBBY, *with basket on her arm, is looking out of door.*

SIBBY. The people are gathering to the door of the Court. The Magistrates will be coming there before long. Here is Timothy Ward coming up the street.

TIMOTHY WARD (*coming to door*). Did you get that summons I left here for you ere yesterday, Mrs. Broderick?

MRS. BRODERICK. I believe it's there in under the canister. (*Takes it out.*) It had my mind tossed looking at it there before me. I know well what is in it if I made no fist of reading it itself. It's no wonder with all I had to go through if the reading and writing got scattered on me.

WARD. You know it is on this day you have to appear in the Court?

MRS. BRODERICK. It isn't easy forget that, though indeed it is hard for me to be keeping anything in my head these times, but maybe remembering to-morrow the thing I was saying to-day.

WARD. Up to one o'clock the magistrates will be able to attend to you, ma'am, before they will go out eating their meal.

MRS. BRODERICK. Haven't I the mean, begrudging creditors now that would put me into the Court? Sure it's a terrible thing to go in it and to be bound to speak nothing but the truth. When people would meet with you after, they would remember your face in the Court. What way would they be certain was it in or outside of the dock?

WARD. It is not in the dock you will be put this time. And there will be no bodily harm done to you, but to seize your furniture and your goods. It's best for me to be going there myself and not to be wasting my time. *(Goes out.)*

MRS. BRODERICK. Many a one taking my goods on credit and I seeing their face no more. But nothing would satisfy the people of this district. Sure the great God Himself when He came down couldn't please everybody.

SIBBY. I am thinking you were talking of some friend, ma'am, might be apt to be coming to your aid.

MRS. BRODERICK. Well able he is to do it if the Lord would but put it in his mind. Isn't it a strange thing the goods of this world to shut up the heart of a brother from his own, the same as Esau and Jacob, and he having a good farm of land in the County Limerick. It is what I heard that in that place the grass does be as thick as grease.

SIBBY. I suppose, ma'am, you wrote giving him an account of your case?

MRS. BRODERICK. Sure, Mr. Nestor, the dear man, has his fingers wore away writing for me, and I telling him all he had or had not to say. At Christmas I wrote, and at Little Christmas, and at St. Brigit's Day, and on the Feast of St. Patrick, and after that again such time as I had news of the summons being about to be served. And you may ask Mrs. Delane at the Post Office am I telling any lie saying I got no word or answer at all. . . . It's long since I saw him, but it is the way he used to be, his eyes on kippeens and some way suspicious in his heart; a dark weighty tempered man.

SIBBY. A person to be crabbed and he young, it is not likely he will grow kind at the latter end.

TOMMY NALLY. That is no less than true now. There are crabbed people and suspicious people to be met with in every place. It is much that I got a pass from the Workhouse this day, the Master making sure when I asked it that I had in my pocket the means of getting drink.

MRS. BRODERICK. It would maybe be best to go join you in the Workhouse, Tommy Nally, when I am out of this, than to go walking the world from end to end.

TOMMY NALLY. Ah, don't be saying that, ma'am; sure you couldn't be happy within those walls if you had the whole world. Clean outside, but very hard within. No rank but all mixed together, the good, the middling and the bad, the well reared and the rough.

MRS. BRODERICK. Sure I'm not asking to go in it. You could never be as stiff in any place as in any sort of little cabin of your own.

TOMMY NALLY. The tea boiled in a boiler, you should close your eyes drinking it, and ne'er a bit of sugar hardly in it at all. And our curses on them that boil the eggs too hard! What use is an egg that is hard to any person on earth? And as to the dinner, what way would a tasty person eat it not having a knife or a fork?

MRS. BRODERICK. That I may live to be in no one's way, but to have some little corner of my own!

TOMMY NALLY. And to come to your end in it, ma'am! If you were the Lady Mayor herself you'd be brought out to the dead-house if it was ten o'clock at night, and not a wash unless it was just a Scotch lick, and nobody to wake you at all!

MRS. BRODERICK. I will not go in it! I would sooner make any shift and die by the side of the wall. Sure heaven is the best place, heaven and this world we're in now!

SIBBY. Don't be giving up now, ma'am. Here is Mr. Nestor coming, and if any one will give you an advice he is the one will do it. Why wouldn't he, he being, as he is, an educated man, and such a great one to be reading books.

MRS. BRODERICK. So he is too, and keeps it in his mind after. It's a wonder to me a man that does be reading to keep any memory at all.

NALLY. It's easy for him to carry things light, and his pension paid regular at springtime and harvest.

(*Nestor comes in reading "Tit-Bits."*)

NESTOR. There was a servant girl in Austria cut off her finger slicing cabbage. . . .

ALL. The poor thing!

NESTOR. And her master stuck it on again with glue. That now was a very foolish thing to do. What use would a finger be stuck with glue that might melt off at any time, and she to be stirring the pot?

SIBBY. That is true indeed.

NESTOR. Now, if I myself had been there, it is what I would have advised . . .

SIBBY. That's what I was saying, Mr. Nestor. It is you are the grand adviser. What now will you say to poor Mrs. Broderick that has a summons out against her this day for up to ten pounds?

NESTOR. It is what I am often saying, it is a very foolish thing to be getting into debt.

MRS. BRODERICK. Sure what way could I help it? It's a very done-up town to be striving to make a living in.

NESTOR. It would be a right thing to be showing a good example.

MRS. BRODERICK. They would want that indeed. There are more die with debts on them in this place than die free from debt.

NESTOR. Many a poor soul has had to suffer from the weight of the debts on him, finding no rest or peace after death.

SIBBY. The Magistrates are gone into the Courthouse, Mrs. Broderick. Why now wouldn't you go up to the bank and ask would the manager advance you a loan?

MRS. BRODERICK. It is likely he would not do it. But maybe it's as good for me go as to be sitting here waiting for the end.

(*Puts on hat and shawl.*)

NESTOR. I now will take charge of the shop for you, Mrs. Broderick.

MRS. BRODERICK. It's little call there'll be to it. The time a person is sunk that's the time the custom will go from her. (*She goes out.*)

NALLY. I'll be taking a ramble into the Court to see what are the lads doing. (*Goes out.*)

SIBBY (*following them*). I might chance some customers there myself.

(*Goes out calling—oranges, good oranges.*)

NESTOR (*taking a paper from his pocket, sitting down, and beginning to read*). "Romantic elopement in high life. A young lady at Aberdeen, Missouri, U.S.A., having been left by her father an immense fortune . . ."

(*Stops to wipe his spectacles, puts them on again and looks for place, which he has lost. Cooney puts his head in at door and draws it out again.*)

NESTOR. Come in, come in!

COONEY (*coming in cautiously and looking round*). Whose house now might this be?

NESTOR. To the Widow Broderick it belongs. She is out in the town presently.

COONEY. I saw her name up over the door.

NESTOR. On business of her own she is gone. It is I am minding the place for her.

COONEY. So I see. I suppose now you have good cause to be minding it?

NESTOR. It would be a pity any of her goods to go to loss.

74

COONEY. I suppose so. Is it to auction them you will or to sell them in bulk?

NESTOR. Not at all. I can sell you any article you will require.

COONEY. It would be no profit to herself now, I suppose, if you did?

NESTOR. What do you mean saying that? Do you think I would defraud her from her due in anything I would sell for her at all?

COONEY. You are not the bailiff so?

NESTOR. Not at all. I wonder any person to take me for a bailiff!

COONEY. You are maybe one of the creditors?

NESTOR. I am not. I am not a man to have a debt upon me to any person on earth.

COONEY. I wonder what it is you are at so, if you have no claim on the goods. Is it any harm now to ask what's this your name is?

NESTOR. One Joseph Nestor I am, there are few in the district but know me. Indeed they all have a great opinion of me. Travelled I did in the army, and attended school and I young, and slept in the one bed with two boys that were learning Greek.

COONEY. What way now can I be rightly sure that you *are* Joseph Nestor?

NESTOR (*pulling out envelope*). There is my pension docket. You will maybe believe that.

COONEY (*examining it*). I suppose you may be him so. I saw your name often before this.

NESTOR. Did you now? I suppose it may have travelled a good distance.

COONEY. It travelled as far as myself anyway at the bottom of letters that were written asking relief for the owner of this house.

NESTOR. I suppose you are her brother so, Michael Cooney?

COONEY. If I am, there are some questions that I want to put and to get answers to before my mind will be satisfied. Tell me this now. Is it a fact Mary Broderick to be living at all?

NESTOR. What would make you think her not to be living and she sending letters to you through the post?

COONEY. I was saying to myself with myself, there was maybe some other one personating her and asking me to send relief for their own ends.

NESTOR. I am in no want of any relief. That is a queer thing to say and a very queer thing. There are many worse off than myself, the Lord be praised!

COONEY. Don't be so quick now starting up to take offence. It is hard to believe the half the things you hear or that will be told to you.

NESTOR. That may be so indeed; unless it is things that would be printed on the papers. But I would think you might trust one of your own blood.

COONEY. I might or I might not. I had it in my mind this long time to come hither and to look around for myself. There are seven generations of the Cooneys trusted nobody living or dead.

NESTOR. Indeed I was reading in some history of one Ulysses that came back from a journey and sent no word before him but slipped in unknown to all but the house dog to see was his wife minding the place, or was she, as she was, scattering his means.

COONEY. So she would be too. If Mary Broderick is in need of relief I will relieve her, but if she is not, I will bring away what I brought with me to its own place again.

NESTOR. Sure here is the summons. You can read that, and if you will look out the door you can see by the stir the Magistrates are sitting in the Court. It is a great welcome she will have before you, and the relief coming at the very nick of time.

COONEY. It is too good a welcome she will give me I am thinking. It is what I am in dread of now, if she thinks I brought her the money so soft and so easy, she will never be leaving me alone, but dragging all I have out of me by little and little.

NESTOR. Maybe you might let her have but the lend of it.

COONEY. Where's the use of calling it a lend when I may be sure I never will see it again? It might be as well for me to earn the value of a charity.

NESTOR. You might do that and not repent of it.

COONEY. It is likely I'll be annoyed with her to the end of my lifetime if she knows I have as much as that to part with. It might be she would be following me to Limerick.

NESTOR. Wait now a minute till I will give you an advice.

COONEY. It is likely my own advice is the best. Look over your own shoulder and do the thing you think right. How can any other person know the reasons I have in my mind?

NESTOR. I will know what is in your mind if you will tell it to me.

COONEY. It would suit me best, she to get the money and not to know at the present time where did it come from. The next time she will write wanting help from me, I will task her with it and ask her to give me an account.

NESTOR. That now would take a great deal of strategy. . . . Wait now till I think. . . . I have it in my mind I was reading in a penny novel . . . no but on the "Gael" . . . about a boy of Kilbecanty that saved his old sweetheart from being evicted.

COONEY. I never heard my sister had any old sweetheart.

NESTOR. It was playing Twenty-five he did it. Played with the husband he did, letting him win up to fifty pounds.

COONEY. Mary Broderick was no cardplayer. And if she was itself she would know me. And it's not fifty pounds I am going to leave with her, or twenty pounds, or a penny more than is needful to free her from the summons to-day.

NESTOR (*excited*). I will make up a plan! I am sure I will think of a good one. It is given in to me there is no person so good at making up a plan as myself on this side of the world, not on this side of the world! I will manage all. Leave here what you have for her before she will come in. I will give it to her in some secret way.

COONEY. I don't know. I will not give it to you before I will get a receipt for it . . . and I'll not leave the town till I'll see did she get it straight and fair. Into the Court I'll go to see her paying it.

(*Sits down and writes out receipt.*)

NESTOR. I was reading on "Home Chat" about a woman put a note for five pounds into her son's prayer book and he going a voyage. And when he came back and was in the church with her it fell out, he never having turned a leaf of the book at all.

COONEY. Let you sign this and you may put it in the prayer book so long as she will get it safe.

(*Nestor signs. Cooney looks suspiciously at signature and compares it with a letter and then gives notes.*)

NESTOR (*signing*). Joseph Nestor.

COONEY. Let me see now is it the same hand-writing I used to be getting on the letters. It is. I have the notes here.

NESTOR. Wait now till I see is there a prayer book. . . . (*Looks on shelf*). Treacle, castor oil, marmalade. . . . I see no books at all.

COONEY. Hurry on now, she will be coming in and finding me.

NESTOR. Here is what will do as well. . . . "Old Moore's Almanac." I will put it here between the leaves. I will ask her the prophecy for the month. You can come back here after she finding it.

COONEY. Amn't I after telling you I wouldn't wish her to have sight of me here at all? What are you at now, I wonder, saying that. I will take my own way to know does she pay the money. It is not my intention to be made a fool of.

(*Goes out.*)

77

NESTOR. You will be satisfied and well satisfied. Let me see now where are the predictions for the month. (*Reads.*) "The angry appearance of Scorpio and the position of the pale Venus and Jupiter presage much danger for England. The heretofore obsequious Orangemen will refuse to respond to the tocsin of landlordism. The scales are beginning to fall from their eyes."

(*Mrs. Broderick comes in without his noticing her. She gives a groan. He drops book and stuffs notes into his pocket.*)

MRS. BRODERICK. Here I am back again and no addition to me since I went.

NESTOR. You gave me a start coming in so noiseless.

MRS. BRODERICK. It is time for me go to the Court, and I give you my word I'd be better pleased going to my burying at the Seven Churches. A nice slab I have there waiting for me, though the man that put it over me I never saw him at all, and he a far off cousin of my own.

NESTOR. Who knows now, Mrs. Broderick, but things might turn out better than you think.

MRS. BRODERICK. What way could they turn out better between this and one o'clock?

NESTOR. (*scratching his head*). I suppose now you wouldn't care to play a game of Twenty-five?

MRS. BRODERICK. I am surprised at you, Mr. Nestor, asking me to go cardplaying on such a day and at such an hour as this.

NESTOR. I wonder might some person come in and give an order for ten pounds' worth of the stock?

MRS. BRODERICK. Much good it would do me. Sure I have the most of it on credit.

NESTOR. Well, there is no knowing. Some well-to-do person now passing the street might have seen you and taken a liking to you and be willing to make an advance or a loan.

MRS. BRODERICK. Ah, who would be taking a liking to me as they might to a young girl in her bloom.

NESTOR. Oh, it's a sort of thing might happen. Sure age didn't catch on to you yet; you are clean and fresh and sound. What's this I was reading in "Answers." (*Looks at it.*) "Romantic elopement . . ."

MRS. BRODERICK. I know of no one would be thinking of me for a wife . . . unless it might be yourself, Mr. Nestor. . . .

NESTOR (*jumping up and speaking fast and running finger up and down paper*). "Performance of Dick Whittington." . . . There now, there is a story that I read in my reading, it was called Whittington and the Cat. It was the cat led to his fortune. There might some person take a fancy to your cat....

MRS. BRODERICK. Ah, let you have done now. I have no cat this good while. I banished it on the head of it threatening the jackdaw.

NESTOR. The jackdaw?

MRS. BRODERICK (*fetches cage from inner room*). Sure I reared it since the time it fell down the chimney and I going into my bed. It is often you should have seen it, in or out of its cage. Hero his name is. Come out now, Hero.

(*Opens cage.*)

NESTOR (*slapping his side*). This is it . . . that's the very thing. Listen to me now, Mrs. Broderick, there are *some* might give a good price for that bird. (*Sitting down to the work.*) It chances now there is a friend of mine in South Africa. A mine owner he is . . . very rich . . . but it is down in the mine he has to live by reason of the Kaffirs . . . it is hard to keep a watch upon them in the half dark, they being black.

MRS. BRODERICK. I suppose. . .

NESTOR. He does be lonesome now and again, and he is longing for a bird to put him in mind of old Ireland . . . but he is in dread it would die in the darkness . . . and it came to his mind that it is a custom with jackdaws to be living in chimneys, and that if any birds would bear the confinement it is they that should do it.

MRS. BRODERICK. And is it to buy jackdaws he is going?

NESTOR. Isn't that what I am coming to. (*He pulls out notes.*) Here now is ten pounds I have to lay out for him. Take them now and good luck go with them, and give me the bird.

MRS. BRODERICK. Notes is it? Is it waking or dreaming I am and I standing up on the floor?

NESTOR. Good notes and ten of them. Look at them! National Bank they are. . . . Count them now, according to your fingers, and see did I tell any lie.

MRS. BRODERICK (*counting*). They are in it sure enough . . . so long as they are good ones and I not made a hare of before the magistrates.

NESTOR. Go out now to the Court and show them to Timothy Ward, and see does he say are they good. Pay them over then, and its likely you will be let off the costs.

MRS. BRODERICK (*taking shawl*). I will go, I will go. Well, you are a great man and a kind man, Joseph Nestor, and that you may live a thousand years for this good deed.

NESTOR. Look here now, ma'am. I wouldn't wish you to be mentioning my name in this business or saying I had any hand in it at all.

MRS. BRODERICK. I will not so long as it's not pleasing to you. Well, it is yourself took a great load off me this day! (*She goes out.*)

NESTOR (*calling after her*). I might as well be putting the jackdaw back into the cage to be ready for the journey. (*Comes into shop.*) I hope now he will be well treated by the sailors and he travelling over the sea. . . . Where is he now. . . . (*Chirrups.*) Here now, come here to me, what's this your name is. . . . Nero! Nero! (*Makes pounces behind counter.*) Ah, bad manners to you, is it under the counter you are gone!

(*Lies flat on floor chirruping and calling, Nero! Nero! NALLY comes in and watches him curiously.*)

NALLY. Is it catching blackbeetles you are, Mr. Nestor? Where are they and I will give you a hand. . . .

NESTOR (*getting up annoyed*). It's that bird I was striving to catch a hold of for to put him back in the cage.

TOMMY NALLY (*making a pounce*). There he is now. (*Puts bird in cage.*) Wait now till I'll fasten the gate.

NESTOR. Just putting everything straight and handy for the widow woman I am before she will come back from the settlement she is making in the Court.

NALLY. What way will she be able to do that?

NESTOR. I gave her advice. A thought I had, something that came from my reading. (*Taps paper.*) Education and reading and going in the army through the kingdoms of the world; that is what fits a man now to be giving out advice.

TOMMY. Indeed, it's good for them to have you, all the poor ignorant people of this town.

COONEY (*coming in hurriedly and knocking against NALLY as he goes out*). What, now, would you say to be the best nesting place in this town. Nests of jackdaws I should say.

NESTOR. There is the old mill should be a good place. To the west of the station it is. Chimneys there are in it. Middling high they are. Wait now till I'll tell you of the great plan I made up. . . .

COONEY. What are you asking for those rakes in the corner? It's no matter, I'll take one on credit, or maybe it is only the lend of it I'll take. . . . I'll be coming back immediately.

(*He goes out with rake.*)

SIBBY (*coming in excitedly*). If you went bird-catching, Mr. Nestor, tell me what way would you go doing it?

NESTOR. It is not long since I was reading some account of that ... lads that made a trade of it ... nets they had and they used to be spreading them in the swamps where the plover do be feeding ...

SIBBY. Ah, sure where's the use of a plover!

NESTOR. And snares they had for putting along the drains where the snipe do be picking up worms. . . . But if I myself saw any person going after things of the sort, it is what I would advise them to stick to the net.

SIBBY. What now is the price of that net in the corner?

NESTOR (*taking it down*). It is but a little bag that is, suitable for carrying small articles; it would become your oranges well. Two pence I believe, Sibby, is what I should charge you for that.

SIBBY (*taking money out of handkerchief*). Give it to me so! Here I'll get the start of you, Timothy Ward, anyway.

(*She takes it and goes out, almost overturning* TIMOTHY WARD, *who is rushing in.*)

NESTOR. Well, Timothy, did you see the Widow Broderick in the Court?

WARD. I did see her. It is in it she is, now, looking as content as in the coffin, and she paying her debt.

NESTOR. Did she give you any account of herself?

WARD. She did to be sure, and to the whole Court; but look here now, I have no time to be talking. I have to be back there when the magistrates will have their lunch taken. Now you being so clever a man, Mr. Nestor, what would you say is the surest way to go catching birds?

NESTOR. It is a strange thing now, I was asked the same question not three minutes ago. I was just searching my mind. It seems to me I have read in some place it is a very good way to go calling to them with calls; made for the purpose they are. You have but to sit under a tree or whatever place they may perch and to whistle ... suppose now it might be for a curlew. . . .

(*Whistles.*)

TIMOTHY WARD. Are there any of those calls in the shop?

NESTOR. I would not say there are any made for the purpose, but there might be something might answer you all the same. Let me see now. . . .

(*Gets down a box of musical toys and turns them over.*)

WARD. Is there anything now has a sound like the croaky screech of a jackdaw?

NESTOR. Here now is what we used to be calling a corncrake. ... (*Turns it.*) Corncrake, corncrake ... but it seems to me now that to give it but the one creak, this way ... it is much like what you would hear in the chimney at the time of the making of nests.

WARD. Give it here to me!

(*Puts a penny on counter and runs out.*)

TOMMY NALLY (*coming in shaking with excitement*). For the love of God, Mr. Nestor, will you give me that live-trap on credit!

NESTOR. A trap? Sure there is no temptation for rats to be settling themselves in the Workhouse.

NALLY. Or a snare itself ... or any sort of a thing that would make the makings of a crib.

NESTOR. What would you want, I wonder, going out fowling with a crib?

NALLY. Why wouldn't I want it? Why wouldn't I have leave to catch a bird the same as every other one?

NESTOR. And what would the likes of you be wanting with a bird?

NALLY. What would I want with it, is it? Why wouldn't I be getting my own ten pounds?

NESTOR. Heaven help your poor head this day!

NALLY. Why wouldn't I get it the same as Mrs. Broderick got it?

NESTOR. Well, listen to me now. You will not get it.

NALLY. Sure that man is buying them will have no objection they to come from one more than another.

NESTOR. Don't be arguing now. It is a queer thing for you, Tommy Nally, to be arguing with a man like myself.

NALLY. Think now all the good it would do me ten pound to be put in my hand! It is not you should be begrudging it to me, Mr. Nestor. Sure it would be a relief upon the rates.

NESTOR. I tell you you will not get ten pound or any pound at all. Can't you give attention to what I say?

NALLY. If I had but the price of the trap you wouldn't refuse it to me. Well, isn't there great hardship upon a man to be bet up and to have no credit in the town at all.

NESTOR (*exasperated, and giving him the cage*). Look here now, I have a right to turn you out into the street. But, as you are silly like and with no great share of wits, I will make you a present of this bird till you try what will you get for it, and till you see will you

82

get as much as will cover its diet for one day only. Go out now looking for customers and maybe you will believe what I say.

NALLY (*seizing it*). That you may be doing the same thing this day fifty years! My fortune's made now! (*Goes out with cage.*)

NESTOR (*sitting down*). My joy go with you, but I'm bothered with the whole of you. Everyone expecting me to do their business and to manage their affairs. That is the drawback of being an educated man!

(*Takes up paper to read.*)

MRS. BRODERICK (*coming in*). I declare I'm as comforted as Job coming free into the house from the Court!

NESTOR. Well, indeed, ma'am, I am well satisfied to be able to do what I did for you, and for my friend from Africa as well, giving him so fine and so handsome a bird.

MRS. BRODERICK. Sure Finn himself that chewed his thumb had not your wisdom, or King Solomon that kept order over his kingdom and his own seven hundred wives. There is neither of them could be put beside you for settling the business of any person at all.

(SIBBY *comes in holding up her netted bag.*)

NESTOR. What is it you have there, Sibby?

SIBBY. Look at them here, look at them here. . . . I wasn't long getting them. Warm they are yet; they will take no injury.

MRS. BRODERICK. What are they at all?

SIBBY. It is eggs they are . . . look at them. Jackdaws' eggs.

NESTOR (*suspiciously*). And what call have you now to be bringing in jackdaws' eggs?

SIBBY. Is it ten pound apiece I will get for them do you think, or is it but ten pound I will get for the whole of them?

NESTOR. Is it drink, or is it tea, or is it some change that is come upon the world that is fitting the people of this place for the asylum in Ballinasloe?

SIBBY. I know of a good clocking hen. I will put the eggs under her. . . . I will rear them when they'll be hatched out.

NESTOR. I suppose now, Mrs. Broderick, you went belling the case through the town?

MRS. BRODERICK. I did not, but to the Magistrates upon the bench that I told it out of respect to, and I never mentioned your name in it at all.

SIBBY. Tell me now, Mrs. Broderick, who have I to apply to?

MRS. BRODERICK. What is it you are wanting to apply about?

SIBBY. Will you tell me where is the man that is after buying your jackdaw?

MRS. BRODERICK (*looking at Nestor*). What's that? Where is he, is it?

NESTOR (*making signs of silence*). How would you know where he is? It is not in a broken little town of this sort such a man would be stopping, and he having his business finished.

SIBBY. Sure he will have to be coming back here for the bird. I will stop till I'll see him drawing near.

NESTOR. It is more likely he will get it consigned to the shipping agent. Mind what I say now, it is best not be speaking of him at all.

(TIMOTHY WARD *comes in triumphantly, croaking his toy. He has a bird in his hand.*)

WARD. I chanced on a starling. It was not with this I tempted him, but a little chap that had him in a crib. Would you say now, Mr. Nestor, would that do as well as a jackdaw? Look now, it's as handsome every bit as the other. And anyway it is likely they will both die before they will reach to their journey's end.

NESTOR (*lifting up his hands*). Of all the foolishness that ever came upon the world!

WARD. Hurry on now, Mrs. Broderick, tell me where will I bring it to the buyer you were speaking of. He is fluttering that hard it is much if I can keep him in my hand. Is it at Noonan's Royal Hotel he is or is it at Mack's?

NESTOR (*shaking his head threateningly*). How can you tell that and you not knowing it yourself?

WARD. Sure you have a right to know what way did he go, and he after going out of this.

MRS. BRODERICK (*her eyes apprehensively on Nestor*). Ah, sure, my mind was tattered on me. I couldn't know did he go east or west. Standing here in this place I was, like a ghost that got a knock upon its head.

WARD. If he is coming back for the bird it is here he will be coming, and if it is to be sent after him it is likely you will have his address.

MRS. BRODERICK. So I should, too, I suppose. Where now did I put it? (*She looks to Nestor for orders, but cannot understand his signs, and turns out pocket.*) That's my specs . . . that's the key of the box . . . that's a bit of root liquorice. . . . Where now at all could I have left down that address?

WARD. There has no train left since he was here. Sure what does it matter so long as he did not go out of this. I'll bring this bird to the railway. Tell me what sort was he till I'll know him.

84

MRS. BRODERICK (*still looking at Nestor*). Well, he was middling tall . . . not very gross . . . about the figure now of Mr. Nestor.

WARD. What aged man was he?

MRS. BRODERICK. I suppose up to sixty years. About the one age, you'd say, with Mr. Nestor.

WARD. Give me some better account now; it is hardly I would make him out by that.

MRS. BRODERICK. A grey beard he has hanging down . . . and a bald poll, and grey hair like a fringe around it . . . just for all the world like Mr. Nestor!

NESTOR (*jumping up*). There is nothing so disagreeable in the world as a woman that has too much talk.

MRS. BRODERICK. Well, let me alone. Where's the use of them all picking at me to say where did I get the money when I am under orders not to tell it?

WARD. Under orders?

MRS. BRODERICK. I am, and strong orders.

WARD. Whose orders are those?

MRS. BRODERICK. What's that to you, I ask you?

WARD. Isn't it a pity now a woman to be so unneighbourly and she after getting profit for herself?

MRS. BRODERICK. Look now, Mr. Nestor, the way they are going on at me, and you saying no word for me at all.

WARD. How would he say any word when he hasn't it to say? The only word could be said by any one is that you are a mean grasping person, gathering what you can for your own profit and keeping yourself so close and so compact. It is back to the Court I am going, and it's no good friend I'll be to you from this out, Mrs. Broderick!

MRS. BRODERICK. Amn't I telling you I was bidden not to tell?

SIBBY. You were. And is it likely it was you yourself bid yourself and gave you that advice, Mrs. Broderick? It is what I think the bird was never bought at all. It is in some other way she got the money. Maybe in a way she does not like to be talking of. Light weights, light fingers! Let us go away so and leave her, herself and her money and her orders! (TIMOTHY WARD *goes out, but* SIBBY *stops at door.*) And much good may they do her.

MRS. BRODERICK. Listen to that, Mr. Nestor! Will you be listening to that, when one word from yourself would clear my character! I leave it now between you and the hearers. Why would I be questioned this way and that way, the same as if I was on the green

table before the judges? You have my heart broke between you.
It's best for me to heat the kettle and wet a drop of tea.

(*Goes to inner room.*)

SIBBY. Tell us the truth now, Mr. Nestor, if you know anything
at all about it.

NESTOR. I know everything about it. It was to myself the notes
were handed in the first place. I am willing to take my oath to you
on that. It was a stranger, I said, came in.

SIBBY. I wish I could see him and know him if I did see him.

NESTOR. It is likely you would know a man of that sort if you
did see him, Sibby Fahy. It is likely you never saw a man yet that
owns riches would buy up the half of this town.

SIBBY. It is not always them that has the most that makes the
most show. But it is likely he will have a good dark suit anyway,
and shining boots, and a gold chain hanging over his chest.

NESTOR (*sarcastically*). He will, and gold rings and pins the same
as the King of France or of Spain.

(*Enter* COONEY, *hatless, streaked with soot and lime, speechless but triumphant. He holds up a nest with nestlings.*)

NESTOR. What has happened you, Mr. Cooney at all?

COONEY. Look now, what I have got!

NESTOR. A nest, is it?

COONEY. Three young ones in it!

NESTOR (*faintly*). Is it what you are going to say they are jackdaws!

COONEY. I followed your direction. . . .

NESTOR. How do you make that out?

COONEY. You said the mill chimneys were full of them. . . .

NESTOR. What has that to do with it?

COONEY. I left my rake after me broken in the loft . . . my hat
went away in the millrace . . . I tore my coat on the stones . . . there
has mortar got into my eye.

NESTOR. The Lord bless and save us!

COONEY. But there is no man can say I did not bring back the
birds, sound and living and in good health. Look now, the open
mouths of them! (*All gather round.*) Three of them safe and living. . . . I lost one climbing the wall. . . . Where now is the man is
going to buy them?

SIBBY (*pointing at* NESTOR). It is he that can tell you that.

COONEY. Make no delay bringing me to him. I'm in dread they
might die on me first.

NESTOR. You should know well that no one is buying them.

SIBBY. No one! Sure it was you yourself told us that there was!

NESTOR. If I did itself there is no such a man.

SIBBY. It's not above two minutes he was telling of the rings and the pins he wore.

NESTOR. He never was in it at all.

COONEY. What plan is he making up now to defraud me and to rob me?

SIBBY. Question him yourself, and you will see what will he say.

COONEY. How can I ask questions of a man that is telling lies?

NESTOR. I am telling no lies. I am well able to answer you and to tell you the truth.

COONEY. Tell me where is the man that will give me cash for these birds, the same as he gave it to the woman of this house?

SIBBY. That's it, that is it. Let him tell it out now.

COONEY. Will you have me ask it as often as the hairs of my head? If I get vexed I will make you answer me.

NESTOR. It seems to me to have set fire to a rick, but I am well able to quench it after. There is no man in South Africa, or that came from South Africa, or that ever owned a mine there at all. Where is the man bought the bird, are you asking? There he is standing among us on this floor. (*Points to* COONEY.) That is himself, the very man!

COONEY (*advancing a step*). What is that you are saying?

NESTOR. I say that no one came in here but yourself.

COONEY. Did he say or not say there was a rich man came in?

SIBBY. He did, surely.

NESTOR. To make up a plan. . . .

COONEY. I know well you have made up a plan.

NESTOR. To give it unknownst. . . .

COONEY. It is to keep it unknownst you are wanting!

NESTOR. The way she would not suspect. . . .

COONEY. It is I myself suspect and have cause to suspect! Give me back my own ten pounds and I'll be satisfied.

NESTOR. What way can I give it back?

COONEY. The same way as you took it, in the palm of your hand.

NESTOR. Sure it is paid away and spent. . . .

COONEY. If it is you'll repay it! I know as well as if I was inside you you are striving to make me your prey! But I'll sober you! It is into the Court I will drag you, and as far as the gaol!

NESTOR. I tell you I gave it to the widow woman. . . .

(MRS. BRODERICK *comes in*.)

COONEY. Let her say now did you.

MRS. BRODERICK. What is it at all? What is happening? Joseph Nestor threatened by a tinker or a tramp!

NESTOR. I would think better of his behaviour if he was a tinker or a tramp.

MRS. BRODERICK. He has drink taken so. Isn't drink the terrible tempter, a man to see flames and punishment upon the one side and drink upon the other, and to turn his face towards the drink!

COONEY. Will you stop your chat, Mary Broderick, till I will drag the truth out of this traitor?

MRS. BRODERICK. Who is that calling me by my name? Och! Is it Michael Cooney is in it? Michael Cooney, my brother! O Michael, what will they think of you coming into the town and much like a rag on a stick would be scaring in the wheatfield through the day?

COONEY (*pointing at* NESTOR). It was going up in the mill I destroyed myself, following the directions of that ruffian!

MRS. BRODERICK. And what call has a man that has drink taken to go climbing up a loft in a mill? A crooked mind you had always, and that's a sort of person drink doesn't suit.

COONEY. I tell you I didn't take a glass over a counter this ten year.

MRS. BRODERICK. You would do well to go learn behaviour from Mr. Nestor.

COONEY. The man that has me plundered and robbed! Tell me this now, if you can tell it. Did you find any pound notes in "Old Moore's Almanac"?

MRS. BRODERICK. I did not to be sure, or in any other place.

NESTOR. She came in at the door and I striving to put them into the book.

COONEY. Look are they in it now, and I will say he is not tricky, but honest.

NESTOR. You needn't be looking. . . .

MRS. BRODERICK (*turning over the leaves*). Ne'er a thing at all in it but the things that will or will not happen, and the days of the changes of the moon.

COONEY (*seizing and shaking it*). Look at that now! (*To* NESTER.) Will you believe me now telling you that you are a rogue?

NESTOR. Will you listen to me, ma'am. . . .

COONEY. No, but listen to myself. I brought the money to you.

NESTOR. If he did he wouldn't trust you with it, ma'am.

COONEY. I intended it for your relief.

NESTOR. In dread he was you would go follow him to Limerick.

MRS. BRODERICK. It is not likely I would be following the like of him to Limerick, a man that left me to the charity of strangers from Africa!

COONEY. I gave the money to him. . . .

NESTOR. And I gave it to yourself paying for the jackdaw. Are you satisfied now, Mary Broderick?

MRS. BRODERICK. Satisfied, is it? It would be a queer thing indeed I to be satisfied. My brother to be spending money on birds, and his sister with a summons on her head. Michael Cooney to be passing himself off as a mine-owner, and I myself being the way I am!

COONEY. What would I want doing that? I tell you I ask no birds, black, blue or white!

MRS. BRODERICK. I wonder at you now saying that, and you with that clutch on your arm! (COONEY *indignantly flings away nest.*) Searching out jackdaws and his sister without the price of a needle in the house! I tell you, Michael Cooney, it is yourself will be wandering after your burying, naked and perishing, through winds and through frosts, in satisfaction for the way you went wasting your money and your means on such vanities, and she that was reared on the one floor with you going knocking at the Workhouse door! What good will jackdaws be to you that time?

COONEY. It is what I would wish to know, what scheme are the whole of you at? It is long till I will trust any one but my own eyes again in the whole of the living world.

(*She wipes her eyes indignantly.* TOMMY NALLY *rushes in the bird and cage still in his hands.*)

NALLY. Where is the bird buyer? It is here he is said to be. It is well for me get here the first. It is the whole of the town will be here within half an hour; they have put a great scatter on themselves hunting and searching in every place, but I am the first!

NESTOR. What is it you are talking about?

NALLY. Not a house in the whole street but is deserted. It is much if the Magistrates themselves didn't quit the bench for the pursuit, the way Tim Ward quitted the place he had a right to be!

NESTOR. It is some curse in the air, or some scourge?

NALLY. Birds they are getting by the score! Old and young! Where is the bird-buyer? Who is it now will give me my price?

(*He holds up the cage.*)

COONEY. There is surely some root for all this. There must be some buyer after all. It's to keep him to themselves they are wanting. (*Goes to door.*) But I'll get my own profit in spite of them.

(*He goes outside door, looking up and down the street.*)

MRS. BRODERICK. Look at what Tommy Nally has. That's my bird.

NALLY. It is not, it's my own!

MRS. BRODERICK. That is my cage!

NALLY. It is not, it is mine!

MRS. BRODERICK. Wouldn't I know my own cage and my own bird? Don't be telling lies that way!

NALLY. It is no lie I am telling. The bird and the cage were made a present to me.

MRS. BRODERICK. Who would make a present to you of the things that belong to myself?

NALLY. It was Mr. Nestor gave them to me.

MRS. BRODERICK. Do you hear what he says, Joseph Nestor? What call have you to be giving a present of my bird?

NESTOR. And wasn't I after buying it from you?

MRS. BRODERICK. If you were it was not for yourself you bought it, but for the poor man in South Africa you bought it, and you defrauding him now, giving it away to a man has no claim to it at all. Well, now, isn't it hard for any man to find a person he can trust?

NESTOR. Didn't you hear me saying I bought it for no person at all?

MRS. BRODERICK. Give it up now, Tommy Nally, or I'll have you in gaol on the head of it.

NALLY. Oh, you wouldn't do such a thing, ma'am, I am sure!

MRS. BRODERICK. Indeed and I will, and have you on the tread-mill for a thief.

NALLY. Oh, oh, oh, look now, Mr. Nestor, the way you have made me a thief and to be lodged in the gaol!

NESTOR. I wish to God you were lodged in it, and we would have less annoyance in this place!

NALLY. Oh, that is a terrible thing for you to be saying! Sure the poorhouse itself is better than the gaol! The nuns preparing you for heaven and the Mass every morning of your life. . . .

NESTOR. If you go on with your talk and your arguments it's to gaol you will surely go.

NALLY. Milk of a Wednesday and a Friday, the potatoes steamed very good. . . . It's the skins of the potatoes they were telling me

you do have to be eating in the gaol. It is what I am thinking, Mr.
Nestor, that bird will lie heavy on you at the last!

NESTOR (*seizing cage and letting the bird out of the door*). Bad
cess and a bad end to it, and that I may never see it or hear of it
again!

MRS. BRODERICK. Look what he is after doing! Get it back for
me! Give it here into my hands I say! Why wouldn't I sell it secondly to the buyer and he to be coming to the door? It is in my
own pocket I will keep the price of it that time!

NALLY. It would have been as good you to have left it with me
as to be sending itself and the worth of it up into the skies!

MRS. BRODERICK (*taking* NESTOR'S *arm*). Get it back for me I
tell you! There it is above in the ash tree, and it flapping its wings
on a bough!

NESTOR. Give me the cage, if that will content you, and I will
strive to entice it to come in.

COONEY (*coming in*). Everyone running this way and that way.
It is for birds they are looking sure enough. Why now would they
go through such hardship if there was not a demand in some place?

NESTOR (*pushing him away*). Let me go now before that bird
will quit the branch where it is.

COONEY (*seizing hold of him*). Is it striving to catch a bird for
yourself you are now?

NESTOR. Let me pass if you please. I have nothing to say to you
at all.

COONEY. Laying down to me they were worth nothing! I knew
well you had made up some plan! The grand adviser is it! It is to
yourself you gave good advice that time!

NESTOR. Let me out I tell you before that uproar you are making will drive it from its perch on the tree.

COONEY. Is it to rob me of my own money you did and to be
keeping me out of the money I earned along with it!

(*Threatens* NESTOR *with* "*Moore's Almanac,*" *which he has
picked up.*)

SIBBY. Take care would there be murder done in this place!

(*She seizes* NESTOR, MRS. BRODERICK *seizes* COONEY.
TOMMY NALLY *wrings his hands.*)

NESTOR. Tommy Nally, will you kindly go and call for the
police.

COONEY. Is it into a den of wild beasts I am come that must go
calling out for the police?

NESTOR. A very unmannerly person indeed!

COONEY. Everyone thinking to take advantage of me and to make their own trap for my ruin.

NESTOR. I don't know what cause has he at all to have taken any umbrage against me.

COONEY. You that had your eye on my notes from the first like a goat in a cabbage garden!

NESTOR. Coming with a gift in the one hand and holding a dagger in the other!

COONEY. If you say that again I will break your collar bone!

NESTOR. O, but you are the terrible wicked man!

COONEY. I'll squeeze satisfaction out of you if I had to hang for it! I will be well satisfied if I'll kill you!

(*Flings "Moore's Almanac" at him.*)

NESTOR (*throwing his bundle of newspapers*). Oh, good jewel!

WARD (*coming in hastily*). Whist the whole of you, I tell you! The Magistrates are coming to the door! (*Comes in and shuts it after him.*)

MRS. BRODERICK. The Lord be between us and harm! What made them go quit the Court?

WARD. The whole of the witnesses and of the prosecution made off bird-catching. The Magistrates sent to invite the great mine-owner to go lunch at Noonan's with themselves.

COONEY. Horses of their own to stick him with they have. I wouldn't doubt them at all.

WARD. He could not be found in any place. They are informed he was never seen leaving this house. They are coming to make an investigation.

NESTOR. Don't be anyway uneasy. I will explain the whole case.

WARD. The police along with them. . . .

COONEY. Is the whole of this district turned into a trap?

WARD. It is what they are thinking, that the stranger was made away with for his gold!

COONEY. And if he was, as sure as you are living, it was done by that blackguard there! (*Points at Nestor.*)

WARD. If he is not found they will arrest all they see upon the premises. . . .

COONEY. It is best for me to quit this. (*Goes to door.*)

WARD. Here they are at the door. Sergeant Carden along with them. Hide yourself, Mr. Nestor, if you've anyway to do it at all.

(*Sounds of feet and talking and knock at the door. COONEY*

hides under counter. NESTOR *lies down on top of bench, spreads his newspaper over him.* MRS. BRODERICK *goes behind counter.*)

NESTOR (*raising paper from his face and looking out.*) Tommy Nally, I will give you five shillings if you will draw "Tit-Bits" over my feet.

Curtain.

THE WORKHOUSE WARD

THE WORKHOUSE WARD

PERSONS

MIKE MCINERNEY   ⎱ *Paupers*
MICHAEL MISKELL   ⎰

MRS. DONOHUE, *a Countrywoman*

SCENE: *A ward in Cloon Workhouse. The two old men in their beds.*

MICHAEL MISKELL. Isn't it a hard case, Mike McInerney, myself and yourself to be left here in the bed, and it the feast day of Saint Colman, and the rest of the ward attending on the Mass.

MIKE MCINERNEY. Is it sitting up by the hearth you are wishful to be, Michael Miskell, with cold in the shoulders and with speckled shins? Let you rise up so, and you well able to do it, not like myself that has pains the same as tin-tacks within in my inside.

MICHAEL MISKELL. If you have pains within in your inside there is no one can see it or know of it the way they can see my own knees that are swelled up with the rheumatism, and my hands that are twisted in ridges the same as an old cabbage stalk. It is easy to be talking about soreness and about pains, and they maybe not to be in it at all.

MIKE MCINERNEY. To open me to analyse me you would know what sort of a pain and a soreness I have in my heart and in my chest. But I'm not one like yourself to be cursing and praying and tormenting the time the nuns are at hand, thinking to get a bigger share than myself of nourishment and of the milk.

MICHAEL MISKELL. That's the way you do be picking at me and faulting me. I had a share and a good share in my early time, and it's well you know that, and the both of us reared in Skehanagh.

MIKE MCINERNEY. You may say that, indeed, we are both of us reared in Skehanagh. Little wonder you to have good nourishment the time we were both rising, and you bringing away my rabbits out of the snare.

MICHAEL MISKELL. And you didn't bring away my own eels, I suppose, I was after spearing in the Turlough? Selling them to the nuns in the convent you did, and letting on they to be your own.

97

For you were always a cheater and a schemer, grabbing every earthly thing for your own profit.

MIKE MCINERNEY. And you were no grabber yourself, I suppose, till your land and all you had grabbed wore away from you!

MICHAEL MISKELL. If I lost it itself, it was through the crosses I met with and I going through the world. I never was a rambler and a cardplayer like yourself, Mike McInerney, that ran through all and lavished it unknown to your mother!

MIKE MCINERNEY. Lavished it, is it? And if I did was it you yourself led me to lavish it or some other one? It is on my own floor I would be to-day and in the face of my family, but for the misfortune I had to be put with a bad next door neighbour that was yourself. What way did my means go from me is it? Spending on fencing, spending on walls, making up gates, putting up doors, that would keep your hens and your ducks from coming in through starvation on my floor, and every four footed beast you had from preying and trespassing on my oats and my mangolds and my little lock of hay!

MICHAEL MISKELL. O to listen to you! And I striving to please you and to be kind to you and to close my ears to the abuse you would be calling and letting out of your mouth. To trespass on your crops is it? It's little temptation there was for my poor beasts to ask to cross the mering. My God Almighty! What had you but a little corner of a field!

MIKE MCINERNEY. And what do you say to my garden that your two pigs had destroyed on me the year of the big tree being knocked, and they making gaps in the wall.

MICHAEL MISKELL. Ah, there does be a great deal of gaps knocked in a twelvemonth. Why wouldn't they be knocked by the thunder, the same as the tree, or some storm that came up from the west?

MIKE MCINERNEY. It was the west wind, I suppose, that devoured my green cabbage? And that rooted up my Champion potatoes? And that ate the gooseberries themselves from off the bush?

MICHAEL MISKELL. What are you saying? The two quietest pigs ever I had, no way wicked and well ringed. They were not ten minutes in it. It would be hard for them eat strawberries in that time, let alone gooseberries that's full of thorns.

MIKE MCINERNEY. They were not quiet, but very ravenous pigs you had that time, as active as a fox they were, killing my young ducks. Once they had blood tasted you couldn't stop them.

MICHAEL MISKELL. And what happened myself the fair day of Esserkelly, the time I was passing your door? Two brazened dogs that rushed out and took a piece of me. I never was the better of it or of the start I got, but wasting from then till now!

MIKE MCINERNEY. Thinking you were a wild beast they did, that had made his escape out of the travelling show, with the red eyes of you and the ugly face of you, and the two crooked legs of you that wouldn't hardly stop a pig in a gap. Sure any dog that had any life in it at all would be roused and stirred seeing the like of you going the road!

MICHAEL MISKELL. I did well taking out a summons against you that time. It is a great wonder you not to have been bound over through your lifetime, but the laws of England is queer.

MIKE MCINERNEY. What ailed me that I did not summons yourself after you stealing away the clutch of eggs I had in the barrel, and I away in Ardrahan searching out a clocking hen.

MICHAEL MISKELL. To steal your eggs is it? Is that what you are saying now? (*Holds up his hands.*) The Lord is in heaven, and Peter and the saints, and yourself that was in Ardrahan that day put a hand on them as soon as myself! Isn't it a bad story for me to be wearing out my days beside you the same as a spancelled goat. Chained I am and tethered I am to a man that is ramsacking his mind for lies!

MIKE MCINERNEY. If it is a bad story for you, Michael Miskell, it is a worse story again for myself. A Miskell to be next and near me through the whole of the four quarters of the year. I never heard there to be any great name on the Miskells as there was on my own race and name.

MICHAEL MISKELL. You didn't, is it? Well, you could hear it if you had but ears to hear it. Go across to Lisheen Crannagh and down to the sea and to Newtown Lynch and the mills of Duras and you'll find a Miskell, and as far as Dublin!

MIKE MCINERNEY. What signifies Crannagh and the mills of Duras? Look at all my own generations that are buried at the Seven Churches. And how many generations of the Miskells are buried in it? Answer me that!

MICHAEL MISKELL. I tell you but for the wheat that was to be sowed there would be more side cars and more common cars at my father's funeral (God rest his soul!) than at any funeral ever left your own door. And as to my mother, she was a Cuffe from Clare-galway, and it's she had the purer blood!

MIKE MCINERNEY. And what do you say to the banshee? Isn't

she apt to have knowledge of the ancient race? Was ever she heard to screech or to cry for the Miskells? Or the Cuffes from Claregalway? She was not, but for the six families, the Hyneses, the Foxes, the Faheys, the Dooleys, the McInerneys. It is of the nature of the McInerneys she is I am thinking, crying them the same as a king's children.

MICHAEL MISKELL. It is a pity the banshee not to be crying for yourself at this minute, and giving you a warning to quit your lies and your chat and your arguing and your contrary ways; for there is no one under the rising sun could stand you. I tell you you are not behaving as in the presence of the Lord!

MIKE MCINERNEY. Is it wishful for my death you are? Let it come and meet me now and welcome so long as it will part me from yourself! And I say, and I would kiss the book on it, I to have one request only to be granted, and I leaving it in my will, it is what I would request, nine furrows of the field, nine ridges of the hills, nine waves of the ocean to be put between your grave and my own grave the time we will be laid in the ground!

MICHAEL MISKELL. Amen to that! Nine ridges, is it? No, but let the whole ridge of the world separate us till the Day of Judgment! I would not be laid anear you at the Seven Churches, I to get Ireland without a divide!

MIKE MCINERNEY. And after that again! I'd sooner than ten pound in my hand, I to know that my shadow and my ghost will not be knocking about with your shadow and your ghost, and the both of us waiting our time. I'd sooner be delayed in Purgatory! Now, have you anything to say?

MICHAEL MISKELL. I have everything to say, if I had but the time to say it!

MIKE MCINERNEY (*sitting up.*) Let me up out of this till I'll choke you!

MICHAEL MISKELL. You scolding pauper you!

MIKE MCINERNEY (*shaking his fist at him*). Wait a while!

MICHAEL MISKELL (*shaking his fist*). Wait a while yourself!

> (MRS. DONOHOE *comes in with a parcel. She is a countrywoman with a frilled cap and a shawl. She stands still a minute. The two old men lie down and compose themselves.*)

MRS. DONOHOE. They bade me come up here by the stair. I never was in this place at all. I don't know am I right. Which now of the two of ye is Mike McInerney?

MIKE MCINERNEY. Who is it is calling me by my name?

MRS. DONOHOE. Sure amn't I your sister, Honor McInerney that was, that is now Honor Donohoe.

MIKE MCINERNEY. So you are, I believe. I didn't know you till you pushed anear me. It is time indeed for you to come see me, and I in this place five year or more. Thinking me to be no credit to you, I suppose, among that tribe of the Donohoes. I wonder they to give you leave to come ask am I living yet or dead?

MRS. DONOHOE. Ah, sure, I buried the whole string of them. Himself was the last to go. (*Wipes her eyes.*) The Lord be praised he got a fine natural death. Sure we must go through our crosses. And he got a lovely funeral; it would delight you to hear the priest reading the Mass. My poor John Donohoe! A nice clean man, you couldn't but be fond of him. Very severe on the tobacco he was, but he wouldn't touch the drink.

MIKE MCINERNEY. And is it in Curranroe you are living yet?

MRS. DONOHOE. It is so. He left all to myself. But it is a lonesome thing the head of a house to have died!

MIKE MCINERNEY. I hope that he has left you a nice way of living?

MRS. DONOHOE. Fair enough, fair enough. A wide lovely house I have; a few acres of grass land . . . the grass does be very sweet that grows among the stones. And as to the sea, there is something from it every day of the year, a handful of periwinkles to make kitchen, or cockles maybe. There is many a thing in the sea is not decent, but cockles is fit to put before the Lord!

MIKE MCINERNEY. You have all that! And you without ere a man in the house?

MRS. DONOHOE. It is what I am thinking, yourself might come and keep me company. It is no credit to me a brother of my own to be in this place at all.

MIKE MCINERNEY. I'll go with you! Let me out of this! It is the name of the McInerneys will be rising on every side!

MRS. DONOHOE. I don't know. I was ignorant of you being kept to the bed.

MIKE MCINERNEY. I am not kept to it, but maybe an odd time when there is a colic rises up within me. My stomach always gets better the time there is a change in the moon. I'd like well to draw anear you. My heavy blessing on you, Honor Donohoe, for the hand you have held out to me this day.

MRS. DONOHOE. Sure you could be keeping the fire in, and stirring the pot with the bit of Indian meal for the hens, and milking the goat and taking the tacklings off the donkey at the door; and maybe putting out the cabbage plants in their time. For when the old man died the garden died.

MIKE MCINERNEY. I could to be sure, and be cutting the potatoes for seed. What luck could there be in a place and a man not to be in it? Is that now a suit of clothes you have brought with you?

MRS. DONOHOE. It is so, the way you will be tasty coming in among the neighbours at Curranroe.

MIKE MCINERNEY. My joy you are! It is well you earned me! Let me up out of this! (*He sits up and spreads out the clothes and tries on coat.*) That now is a good frieze coat . . . and a hat in the fashion . . . (*He puts on hat.*)

MICHAEL MISKELL (*alarmed*). And is it going out of this you are, Mike McInerney?

MIKE MCINERNEY. Don't you hear I am going? To Curranroe I am going. Going I am to a place where I will get every good thing!

MICHAEL MISKELL. And is it to leave me here after you you will?

MIKE MCINERNEY (*in a rising chant*). Every good thing! The goat and the kid are there, the sheep and the lamb are there, the cow does be running and she coming to be milked! Ploughing and seed sowing, blossom at Christmas time, the cuckoo speaking through the dark days of the year! Ah, what are you talking about? Wheat high in hedges, no talk about the rent! Salmon in the rivers as plenty as turf! Spending and getting and nothing scarce! Sport and pleasure, and music on the strings! Age will go from me and I will be young again. Geese and turkeys for the hundreds and drink for the whole world!

MICHAEL MISKELL. Ah, Mike, is it truth you are saying, you to go from me and to leave me with rude people and with townspeople, and with people of every parish in the union, and they having no respect for me or no wish for me at all!

MIKE MCINERNEY. Whist now and I'll leave you . . . my pipe (*hands it over*); and I'll engage it is Honor Donohoe won't refuse to be sending you a few ounces of tobacco an odd time, and neighbours coming to the fair in November or in the month of May.

MICHAEL MISKELL. Ah, what signifies tobacco? All that I am craving is the talk. There to be no one at all to say out to whatever thought might be rising in my innate mind! To be lying here and no conversible person in it would be the abomination of misery!

MIKE MCINERNEY. Look now, Honor. . . . It is what I often heard said, two to be better than one. . . . Sure if you had an old trouser was full of holes . . . or a skirt . . . wouldn't you put another in under it that might be as tattered as itself, and the two of them together would make some sort of a decent show?

MRS. DONOHOE. Ah, what are you saying? There is no holes in that suit I brought you now, but as sound it is as the day I spun it for himself.

MIKE MCINERNEY. It is what I am thinking, Honor . . . I do be weak an odd time. . . any load I would carry, it preys upon my side . . . and this man does be weak an odd time with the swelling in his knees . . but the two of us together it's not likely it is at the one time we would fail. Bring the both of us with you, Honor, and the height of the castle of luck on you, and the both of us together will make one good hardy man!

MRS. DONOHOE. I'd like my job! Is it queer in the head you are grown asking me to bring in a stranger off the road?

MICHAEL MISKELL. I am not, ma'am, but an old neighbour I am. If I had forecasted this asking I would have asked it myself. Michael Miskell I am, that was in the next house to you in Skehanagh!

MRS. DONOHUE. For pity's sake! Michael Miskell is it? That's worse again. Yourself and Mike that never left fighting and scolding and attacking one another! Sparring at one another like two young pups you were, and threatening one another after like two grown dogs!

MIKE MCINERNEY. All the quarrelling was ever in the place it was myself did it. Sure his anger rises fast and goes away like the wind. Bring him out with myself now, Honor Donohoe, and God bless you.

MRS. DONOHOE. Well, then, I will not bring him out, and I will not bring yourself out, and you not to learn better sense. Are you making yourself ready to come?

MIKE MCINERNEY. I am thinking, maybe . . . it is a mean thing for a man that is shivering into seventy years to go changing from place to place.

MRS. DONOHUE. Well, take your luck or leave it. All I asked was to save you from the hurt and the harm of the year.

MIKE MCINERNEY. Bring the both of us with you or I will not stir out of this.

MRS. DONOHOE. Give me back my fine suit so (*begins gathering up the clothes*), till I'll go look for a man of my own!

MIKE MCINERNEY. Let you go so, as you are so unnatural and so disobliging, and look for some man of your own, God help him! For I will not go with you at all!

MRS. DONOHOE. It is too much time I lost with you, and dark night waiting to overtake me on the road. Let the two of you stop together, and the back of my hand to you. It is I will leave you there the same as God left the Jews!

(*She goes out. The old men lie down and are silent for a moment.*)

MICHAEL MISKELL. Maybe the house is not so wide as what she says.

MIKE MCINERNEY. Why wouldn't it be wide?

MICHAEL MISKELL. Ah, there does be a good deal of middling poor houses down by the sea.

MIKE MCINERNEY. What would you know about wide houses? Whatever sort of a house you had yourself it was too wide for the provision you had into it.

MICHAEL MISKELL. Whatever provision I had in my house it was wholesome provision and natural provision. Herself and her periwinkles! Periwinkles is a hungry sort of food.

MIKE MCINERNEY. Stop your impudence and your chat or it will be the worse for you. I'd bear with my own father and mother as long as any man would, but if they'd vex me I would give them the length of a rope as soon as another!

MICHAEL MISKELL. I would never ask at all to go eating periwinkles.

MIKE MCINERNEY (*sitting up*). Have you anyone to fight me?

MICHAEL MISKELL (*whimpering*). I have not, only the Lord!

MIKE MCINERNEY. Let you leave putting insults on me so, and death picking at you!

MICHAEL MISKELL. Sure I am saying nothing at all to displease you. It is why I wouldn't go eating periwinkles, I'm in dread I might swallow the pin.

MIKE MCINERNEY. Who in the world wide is asking you to eat them? You're as tricky as a fish in the full tide!

MICHAEL MISKELL. Tricky is it! Oh, my curse and the curse of the four and twenty men upon you!

MIKE MCINERNEY. That the worm may chew you from skin to marrow bone! (*Seizes his pillow.*)

MICHAEL MISKELL (*seizing his own pillow*). I'll leave my death on you, you scheming vagabone!

MIKE MCINERNEY. By cripes! I'll pull out your pin feathers! (*Throwing pillow.*)

MICHAEL MISKELL (*throwing pillow*). You tyrant! You big bully you!

MIKE MCINERNEY (*throwing pillow and seizing mug*). Take this so, you stobbing ruffian you!

(*They throw all within their reach at one another, mugs, prayer books, pipes, etc.*)

Curtain.

THE BOGIE MEN

THE BOGIE MEN

PERSONS

    TAIG O'HARRAGHA

    DARBY MELODY   }   *both Chimney Sweeps*

SCENE: *A Shed near where a coach stops.* DARBY *comes in. Has a tin can of water in one hand, a sweep's bag and brush in the other. He lays down bag on an empty box and puts can on the floor. Is taking a showy suit of clothes out of bag and admiring them and is about to put them on when he hears some one coming and hurriedly puts them back into the bag.*

TAIG (*at door*). God save all here!

DARBY. God save you. A sweep is it? (*Suspiciously.*) What brought you following me?

TAIG. Why wouldn't I be a sweep as good as yourself?

DARBY. It is not one of my own trade I came looking to meet with. It is a shelter I was searching out, where I could put on a decent appearance, rinsing my head and my features in a tin can of water.

TAIG. Is it long till the coach will be passing by the cross-road beyond?

DARBY. Within about a half an hour they were telling me.

TAIG. There does be much people travelling to this place?

DARBY. I suppose there might, and it being the high road from the town of Ennis.

TAIG. It should be in this town you follow your trade?

DARBY. It is not in the towns I do be.

TAIG. There's nothing but the towns, since the farmers in the country clear out their own chimneys with a bush under and a bush overhead.

DARBY. I travel only gentlemen's houses.

TAIG. There does be more of company in the streets than you'd find on the bare road.

DARBY. It isn't easy get company for a person has but two empty hands.

TAIG. Wealth to be in the family it is all one nearly with having a grip of it in your own palm.

DARBY. I wish to the Lord it was the one thing.

TAIG. You to know what I know——

DARBY. What is it that you know?

TAIG. It is dealing out cards through the night time I will be from this out, and making bets on racehorses and fighting-cocks through all the hours of the day.

DARBY. I would sooner to be sleeping in feathers and to do no hand's turn at all, day or night.

TAIG. If I came paddling along through every place this day and the road hard under my feet, it is likely I will have my choice way leaving it.

DARBY. How is that now?

TAIG. A horse maybe and a car or two horses, or maybe to go in the coach, and I myself sitting alongside the man came in it.

DARBY. Is it that he is taking you into his service?

TAIG. Not at all! And I being of his own family and his blood.

DARBY. Of his blood now?

TAIG. A relation I have, that is full up of money and of every whole thing.

DARBY. A relation?

TAIG. A first cousin, by the side of the mother.

DARBY. Well, I am not without having a first cousin of my own.

TAIG. I wouldn't think he'd be much. To be listening to my mother giving out a report of my one's ways, you would maybe believe it is no empty skin of a man he is.

DARBY. My own mother was not without giving out a report of my man's ways.

TAIG. Did she see him?

DARBY. She did, I suppose, or the thing was near him. She never was tired talking of him.

TAIG. It is often my own mother would have Dermot pictured to myself.

DARBY. It is often the likeness of Timothy was laid down to me by the teaching of my mother's mouth, since I was able to walk the floor. She thought the whole world of him.

TAIG. A bright scholar she laid Dermot down to be. A good doing fellow for himself. A man would be well able to go up to his promise.

DARBY. That is the same account used to be given out of Timothy.

TAIG. To some trade of merchandise it is likely Dermot was reared. A good living man that was never any cost on his mother.

DARBY. To own an estate before he would go far in age Timothy was on the road.

TAIG. To have the handling of silks and jewelleries and to be free of them, and of suits and the making of suits, that is the way with the big merchants of the world.

DARBY. It is letting out his land to grass farmers a man owning acres does be making his profit.

TAIG. A queer thing you to be the way you are, and he to be an upstanding gentleman.

DARBY. It is the way I went down; my mother used to be faulting me and I not being the equal of him. Tormenting and picking at me and shouting me on the road. "You thraneen," she'd say, "you little trifle of a son! You stumbling over the threshold as if in slumber, and Timothy being as swift as a bee!"

TAIG. So my own mother used to be going on at myself, and be letting out shrieks and screeches. "What now would your cousin Dermot be saying?" every time there would come a new rent in my rags.

DARBY. "Little he'd think of you," she'd say; "you without body and puny, not fit to lift scraws from off the field, and Timothy bringing in profit to his mother's hand, and earning prizes and rewards."

TAIG. The time it would fail me to follow my book or to say off my A,B, ab, to draw Dermot down on me she would. "Before he was up to your age," she would lay down, "he was fitted to say off Catechisms and to read newses. You have no more intellect beside him," she'd say, "than a chicken has its head yet in the shell."

DARBY. "Let you hold up the same as Timothy," she'd give out, and I to stoop my shoulders the time the sun would prey upon my head. "He that is as straight and as clean as a green rush on the brink of the bog."

TAIG. "It is you will be fit but to blow the bellows," my mother would say, "the time Dermot will be forging gold." I let on the book to have gone astray on me at the last. Why would I go crush and bruise myself under a weight of learning, and there being one in the family well able to take my cost and my support whatever way it might go? Dermot that would feel my keep no more than the lake would feel the weight of the duck.

DARBY. I seen no use to be going sweating after farmers, striving to plough or to scatter seed, when I never could come anear

Timothy in any sort of a way, and he, by what she was saying, able to thrash out a rick of oats in the day. So it fell out I was thrown on the ways of the world, having no skill in any trade, till there came a demand for me going aloft in chimneys, I being as thin as a needle and shrunken with weakness and want of food.

TAIG. I got my living for a while by miracle and trafficking in rabbit skins, till a sweep from Limerick bound me to himself one time I was skinned with the winter. Great cruelty he gave me till I ran from him with the brush and the bag, and went foraging around for myself.

DARBY. So am I going around by myself. I never had a comrade lad.

TAIG. My mother that would hit me a crack if I made free with any of the chaps of the village, saying that would not serve me with Dermot, that had a good top-coat and was brought up to manners and behaviour.

DARBY. My own mother that drew down Timothy on me the time she'd catch me going with the lads that had their pleasure out of the world, slashing tops and pebbles, throwing and going on with games.

TAIG. I took my own way after, fitting myself for sports and funning, against the time the rich man would stretch out his hand. Going with wild lads and poachers I was, till they left me carrying their snares in under my coat, that I was lodged for three months in the gaol.

DARBY. The neighbours had it against me after, I not being friendly when we were small. The most time I am going the road it is a lonesome shadow I cast before me.

TAIG (*looking out of the door*). It is on this day I will be making acquaintance with himself. My mother that sent him a request to come meet me in this town on this day, it being the first of the summer.

DARBY. My own mother that did no less, telling me she got word from Timothy he would come meet here with myself. It is certain he will bring me into his house, she having wedded secondly with a labouring man has got a job at Golden Hill in Lancashire. I would not recognise him beyond any other one.

TAIG. I would recognise the signs of a big man. I wish I was within in his kitchen. There is a pinch of hunger within in my heart.

DARBY. So there is within in myself.

TAIG. Is there nothing at all in the bag?

DARBY. It is a bit of a salted herring.

TAIG. Why wouldn't you use it?

DARBY. I would be delicate coming before him and the smell of it to be on me, and all the grand meats will be at his table.

TAIG (*showing a bottle*). The full of a pint I have of porter, that fell from a tinker's car.

DARBY. I wonder you would not swallow it down for to keep courage in your mind.

TAIG. It is what I am thinking, I to take it fasting, it might put confusion and wildness in my head. I would wish, and I meeting with him, my wits to be of the one clearness with his own. It is not long to be waiting; it is in claret I will be quenching my thirst to-night, or in punch!

DARBY (*looking out*). I am nearly in dread meeting Timothy, fearing I will not be pleasing to him, and I not acquainted with his habits.

TAIG. I would not be afeared, and Dermot to come sparkling in, and seven horses in his coach.

DARBY. What way can I come before him at all? I would be better pleased you to personate me and to stand up to him in my place.

TAIG. Any person to put orders on me, or to bid me change my habits, I'd give no heed! I'd stand up to him in the spite of his teeth!

DARBY. If it wasn't for the hearthfires to be slackened with the springtime, and my work to be lessened with the strengthening of the sun, I'd sooner not see him till another moon is passed, or two moons.

TAIG. He to bid me read out the news of the world, taking me to be a scholar, I'd give him words that are in no books! I'd give him newses! I'd knock rights out of him or any one I ever seen.

DARBY. I could speak only of my trade. The boundaries of the world to be between us, I'm thinking I'd never ask to go cross them at all.

TAIG. He to go into Court swearing witnesses and to bring me along with him to face the judges and the whole troop of the police, I'd go bail I'll be no way daunted or scared.

DARBY. What way can I keep company with him? I that was partly reared in the workhouse. And he having a star on his hat and a golden apple in his hand. He will maybe be bidding me to scour myself with soapy water all the Sundays and Holy days of the year!

I tell you I am getting low hearted. I pray to the Lord to forgive me where I did not go under the schoolmaster's rod!

TAIG. I that will shape crampy words the same as any scholar at all! I'll let on to be a master of learning and of Latin!

DARBY. Ah, what letting on? It is Timothy will look through me the same as if my eyes were windows, and my thoughts standing as plain as cattle under the risen sun! It is easier letting on to have knowledge than to put on manners and behaviour.

TAIG. Ah, what's manners but to refuse no man a share of your bite and to keep back your hand from throwing stones?

DARBY. I tell you I'm in shivers! My heart that is shaking like an ivy leaf! My bones that are loosened and slackened in the similitude of a rope of tow! I'd sooner meet with a lion of the wilderness or the wickedest wind of the hills! I thought it never would come to pass. I'd sooner go into the pettiest house, the wildest home and the worst! Look at here now. Let me stop along with yourself. I never let out so much of my heart to any one at all till this day. It's a pity we should be parted!

TAIG. Is it to come following after me you would, before the face of Dermot?

DARBY. I'd feel no dread and you being at my side.

TAIG. Dermot to see me in company with the like of you! I wouldn't for the whole world he should be aware I had ever any traffic with chimneys or with soot. It would not be for his honour you to draw anear him!

DARBY (indignantly). No but Timothy that would make objection to yourself! He that would whip the world for manners and behaviour!

TAIG. Dermot that is better again. He that would write and dictate to you at the one time!

DARBY. What is that beside owning tillage, and to need no education, but to take rents into your hand?

TAIG. I would never believe him to own an estate.

DARBY. Why wouldn't he own it? "The biggest thing and the grandest," my mother would say when I would ask her what was he doing.

TAIG. Ah, what could be before selling out silks and satins. There is many an estated lord couldn't reach you out a fourpenny bit.

DARBY. The grandest house around the seas of Ireland he should have, beautifully made up! You would nearly go astray in it! It wouldn't be known what you could make of it at all! You wouldn't have it walked in a month!

TAIG. What is that beside having a range of shops as wide maybe as the street beyond?

DARBY. A house would be the capital of the county! One door for the rich, one door for the common! Velvet carpets rolled up, the way there would no dust from the chimney fall upon them. A hundred wouldn't be many standing in a corner of that place! A high bed of feathers, curled hair mattresses. A cover laid on it would be flowery with blossoms of gold!

TAIG. Muslin and gauze, cambric and linen! Canton crossbar! Glass windows full up of ribbons as gaudy as the crooked bow in the sky! Sovereigns and shillings in and out as plenty as to riddle rape seed. Sure them that do be selling in shops die leaving millions.

DARBY. Your man is not so good as mine in his office or in his billet.

TAIG. There is the horn of the coach. Get out now till I'll prepare myself. He might chance to come seeking for me here.

DARBY. There's a lather of sweat on myself. That's my tin can of water!

TAIG (holding can from him). Get out I tell you! I wouldn't wish him to feel the smell of you on the breeze.

DARBY. You are a mean savage to go keeping from me my tin can and my rag!

TAIG. What are you beside me? (taking clothes out of bag and putting them on). I have good clothes to put on me, that you haven't got.

DARBY (unpacking his bag). So have I good clothes! (Putting them on.) A body-coat my mother made out. She lost up to three shilling on it. And a speckled blue cravat!

TAIG (having washed face is putting on hat, sings).

All round my hat I wore a green ribbon
All round my hat for a year and a day;
And if anyone asks me the reason I wore it
I'll say that my true love went over the sea!

DARBY (washing face, sings).

All in my hat I will stick a blue feather
The same as the birds do be up in the tree;
And if you would ask me the reason I do it
I'll tell you my true love is come back to me!

(*He looks at reflection in tin can.*) Well that's a lovely picture of a man: would you ever say it now to be Dermot Melody!

TAIG. What's that you're saying?

DARBY. Looking I am at my image in the glass.

TAIG. What call have you to go call down the name of Melody?

DARBY. Every call. My father's name that was Melody till he lost his life in the year of the black potatoes.

TAIG. No but the name is it of my own big man. Funning me you are. Striving to put ridicule on me—Dermot Melody!

DARBY. That is my own full name but Darby is the name I am called.

TAIG. Humbugging and making a mock of me! Striving to make out it was my cousin Dermot's lot to go through the world as a tramp! Casting up my trade against me you would, bringing down on me chimneys and soot.

DARBY. Why wouldn't I call myself by my own name?

TAIG. Mocking and making short of me! That is very bad acting behaviour.

DARBY. I tell you I am Dermot Melody!

TAIG (*seizing and shaking him*). Are you a man owning riches and ships and merchandise?

DARBY. I am not, or anything of the sort.

TAIG. Have you teems of money in the bank?

DARBY. If I had would I be carrying this brush?

TAIG. You thief you!

DARBY. Thief yourself! (*hurls him down.*) Give out now your own ugly name!

TAIG (*whimpering*). Timothy O'Harragha.

DARBY (*kicking him*). Timothy O'Harragha. Is it thus you are personating my mother's sister's son?

TAIG. I am personating no one but myself.

DARBY. Giving out news you were an estated magistrate and such a great generation of a man. And you not owning so much as a rood of ridges.

TAIG. No but you covering yourself with choice clothing for to deceive me and lead me astray: you that are but the cull and the weakling of a race!

DARBY. Putting on your head a fine glossy hat the way I'd think you to have come with the spring tide and to have had luck through your life!

TAIG. It's a queer game you played on me and a crooked game.

You surely have a heart of marble. I never would have brought my legs so far to meet with the sooty likes of you!

DARBY (*threatening him*). I'll take no more talk from you. I to be twenty two degrees lower than the Hottentots! And you letting on to be my poor Timothy O'Harragha!

TAIG (*muttering to himself*). I never was called but Taig. Timothy was a sort of a holy day name.

DARBY. Where now are our two fine cousins, or is it that the both of us are cracked?

TAIG. It is, or our mothers before us.

DARBY. My mother was a McGarrity woman from Loughrea. It is Mary was her Christened name.

TAIG. So was my own mother of the McGarritys. It is sisters they were sure enough.

DARBY. That makes us out to be full cousins in the heel.

TAIG. You no better than myself! And the prayers I used to be saying for you, and you but a sketch and an excuse of a man!

DARBY. Ah, I am thinking people put more in their prayers than was ever put in them by God.

TAIG. Our mothers picturing us to one another as if we were the best in the world.

DARBY. Lies I suppose they were drawing down, for to startle us into good behaviour.

TAIG. Wouldn't you say now mothers to be a terror?

DARBY. And we nothing at all after but two chimney sweepers and two harmless drifty lads.

TAIG. Where is the great quality dinner yourself was to give me, having seven sorts of dressed meat? Pullets and bacon I was looking for, and to fall on an easy life.

DARBY. Gone like the clouds of the winter's fog. We rose out of it the same as we went in.

TAIG. We have nothing to do but to starve with the hunger, and you being as bare as myself.

DARBY. We are in a bad shift surely. We must perish with the want of support. It is one of the tricks of the world does be played upon the children of Adam.

TAIG. All we have to do is to crawl to the poorhouse gate. Or to go dig a pit in the graveyard, as it is short till we'll be stretched there with the want of food.

DARBY. Food is it? There is nothing at this time against me eating my bit of a herring. (*Seizes it and takes a bite.*)

TAIG. Give me a divide of it.

DARBY. Give me a drop of your own porter so, is in the bottle. There need be no dread on you now, of you being no match for your grand man.

TAIG. That is so. (*Drinks.*) I'll strive no more to fit myself for high quality relations. I am free from patterns of high up cousins from this out. I'll be a pattern to myself.

DARBY. I am well content being free of you, the way you were pictured to be. I declare to my goodness, the name of you put terror on me through the whole of my lifetime, and your image to be clogging and checking me on every side.

TAIG. To be thinking of you being in the world was a holy terror to myself. I give you my word you came through my sleep the same as a scarecrow or a dragon.

DARBY. It is great things I will be doing from this out, we two having nothing to cast up against one another. To be quit of Timothy the bogie and to get Taig for a comrade, I'm as proud as the Crown of France!

TAIG. I'm in dread of neither bumble or bagman or bugaboo! I will regulate things from myself from this out.

DARBY. There to be fineness of living in the world, why wouldn't I make it out for myself?

TAIG. It is to the harbours of America we will work our way across the wideness of the sea. It is well able we should be to go mounting up aloft in ropes. Come on Darby out of this!

DARBY. There is magic and mastery come into me! This day has put wings to my heart!

TAIG. Be easy now. We are maybe not clear of the chimneys yet.

DARBY. What signifies chimneys? We'll go up in them till we'll take a view of the Seven Stars! It is out beyond the hills of Burren I will cast my eye, till I'll see the three gates of Heaven!

TAIG. It's like enough, luck will flow to you. The way most people fail is in not keeping up the heart. Faith, it's well you have myself to mind you. Gather up now your brush and your bag.

(*They go to the door holding each other's hands and singing: "All in my hat I will stick a blue feather," etc.*)

Curtain.

COATS

COATS

PERSONS
HAZEL. *Editor of "Champion."*
MINEOG. *Editor of "Tribune."*
JOHN. *A waiter.*

SCENE. *Dining room of Royal Hotel, Cloonmore.*

HAZEL (*coming in*). Did Mr. Mineog come yet, John?

JOHN. He did not, Mr. Hazel. Ah, he won't be long coming. It's seldom he does be late.

HAZEL. Is the dinner ready?

JOHN. It is, sir. Boiled beef and parsnips, the same as every Monday for all comers, and an apple pie for yourself and Mr. Mineog.

MINEOG (*coming in*). Mr. Hazel is the first to-night. I'm glad to see you looking so good.

(*They take off coats and give to* WAITER.)

MINEOG. Put that on its own peg.

HAZEL. And mine on its own peg to the rear.

JOHN. I will, sir. (*He drops coats in putting them up. Then notices broken pane in window and picks up the coats hurriedly, putting them on wrong pegs.* HAZEL *and* MINEOG *have sat down.*)

HAZEL. Have you any strange news?

MINEOG. I have but the same news I always have, that it is quick Monday comes around, and that it is hard make provision for to fill up the four sheets of the *Tribune*, and nothing happening in these parts worth while. There would seem to be no news on this day beyond all days of the year.

HAZEL. Sure there is the same care and the same burden on myself. I wish I didn't put a supplement to the *Champion*. The dear knows what way will I fill it between this and Thursday, or in what place I can go questing after news!

MINEOG. Last week passed without anything doing. It is a very backward place to give information for two papers. If it was not for the league is between us, and for us meeting here on every Monday to make sure we are taking different sides on every question may turn up, and giving every abuse to one another in print, there is no person would pay his penny for the two of them, or it may be for the one of them.

HAZEL. That is so. And the worst is, there is no question ever rises that we do not agree on, or that would have power to make us fall out in earnest. It was different in my early time. The questions used to rise up then were worth fighting for.

MINEOG. There are some people so cantankerous they will heat themselves in argument as to which side might be right or wrong in a war, or if wars should be in it at all, or hangings.

HAZEL. Ah, when they are as long on the road as we are, they'll take things easy.

MINEOG. Now all the kingdoms of the earth to go struggling on one wrong side or another, or to bring themselves down to dust and ashes, it would not break our friendship. In all the years past there never did a cross word rise between us.

HAZEL. There never will. What are the fights of politics and parties beside living neighbourly with one another, and to go peaceable to the grave, our selves that are the oldest residents in the Square.

MINEOG. It will be long indeed before you will be followed to the grave. You didn't live no length yet. You are too fresh to go out and to forsake your wife and your family.

HAZEL. Ah, when the age would be getting up on you, you wouldn't be getting younger. But it's yourself that is as full of spirit as a four-year-old. I wish I had a sovereign for every year you will reign after me in the Square.

MINEOG (*sneezes*). There is a draught of air coming in the window.

HAZEL (*rising*). Take care might it be open—no, but a pane that is out. There is a very chilly breeze sweeping in.

MINEOG (*rising*). I will put on my coat so. There is no use giving provocation to a cold.

HAZEL. I'll do the same myself. It is hard to banish a sore throat.

(*They put on coats.* JOHN *brings in dinner. They sit down.*)

MINEOG. See can you baffle that draught of air, John.

JOHN. I'll go in search of something to stop it, sir. This bit of a board I brought is too unshapely.

MINEOG. Two columns of the *Tribune* as empty yet as anything you could see. I had them kept free for the Bishop's speech and he didn't come after.

HAZEL. That's the same cause has left myself with so wide a gap.

MINEOG. In the years past there used always to be something

happening such as famines, or the invention of printing. The whole world has got very slack.

HAZEL. You are a better hand than what I am at filling odd spaces would be left bare. It is often I think the news you put out comes partly from your own brain, and the prophecies you lay down about the weather and the crops.

MINEOG. Ah, I might stick in a bit of invention sometimes, when I'm put to the pin of my collar.

HAZEL. I might maybe make an attack on the *Tribune* for that.

MINEOG. Ah, what is it but a white sin. Sure it tells every person the same thing. It doesn't tell many lies, it goes somewhere anear it.

HAZEL. I spent a good while this evening searching through the shelves of the press I have in the office. I write an article an odd time, when there is nothing doing, that might come handy in a hurry.

MINEOG. So have I a press of the sort, and shelves in it. I am after going through them to-day.

HAZEL. But it's hard find a thing would be suitable, unless you might dress it up again someway fresh.

MINEOG. I made a thought and I searching a while ago. I was thinking it would be a very nice thing to show respect to yourself, and friendliness, putting down a short account of you and of all you have done for your family and for the town.

HAZEL. That is a strange thing now! I had it in my mind to do the very same service to yourself.

MINEOG. Is that so?

HAZEL. Your worth and your generosity and the way you have worked the *Tribune* for your own and for the public good.

MINEOG. And another thing. I not only thought to write it but I am after writing it.

HAZEL (*suspiciously*). You had not much time for that.

MINEOG. I never was one to spare myself in anything that could benefit a friend.

HAZEL. Neither would I spare myself. I have my article wrote.

MINEOG. I have a mind to read my own one to you, the way you will know there is nothing in it but what is friendly and is kind.

HAZEL. I will do the same thing. There's nothing I have said in it but what you will like to be hearing.

MINEOG (*who has rummaged pockets*). I thought I put it in the inside pocket—— No matter—here it is.

HAZEL (*rummaging*). Here is my one. I was thinking I had it lost.

MINEOG (*reading, after he has turned over a couple of sheets rapidly*). "Born and bred in this Square, he took his chief pride in his native town."

HAZEL (*turning over two sheets*). "It was in this parish and district he spent the most part of his promising youth—— Richly stored with world-wide knowledge."

MINEOG. "Well able to give out an opinion on any matter at all."

HAZEL. "To lay down his mind on paper it would be hard to beat him."

MINEOG. "With all that, humble that he would halt and speak to you the same as a child——" I'm maybe putting it down a bit too simple, but the printer will give it a little shaping after.

HAZEL. So will my own printer be lengthening out the words for me according to the type and the letters of the alphabet he will have plentiful and to spare.

MINEOG. "Well looking and well thought of. A true Irishman in supporting all forms of sport."

HAZEL. What's that? I never was one for betting on races or gaining prizes for riddles.

MINEOG. It is strange now I have no recollection of putting that down. It is I myself in the days gone by would put an odd shilling on a horse.

HAZEL. These typewriters would bother the world. Wait now— let me throw an eye on those papers you have in your hand.

MINEOG. Not at all. I would sooner be giving it out to you myself.

HAZEL. Of course it is very pleasing to be listening to so nice an account—but lend it a minute. (*Puts out hand.*)

MINEOG. Bring me now a bottle of wine, John—you know the sort—till I'll drink to Mr. Hazel's good health.

JOHN. I will, sir.

HAZEL. No, but bring it at my own expense till I will drink to Mr. Mineog. Just give me a hold of that paper for one minute only.

MINEOG. Keep patience now. I will go through it with no delay.

HAZEL (*making a snap*). Just for one minute.

MINEOG (*clapping his hand on it*). What a hurry you are in! Stop now till I'll find the place. "Very rarely indeed has been met with so fair and so neighbourly a man."

HAZEL. Give me a look at it.

MINEOG. What is it ails you? You are uneasy about something. What is it you are hiding from me?

HAZEL. What would I have to hide but that the papers got

mixed in some way, and you have in your hand what I wrote about yourself, and not what you wrote about myself?

MINEOG. What way did they get into the wrong pocket now?

HAZEL (*putting MS. in his pocket*). Give me back my own and I will give you back your own.

MINEOG. I don't know. You are putting it in my mind there might be something underhand. I would like to make sure what did you say about me in the heel. (*Turns over.*) "He was honest and widely respected." *Was* honest—are you saying me to be a rogue at this time?

HAZEL. That's not fair dealing to be searching through it against my will.

MINEOG. "He was trusted through the whole townland." *Was* trusted—is it that you are making me out to be a thief?

HAZEL. Well, follow your own road and take your own way.

MINEOG. "—— Mr. Mineog leaves no family to lament his loss, but along with the *Tribune*, which he fostered with the care of a father, we offer up prayers for the repose of his soul." (*Stands up.*) It is a notice of my death you are after writing!

HAZEL. You should understand that.

MIENOG. An obituary notice! Of myself! Is it that you expect me to quit the living world between this and Thursday?

HAZEL. I had no thought of the kind.

MINEOG. I'm not stretched yet! What call have you to go offer prayers for me?

HAZEL. I tell you I had it put by this long time till I would have occasion to use it.

MINEOG. Is it this long time, so, you have been waiting for my death?

HAZEL. Not at all.

MINEOG. You to kill me to-day and to think to bury me to-morrow!

HAZEL. Can't you listen? I was wanting something to fill space.

MINEOG. Would nothing serve you to fill space but only my own corpse? To go set my coffin making and to put nettles growing on my heart! Wouldn't it be enough to rob my house or to make an attack upon my means? Wouldn't that fill up the gap?

HAZEL. Let you not twist it that way!

MINEOG. The time I was in the face of my little dinner to go startle me with a thing of the sort! I'm not worth the ground I stand on! For the *Champion* of next Thursday! I to be dead ere Thursday!

HAZEL. I looked for no such thing.

MINEOG. What is it makes you say me to be done and dying? Am I reduced in the face?

HAZEL. You are not.

MINEOG. Am I yellow and pale and shrunken?

HAZEL. Why would you be?

MINEOG. Would you say me to be crampy in the body? Am I staggery in the legs?

HAZEL. I see no such signs.

MINEOG. Is it in my hand you see them? Is it lame or is it freezed-brittle like ice?

HAZEL. It is as warm and as good as my own.

MINEOG. Let me take a hold of you till you will tell me has it the feel of a dead man's grip.

HAZEL. I know that it has not.

MINEOG. Is it shaking like a bunch of timber shavings?

HAZEL. Not at all, not at all.

MINEOG. It should be my hearing that is failing from me, or that I am crippled and have lost my walk.

HAZEL. You are roaring and bawling without sense.

MINEOG. Let the *Champion* go to flitters before I will die to please it! I will not give in to it driving me out of the world before my hour is spent! It would hardly ask that of a man would be of no use and no account, or even of a beast of any consequence.

HAZEL. Who is asking you to die?

MINEOG. Giving no time hardly for the priest to overtake me and to give me the rites of the Church!

HAZEL. I tell you there is no danger of you giving up at all! Every person knows there must some sickness come before death. Some take it from a neighbour and it is put on others by God.

MINEOG. Even so, it's hard say.

HAZEL. You have not a ha'p'orth on you. No complaint in the world wide.

MINEOG. That's nothing! Sickness comes upon some as sudden as to clap their hands.

HAZEL. What are you talking about? You are thinking us to be in the days of the cholera yet!

MINEOG. There are yet other diseases besides that.

HAZEL. You put the measles over you and we going the road to school.

MINEOG. There is more than measles has power bring a man down.

HAZEL. You had the chin-cough passed and you rising. We were cut at the one time for the pock.

MINEOG. A disease to be allotted to you it would find you out, and you maybe up twenty mile in the air!

HAZEL. Ah, what disease could have you swept in the course of the next two days?

MINEOG. That is what I'm after saying—unless you might have murder in your mind.

HAZEL. Ah, what murder!

MINEOG. What way are you thinking to do away with me? To shoot me with the trigger of a gun and to give me shortening of life?

HAZEL. The trigger of a gun! God bless it, I never fingered such a thing in the length of my life!

MINEOG. To take aim at me and destroy me; to shoot me in forty halves like a crow in the time of the wheat!

HAZEL. Oh, now, don't say a thing like that!

MINEOG. Or to drown me maybe in the river, enticing me across the rotten plank of the bridge. (*Seizing bottle.*) Will you tell me on the virtue of your oath, is death lurking in that sherry wine?

HAZEL (*pulling out paper*). Ah, God bless your jig! And how would I know is it a notice of my own death has come into my hand in the pocket of this coat I put on me through a mistake?

MINEOG. Give it here. That's my property!

HAZEL (*reading*). "We sympathise with Mrs. Hazel and the family." There is proof now. Is it that you would go grieving with my wife and I to be living yet?

MINEOG. I didn't follow you out beyond this world with craving for the repose of your soul. It is nothing at all beside what you wrote.

HAZEL. Oh, I bear no grudge at all against you. I am not huffy and crabbed like yourself to go taking offence. Sure Kings and big people of the sort are used to see their dead-notices made ready from the hour of their birth out. And it is not anything printed on papers or any flight of words on the *Tribune* could give me any concern at all. See now will I be put out. (*Reads*) What now is this? "Mr. Hazel was of good race, having in him the old stock of the country, the Mahons, the O'Hagans, the Casserlys——." Where now did you get that? I never heard before, a Casserly to be in my fathers.

MINEOG. It might be on the side of the mother.

HAZEL. It was not. My mother was a girl of the Hessians that was born in the year of the French. My grandmother was Winefred Kane.

MINEOG. What is being out in one name towards drawing down the forecast of all classes of deaths upon myself?

HAZEL. There are twenty thousand things you might lay down and I would give them no leave to annoy me. But I have no mind any strange family to be mixed through me, but to go my own road and to carry my own character.

MINEOG. I would say you to be very crabbed to be making much of a small little mistake of the sort.

HAZEL. I will not have blood put in my veins that never rose up in them by birth. You to have put a slur maybe on the whole of my posterity for ever. That now is a thing out of measure.

MINEOG. It might be the Casserlys are as fair as the Hessians, and as well looking and as well reared.

HAZEL. There's no one can know that. What place owns them? My tribe didn't come inside the province. Every generation was born and bred in this or in some neighbouring townland.

MINEOG. Sure you will be but yourself whatever family may be laying claim to you.

HAZEL. Any person of the Casserlys to have done a wrong deed at any time, the neighbours would be watching and probing my own brood till they would see might the track of it break out in any way. It ran through our race to be hard tempered, from the Kanes that are very hot.

MINEOG. Why would the family of the Casserlys go doing wrong deeds more than another?

HAZEL. I would never forgive it, if it was the highest man in Connacht said it.

MINEOG. I tell you there to be any flaw in them, it would have worked itself out in yourself ere this.

HAZEL. Putting on me the weight of a family I never knew or never heard the name of at all. It is that is killing me entirely.

MINEOG. Neither did I ever hear their name or if they ever lived in the world, or did any deed good or bad in it at all.

HAZEL. What made you drag them hither for to write them in my genealogies so?

MINEOG. I did not drag them hither—— Give me that paper. (*Takes MS. and looks at it.*) What would it be but a misprint? Hessian, Casserly. There does be great resemblance in the sound of a double S.

HAZEL. Whether or no, you have a great wrong done me! The

person I had most dependence on to be the most person to annoy me! If it was a man from the County Mayo I wouldn't see him treated that way!

MINSOG. Have sense now! What would signify anything might be wrote about you, and the green scraws being over your head?

HAZEL. That's the worst! I give you my oath I would not go miching from death or be in terror of the sharpness of his bones, and he coming as at the Flood to sweep the living world along with me, and leave no man on earth having penmanship to handle my deeds, or to put his own skin on my story!

MINEOG. Ah it's likely the both of us will be forgotten and our names along with us, and we out in the meadow of the dead.

HAZEL. I will not be forgotten! I have posterity will put a good slab over me. Not like some would be left without a monument, unless it might be the rags of a cast waistcoat would be put on sticks in a barley garden, to go flapping at the thieves of the air.

MINEOG. Let the birds or the neighbours go screech after me and welcome, and I not in it to hear or to be annoyed.

HAZEL. Why wouldn't we hear? I'm in dread it's too much I'll hear, and you yourself sending such news to travel abroad, that there is blood in me I concealed through my lifetime!

MINEOG. What you are saying now has not the sense of reason.

HAZEL. Tom Mineog to say that of me, that was my trusty comrade and friend, what at all will strangers be putting out about me?

MINEOG. Ah, what call have you to go lamenting as if you had lost all on this side of the sea!

HAZEL. You to have brought that annoyance on me, what would enemies be saying of me? That it was in my breed to be cracked or to have a thorn in the tongue. There's a generation of families would be great with you, and behind you they would be backbiting you.

MINEOG. They will not. You are of a family doesn't know how to say a wrong word.

HAZEL. A rabbit mushroom they might say me to be, with no memory behind or around me!

MINEOG. Not at all. The world knows you to be civil and brought up to mannerly ways.

HAZEL. They might say me to have been a foreigner or a Jew man!

MINEOG. I can bear witness you have no such yellow look. And Hazel is a natural name.

HAZEL. It's likely they'll say I was a sheep-stealer or a tinker that went foraging around after food!

MINEOG. You that never put your hand on a rabbit burrow or stood before a magistrate or a judge!

HAZEL. They'll put me down as a grabber that was ready to quench a widow's fire!

MINEOG. Oh, where are you running to at all my dear man!

HAZEL. And I not to be able at that time to rise up and to get satisfaction! I to be wandering as a shadow and to see some schemer spilling out his lies! That would be the most grief in death! I to hit him a blow of my fist and he maybe not to feel it or to think it to be but a breeze of wind!

MINEOG. You are going too far entirely!

HAZEL. I to give out a strong curse on him and on his posterity and his land. It would kill my heart if he would take it to be no human voice, but some vanity like the hissing of geese!

MINEOG. I myself would recognise your voice, and you to be living or dead.

HAZEL. You say that now. But my ghost to come calling to you in the night time to rise up and to clear my character, you would run shivering to the priest as from some unnatural thing. You would call to him to come banish me with a Mass!

MINEOG. The Lord be between us and harm.

HAZEL. To have no power of revenge after death! My strength to go nourish weeds and grass! A lie to be told and I living I could go lay my case before the courts. So I will too! I'll silence you! I'll learn you to have done with misspellings and with death notices! I'll hinder you bringing in Casserlys! I go take advice from the lawyer! (*Goes towards door.*)

MINEOG. I'll go lay down my own case and the way that you have my life threatened!

HAZEL. I'll get justice and a hearing. The Judge will give in to my say!

MINEOG. I that will put you under bail! I'll bind you over to quit prophesying!

HAZEL. I'll break the bail of the sun and moon before I'll give you leave to go brand me with strange names the same as you would tar-brand a sheep! I'll put yourself and your *Tribune* under the law of libel!

MINEOG. I'll make a world's wonder of you! I'll give plenty and enough to the *Champion* to fill out its windy pages that time!

HAZEL (*at door*). I will lay my information before you will overtake me!

MINEOG (*seizing him*). I will lay my information against you for theft and you bringing away my coat!

HAZEL. I have no intention of bringing it away!

MINEOG. Is it that you will deny it? Don't I know that spot of grease on the sleeve?

HAZEL. Did I never carve a goose? Why wouldn't there be a spot of grease on my own sleeve?

MINEOG. Strip it off of you this minute!

HAZEL. Give me back my own coat, so!

MINEOG. What are you talking about! That's a great wonder now. So it is not my own coat.

HAZEL. Strip it off before you will quit the room!

MINEOG. I'll be well pleased casting it off!

HAZEL. You will not cast it on the dust and the dirt of the floor! (*Helps him.*) Go easy now—— That's it—— (*Takes it off gently and places it on chair.*)

MINEOG. Give me now my own coat!

HAZEL (*struggling with it*). It fails me to get it off.

MINEOG. What way did you get it on?

HAZEL. It is that it is too narrow.

MINEOG. No, but yourself that has too much bulk.

HAZEL (*struggling*). There now is a tear!

MINEOG (*taking his arm*). Mind now, you'll have it destroyed.

HAZEL. Give me a hand, so.

MINEOG (*helping him gently*). Have a care—it's a bit tender in the seams—— Give me here your hand—it is caught in the rip of the lining.

JOHN (*coming in, puts pie on table*). Wait now, sir, till I'll aid you to handle Mr. Hazel's coat. (*Whips off coat, takes up other coat, hangs both on pegs.*) The apple pie, Sir.

(HAZEL *sits down, gasping and wiping his face.* MINEOG *turns his back.*)

JOHN. Is there anything after happening, Mr. Hazel?

HAZEL. There is not—unless some sort of a battle.

JOHN. Ah, what signifies? There to be more of battles in the world there would be less of wars. (*He pushes Mineog's chair to table.*)

HAZEL (*after a pause*). Apple pie?

MINEOG (*sitting down*). Indeed, I am not any way inclined for eating.

(*Takes plate.* JOHN *stuffs a cushion into window pane and picks up MSS.*)

JOHN. Are these belonging to you, Mr. Mineog?

MINEOG. Let you throw them on the coals of the fire, where we have no use for them presently.

HAZEL (*stopping* JOHN *and taking them*). Thursday is very near at hand. Two empty columns is a large space to go fill.

MINEOG. Indeed I am feeling no way fit to go writing columns.

HAZEL (*putting his MS. in his pocket*). There is nothing ails them only to begin a good way after the start, and to stop before the finish.

MINEOG (*putting his MS. in his pocket*). We'll do that. We can put such part of them as we do not need at this time back in the shelf of the press.

HAZEL (*filling glasses and lifting his*). That it may be long before they will be needed!

MINEOG (*lifting glass*). That they may *never* be neded!

Curtain.

DAMER'S GOLD

DAMER'S GOLD

ACT I

PERSONS
   PATRICK KIRWAN. *Called Damer.*
   STAFFY KIRWAN. *His brother.*
   DELIA HESSIAN. *His sister.*
   RALPH HESSIAN. *Her husband.*
   SIMON NILAND. *Their nephew.*

SCENE. *The kitchen in* DAMER'S *house. Outer door at back. Door leading to an inner room to right. A dresser, a table, and a couple of chairs. An old coat and hat hanging on the wall. A knocking is heard at door at back. It is unlatched from outside.* DELIA *comes in.*

DELIA (*looking round cautiously and going back to door*). You may come in, Staffy and Ralph. There would seem to be no person here.

STAFFY. Take care would Damer ask us to cross the threshold at all. I would not ask to go pushing on him, but to wait till he would call to us himself. He is not an easy led man.

DELIA (*crossing and knocking at inner door*). He is not in it. He is likely slipped out unknownst.

RALPH. Herself that thought to find him at the brink of death and nearing his last leap, after what happened with the jennet. We heard tell of it as far as we were.

DELIA. What ailed him to go own a jennet, he that has means to stable a bay horse would set the windows rattling on the public road, and it sparkling over the flintstones after dark?

STAFFY. Sure he owns no fourfooted beast only the dog abroad in its box. To make its way into the haggard the jennet did, the time it staggered him with a kick. To forage out some grazing it thought to do, beyond dirt and scutchgrass among the stones. Very cross jennets do be, as it is a cross man it met with.

DELIA. A queer sort of a brother he is. To go searching Ireland you wouldn't find queerer. But as soon as I got word what happened I bade Ralph to put the tacklings on the ass. We must have nature about us some way. There was silence between us long enough.

RALPH. She was thinking it might be the cause of him getting his death sooner than God has it promised to him, and that it might turn his mind more friendly like towards us, he knowing us to be at hand for to settle out his burying.

DELIA. Why wouldn't it, and we being all the brothers and sisters ever he had, since Jane Niland, God rest her soul, went out last Little Christmas from the troubles and torments of the world.

STAFFY. There is nothing left of that marriage now, only one young lad is said to be mostly a fool.

DELIA. It is ourselves can bear witness to that, where he came into the house ere yesterday, having no way of living, since death and misfortune scattered him, but as if he was left down out of the skies.

RALPH. He has not, unless the pound piece the mother put into his hand at the last. It is much she had that itself. The time Tom Niland died from her, he didn't leave her hardly the cat.

STAFFY. The lad to have any wit around him he would have come travelling hither along with yourselves, to see would he knock any kindness out of Damer.

RALPH. It is what herself was saying, it would be no advantage to him to be coming here at all, he being as he is half light, where there is nothing only will or wit could pick any profit out of Damer. She did not let on to him what side were we facing, and we travelling out from Loughtyshassy.

STAFFY. It is likely he will get tidings as good as yourself. It is said, and said largely, Damer has a full gallon jar of gold.

RALPH. There is no one could lift it—God bless it—they were telling me. Filled up it is and brimmed to the very brink.

STAFFY. His heart and his soul gone into it. He is death on that gallon of gold.

DELIA. He would give leave to the poorhouse to bury him, if he could but put in his will they should leave it down with his bones.

STAFFY. A man could live an easy life surely and that much being in the house.

DELIA. There is no more grasping man within the four walls of the world. A strange thing he turning to be so ugly and prone to misery, where he was reared along with myself. I have the first covetous person yet to meet I would like! I never would go thrusting after gold, I to get all Lord Clanricarde's estate.

RALPH. She never would, only at a time she might have her own means spent and consumed.

STAFFY. The house is very racked beside what it was. The hungriest cabin in the whole ring of Connemara would not show out so empty and so bare.

DELIA (*taking up a jug*). No sign in this vessel of anything that would leave a sign. I'll go bail he takes his tea in a black state, and the milk to be rotting in the churn.

RALPH (*handling a coat and hat hanging on a nail*). That's a queer cut of a hat. That now should have been a good top-coat in its time.

DELIA. For pity's sake! That is the top-coat and the hat he used to be wearing and he riding his long-tailed pony to every racecourse from this to the Curragh of Kildare. A good class of cloth it should be to last out through seventeen years.

STAFFY. The time he was young and fundless he had not a bad reaching hand. He never was thrifty but lavish till he came into the ownership of the land. It is as if his luck left him, he growing timid at the time he had means to lose.

DELIA. Every horse he would back at that time it would surely win all before it. I saw the people thronging him one time, taking him in their arms for joy, and the winnings coming into his hand. It is likely they ran out through the fingers as swift nearly as they flowed in.

STAFFY. He grew to be very dark and crabbed from the time of the father's death. His mind was on his halfpenny ever since.

DELIA (*looking at dresser*). Spiders' webs heaped in ridges the same as windrows in a bleach of hay. What now is that there above on the upper shelf?

RALPH (*taking it from top shelf*). It is but a pack of cards.

STAFFY. They should maybe be the very same that brought him profit in his wild days. He always had a lucky hand.

DELIA (*dusting them*). You would give your seven oaths the dust to have been gathering on them since the time of the Hebrews' Flood. I'll tell you now a thing to do. We being here before him in the house, why wouldn't we ready it and put some sort of face upon it, the way he would be in humour with us coming in.

RALPH. And the way he might incline to put into our hand some good promise or some gift.

DELIA (*dusting*). I would wish no gift from any person at all, but that my mind is set at this time on a fleet of white goats and a guinea-hen are to be canted out from the Spanish woman at Lisatuwna cross by reason of the hanging gale.

STAFFY. That was the way with you, Delia, from the time you could look out from the half-door, to be coveting pictures and fooleries, that would shape themselves in your mind.

DELIA. There is no sin coveting things are of no great use or profit, but would show out good and have some grandeur around them. Those goats now! Browsing on the blossoms of the bushes they would be, or the herbs that give out a sweet smell. Stir yourself, Staffy, and throw your eye on that turf beyond in the corner. It is that wet you could wring from it splashes and streams. Let you rise the ashes from the sods are on the hearth and redden them with a goosewing, if there is a goosewing to be found. There is no greater beauty to be met with than the leaping of a little yellow flame.

STAFFY. In my opinion there will no pay-day come for this work, but only a thank-you job; a County Clare payment, 'God spare you the health!'

DELIA. Let you do it, Ralph so. (*Takes potatoes from a sieve.*) A roasted potato would be a nice thing to put before him, in the place of this old crust of a loaf. Put them in now around the sods, the way they will be crispy before him.

RALPH (*taking them*). And the way he will see you are a good housekeeper and will mind well anything he might think fit to give.

DELIA (*at clock*). I'll set to the right time of day the two hands of the clock are pointing a full hour before the sun. Take, Staffy, that pair of shoes and lessen from them the clay of the land. That much of doing will not break your heart. He will be as proud as the fallen angels seeing the way we have all set out before him.

(*A harsh laugh is heard at inner door. They turn and see* DAMER *watching them.*)

RALPH. Glory be to God!

DELIA. It is Damer was within all the time!

STAFFY. What are you talking about, Delia? It is Patrick you were meaning to say.

DAMER. Let her go on prattling out Damer to my face, as it is often she called it behind my shoulders. Damer the chandler, the miser got the spoil of the Danes, that was mocked at since the time of the Danes. I know well herself and the world have me christened with that nickname.

RALPH. Ah, it is not to dispraise you they put it on you, but to show you out so wealthy and so rich.

DAMER. I am thinking it is not love of my four bones brings you on this day under my thatch?

STAFFY. We heard tell you were after being destroyed with a jennet.

DAMER. Picking up newses and tidings of me ye do be. It is short the delay was on you coming.

DELIA. And I after travelling through the most of the day on the head of you being wounded and hurt, thinking you to be grieving to see one of your own! And I in dread of my life stealing past your wicked dog.

DAMER. My joy he is, scaring you with his bark! If it wasn't for him you would have me clogged and tormented, coming in and bothering me every whole minute.

DELIA. There is no person in Ireland only yourself but would have as much welcome for me to-day as on the first day ever they saw me!

DAMER. What's that you are doing with my broom?

DELIA. To do away with the spider's webs I did, where the shelves were looped with them and smothered. Look at all that came off of that pack of cards.

DAMER. What call had you to do away with them, and they belonging to myself? Is it to bleed to death I should and I to get a tip of a billhook or a slasher? You and your vagaries to have left me bare, that I would be without means to quench the blood, and it to rise up from my veins and to scatter on every side!

DELIA. Is it that you are without e'er a rag, and that ancient coat to be hanging on the wall?

DAMER. The place swept to flitters! What is that man of yours doing and he handling my turf?

RALPH. It was herself thought to be serviceable to you, setting out the fuel that was full of dampness where it would get an air of the fire.

DAMER. To dry it is it? (*Seizes sods and takes them from the hearth.*) And what length would it be without being burned and consumed and it not to be wet putting it on? (*Pours water over it.*) And I after stacking it purposely in the corner where there does be a drip from the thatch.

RALPH. She but thought it would be more answerable to you being dry.

DAMER. What way could I bear the expense of a fire on the hearth and it to leave smouldering and to break out into a blaze? A month's cutting maybe to go to ashes within three minutes, and into wisps of smoke. And the price of turf in this year gone wild out of measure, and it packed so roguish you could read the printed speeches on the paper through the sods you do be buying in the creel.

STAFFY. I was saying myself not to meddle with it. It is hurry is a worse friend than delay.

DAMER. Where did you get those spuds are roasting there upon the hearth?

RALPH. Herself that brought them out from the sieve, thinking to make ready your meal.

DAMER. My seed potatoes! Samples I got from the guardians and asked in the shops and in stores till I'd gather enough to set a few ridges in the gardens would serve me through the length of the year!

DELIA. Let you be satisfied so with your mouldy bit of loaf. (*Breaks a bit from it and hands it to him.*)

DAMER. Do not be breaking it so wasteful! The mice to have news there was as much as that of crumbs in the house, they would be running the same as chickens around the floor.

RALPH. Thinking to be comfortable to you she was, the way you would make us welcome from this out.

DAMER. Which of ye is after meddling with my clock?

DELIA. It was a full hour before its time.

DAMER. It to be beyond its time, wouldn't that save fire and candles sending me to my bed early in the night? Leave down those boots! (*Takes them from Staffy.*) Is it that you are wearing out the uppers with scraping at them and scratching! Is it to rob me ye are come into this place?

DELIA. I tell you we only came in getting word that you were done and dying.

DAMER. Ha! Is it to think I was dying ye did? Well, I am not. I am not so easy quenched. Strength and courage I have, to keep a fast grip of what I own.

DELIA. Let you not be talking that way! We are no grabbers and no thieves!

DAMER. I have it in my mind that ye are. Very ravenous to run through my money ye are.

DELIA. The world knows I am not ravenous! I never gave my heart to silver or to gold but only to the thing it would bring in. But to hold from me the thing my heart is craving after, you might as well blacken the hearth.

140

DAMER. Striving to scare me out of my courage and my wits, the way I'll give in to go making my will.

RALPH. She would not be wishful you to do that the time your mind would be vexed.

DAMER. I'll make it, sick or sound, if I have a mind to make it.

DELIA. Little thanks you'll get from me if you make it or do not make it. That is the naked truth.

DAMER. The whole of ye think yourselves to be very managing and very wise!

DELIA. Let you go will it so to an asylum for fools.

DAMER. Why wouldn't I? It is in the asylums all the sense is these times. There is only the fools left outside.

DELIA. You to bestow it outside of your own kindred for to benefit and comfort your soul, all the world will say it is that you had it gathered together by fraud.

STAFFY. Do not be annoying him now.

DELIA. I will not. But the time he will be lying under the flag-stone, it is holly rods and brambles will spring up from out of his thorny heart.

DAMER. A hasty, cranky woman in the house is worse than you to lay your hand upon red coals! I know well your tongue that is as sharp as the sickle of the moon!

DELIA. The character you will leave after you will be worse out and out than Herod's!

DAMER. The devil upon the winds she is! That one was born into the world having the use of the bow and arrows!

DELIA. You not to give fair play to your own, it is a pitiful ghost will appear in your image, questing and craving our prayers!

DAMER. I know well what is your aim and your drift!

DELIA. I say any man has a right to give thanks to the heavens, and he having decent people to will his means to, in place of people having no call to it.

DAMER. Whoever I'll will it to will have call to it!

DELIA. Or to part with it to low people and to mean people, and you having it to give.

DAMER. Having it to give is it? Do you see that lock on the door?

DELIA. I do see it and have eyes to see it.

DAMER. Can you make any guess what is inside of it?

DELIA. It is likely it is what there is so much talk about, your own full gallon of gold.

(RALPH *takes off his hat*.)

DAMER. Lay now your eye to that lock hole.

RALPH (*looking through keyhole*). It is all dusky within. It fails me to see any shining thing. (STAFFY *and* DELIA *put their eyes to keyhole but draw back disappointed*.)

DAMER. If you cannot see it, try can you get the smell of it. Take a good draw of it now; lay your head along the hinges of the door. So now ye may quit and scamper out of this, the whole throng of ye, robbers and hangmen and bankbreakers, bargers and bad characters, and you may believe me telling you that is the nearest ye ever will come to my gold! (*He bangs back into room locking door after him*.)

DELIA. He has no more nature than the brutes of the field, hunting and howling after us.

STAFFY. Yourself that rose him out of his wits and his senses. We will sup sorrow for this day's work where he will put curses after us. It is best for us go back to my place. It may be tomorrow that his anger will be cured up.

RALPH. I thought it was to lay him out with candles we were brought here. I declare I came nearer furnishing out a corpse myself with the start I got.

DELIA. There is no dread on me. When he gets in humour I will tackle up again to him. It is too far I came to be facing back to Loughtyshassy and I fasting from the price of my goats! Little collars I was thinking to buckle around their neck the same as a lady's lapdog, and maybe so far as a small clear-sounding bell.

(*They go out,* DAMER *comes back. He puts on clock, rakes out fire, picks up potatoes and puts them back in sieve, takes bread into his room. There is a knock at the door. Then it is cautiously opened and* SIMON NILAND *comes in, and stands near the hearth.* DAMER *comes back and sees him*.)

DAMER. What are you looking for?

SIMON. For what I won't get seemingly, that is a welcome.

DAMER. Maybe it's for fists you are looking?

SIMON. It is not, before I will get my rest. I couldn't box to-night if I was the Queen of England.

DAMER. Have you any traffic with that congregation is after going out?

SIMON. I seen no person good or bad, but a dog and it on the chain.

DAMER. You to have in you any of the breed of the Kirwans that is my own, I'd rise the tongs and pitch you out from the door!

SIMON. I suppose you would not begrudge me to rest myself for a while. (*Sits down.*)

DAMER. I'll give leave to no strolling vagabond to sit in any place at all.

SIMON. All right so. (*Tosses a coin he takes from his pocket, tied in a spotted handkerchief.*)

DAMER. What's that you're doing?

SIMON. Pitching a coin I was to see would it bid me go west or east.

DAMER. Go toss outside so.

SIMON (*stooping and groping*). I will after I will find it.

DAMER. Hurry on now.

SIMON. Wait till I kindle a match. (*Lights one and picks up coin.*)

DAMER. What is that in your hand?

SIMON. You should know.

DAMER. Is it gold it is?

SIMON. It is all I have of means in the world. I never handled a coin before it, but my bite to be given me and my bed.

DAMER. You'll mind it well if you have sense.

SIMON. It is towards the east it bade me go. I'll travel as far as the races of Knockbarron to-morrow.

DAMER. You'll be apt to lose it going to races.

SIMON. I'll go bet with it, and see what way will it turn out.

DAMER. You to set all you own upon a horse that might fail at the leaps! It is a very foolish thing doing that.

SIMON. It might not. Some have luck and are born lucky and more have run through their luck. If I lose it, it is lost. It would not keep me long anyway. I to win, I will have more and plenty.

DAMER. You will surely lose it.

SIMON. If I do I have nothing to get or to fall back on. It is some other one must take my charges.

DAMER. A great pity to go lose a gold sovereign to some schemer you never saw before.

SIMON. Sure you must take some risk. You cannot put your hands around the world.

DAMER. It to be swept by a trick of the loop man!

SIMON. It is not with that class I will make free.

DAMER. To go lose the whole of it in one second of time!

SIMON. I will make four divides of it.

DAMER. To go change it into silver and into copper! That would be the most pity in the world.

SIMON. I'll chance it all upon the one jock so.

DAMER. Gold! Believe me it is a good thing to hold and a very heartbreak the time it is lost. (*Takes it in his hand.*) Pure gold! There is not a thing to be got with it as worthy as what it is itself! There is no comfort in any place and it not in it. The Queen's image on it and her crown. Solid between the fingers; weighty in the palm of the hand; as beautiful as ever I saw.

SIMON. It is likely it is the same nearly as any other one.

DAMER. Gold! My darling it is! From the hollows of the world to the heights of the world there is no grander thing to be found. My bone and my marrow! Let me have the full of my arms of it and I'll not ask the flowers of field or fallow or the dancing of the Easter sun!

SIMON. I am thinking you should be Damer. I heard said Damer has a full crock of gold.

DAMER. He has not! He has not!

SIMON. That is what the world says anyway. I heard it as far as the seaside.

DAMER. I wish to my God it was true!

SIMON. Full and brimming to the brink. That is the way it was told.

DAMER. It is not full! It is not! Whisper now. It is many a time I thought it to be full, full at last, full at last!

SIMON. And it wasn't after?

DAMER. To take it and to shake it I do. It is often I gave myself a promise the time there will be no sound from it, I will give in to nourish myself, I will rise out of misery. But every time I will try it, I will hear a little clatter that tells me there is some space left; some small little hole or gap.

SIMON. What signifies that when you have so much in it?

DAMER. Weightier it gets and weightier, but there will always be that little sound. I thought to stop it one time, putting in a fistful of hayseed; but I felt in my heart that was not dealing fair and honest with myself, and I rose up and shook it out again, rising up from my bed in the night time. I near got my death with the cold and the draught fell on me doing that.

SIMON. It is best for me be going on where I might find my bed.

DAMER. Hearken now. I am old and the long road behind me. You are young and in your strength. It is you is rich, it is I myself that is poor. You know well, you to get the offer, you would not change your lot with my own.

SIMON. I suppose I might not. I'd as lief keep my countenance and my run.

DAMER. Isn't it a great pity there to be that hollow within in my gallon, and the little coin that would likely just fill it up, to be going out of the house?

SIMON. Is it that you are asking it of me?

DAMER. You might never find so good a way to open Heaven to yourself with a charity. To be bringing peace to an old man that has not long to live in the world! You wouldn't think now how quiet I would sleep, and the good dreams would be going through me, and that gallon jar to be full and to make no sound the time I would roll it on the floor. That would be a great deed for one little pound piece to do!

SIMON. I'll toss you for it.

DAMER. I would not dare put anything at all upon a chance.

SIMON. Leave it alone so. (*Turns away.*)

DAMER (*seizing him*). It would make such a good appearance in the little gap!

SIMON. Head or harp?

DAMER. No, I'm in dread I might lose.

SIMON. Take your chance or leave it.

DAMER. I to lose, you may kill me on the moment! My heart is driven down in the sole of my shoe!

SIMON. That is poor courage.

DAMER. There is some shiver forewarning me I will lose! I made a strong oath I never would give in again to try any sort of chance.

SIMON. You didn't make it but with yourself.

DAMER. It was through my luck leaving me I swore against betting and gaming.

SIMON. It might turn back fresh and hearty where you gave it so long a rest.

DAMER. Well—maybe——

SIMON. Here now.

DAMER. I dare not.

SIMON (*going to door*). I'll make my bet so according to a dream I had. It is on a red horse I will put it to-morrow.

DAMER. No—stop—wait a minute.

SIMON. I'll win surely following my dream.

DAMER. I might not lose.

SIMON. I'm in dread of that. All turns to the man is rich.

DAMER. I'll chance it!

SIMON. You said no and I'll take no.

DAMER. You cannot go back on your word.

SIMON. Let me go out from you tempting me.

DAMER (*seizing him*). Heads! I say heads!

SIMON. Harps it is. I win.

DAMER. My bitter grief! Ochone!

SIMON. I'll toss you for another.

DAMER. You will not. What's tosses? Look at here what is put in my way! (*Holds up pack of cards.*)

SIMON. Where's the stakes?

DAMER. Wait a second. (*Goes into room.*)

SIMON. Hurry on or I won't stop.

DAMER. Let you not stir out of that! (*Comes back and throws money on table.*)

SIMON. Come on so. (*Shuffles cards.*)

DAMER. Give me the pack. (*Cuts.*) I didn't feel a card between my fingers this seven and a half-score years!

SIMON. Spades are trumps.

DAMER (*lighting candle*). I'll win it back! I won't begrudge spending a penny candle, no, or two penny candles! I'll play you to the brink of day!

ACT II

The next morning. The same kitchen. Simon Niland is lying asleep on the hearth. Ralph and Staffy are looking at him.

STAFFY. Who is it at all is in it?

RALPH. Who would it be but Simon Niland, that is come following after us.

STAFFY. Stretched and sleeping all the same as if there was a pin of slumber in his hair, as in the early times of the world. The day passing without anything doing. That one will never win to a fortune.

RALPH. It would be as well for ourselves maybe he not to be too great with Damer.

STAFFY. Will Delia make any headway I wonder. She had good courage to go face him, and he abroad on the land, sitting stooped on the bent body of a bush.

RALPH. I wonder what way did that lad make his way into this place. Wait now till I'll waken and question him. (*Shakes* SIMON.)

SIMON (*drowsily*). Who is that stirring me?

RALPH. Rouse yourself up now.

SIMON. Do not be rousing me, where I am striving to catch a hold of the tail of my last dream.

STAFFY. Is it seeking for a share of Damer's wealth you are come?

SIMON. I never asked and never looked for it.

STAFFY. You are going the wrong road to reach to it.

SIMON. A bald cat there was in the dream, was keeping watch over jewelleries in a cave.

STAFFY. No person at all would stretch out his hand to a lad would be rambling and walking the world, and it in its darkness and sleep, and be drowsing and miching from labour through the hours the sun has command of.

DELIA (*at the door*). Is it that ye are within, Staffy and Ralph?

RALPH. We are, and another along with us.

DELIA. Put him out the door!

RALPH. Ah, there's no danger of him coming around Damer. He is simple and has queer talk too.

DELIA. Put him out I say! (*Pushes Simon to door.*) Let him drowse out the day in the car shed! I tell you Damer is at hand!

RALPH. Has he the frown on him yet?

STAFFY. Did his anger anyway cool down?

DELIA. He is coming I say. I am partly in dread of him. I am afeard and affrighted!

RALPH. He should be in terrible rages so. There was no dread on you yesterday, and he cursing and roaring the way he was.

DELIA. He is mad this time out and out. Wait now till you'll see!
(*She goes behind dresser. Damer comes to the door.* STAFFY *goes behind a chair.* RALPH *seizes a broom.*)

DAMER (*at door*). Are you acquainted with any person, Ralph Hessian, is in need of a savage dog?

STAFFY. Is it that you are about to part Jubair your dog?

DAMER. I have no use for him presently.

STAFFY. Is it that you are without dread of robbers coming for to knock in your skull with a stone? Or maybe out in the night it is to burn you out of the house they would.

DAMER. What signifies, what signifies? All must die, all must die. The longest person that will live in the world, he is bound to go in the heel. Life is a long road to travel and a hard rough track under the feet.

STAFFY. Mike Merrick the huckster has an apple garden bought

147

against the harvest. He should likely be seeking for a dog. There do be little lads passing to the school.

DAMER. He might want him, he might want him. (*He leans upon half-door.*)

STAFFY. Is it that you are tired and wore out carrying the load of your wealth?

DAMER. It is a bad load surely. It was the love of money destroyed Buonaparte where he went robbing a church, without the men of learning are telling lies.

STAFFY. I would never go so far as robbery, but to bid it welcome I would, and it coming fair and easy into my hand.

DAMER. There was a king out in Foreign went astray through the same sin. His people that made a mockery of him after his death, filling up his jaws with rendered gold. Believe me, any person goes coveting after riches puts himself under a bad master.

STAFFY. That is a master I'd be willing to engage with, he to give me my victuals and my ease.

DAMER. In my opinion it was to keep temptation from our path the gold of the world was covered under rocks and in the depths of the streams. Believe me it is best leave it where it is, and not to meddle with the Almighty.

STAFFY. You'd be best without it. It is the weight of it is bowing you to your grave. When things are vexing your mind and you are trouble minded they'll be going through your head in the night time. There is a big shift and a great change in you since yesterday. There is not the half of you in it. You have the cut of the misfortune.

DAMER. I am under misfortune indeed.

STAFFY. Give over now your load to myself before the coming of the dusk. The way you are there'll be nothing left of you within three days. There is no way with you but death.

DELIA (*to* RALPH). Let you raise your voice now, and come around him on my own behalf.

RALPH. It is what herself is saying, you to be quitting the world as it seems, it is as good for you make over to her your crock of gold.

DAMER. I would not wish, for all the glories of Ireland, to leave temptation in the path of my own sister or my kin, or to twist a gad for their neck.

DELIA (*to* RALPH). Tell him I'll chance it.

DAMER. At the time of the judgment of the mountain, when the sun and moon will be all one with two blackberries, it is not being pampered with plenty will serve you, beside being great with the angels!

DELIA (*shrinking back*). I would as soon nearly not get it at all, where it might bring me to the wretched state of Damer! (*Dog heard barking.*)

DAMER. I'll go bring my poor Jubair out of this. A great sin and a great pity to be losing provision with a dog, and the image of the saints maybe to be going hungry and bare. How do I know what troop might be bearing witness against me before the gate of heaven? To be cherishing a ravenous beast might be setting his teeth in their limbs! To give charity to the poor is the best religion in Ireland. Didn't our Lord Himself go beg through three and thirty years? (*He goes.*)

DELIA (*coming forward*). Will you believe me now telling you he is gone unsteady in the head?

STAFFY. I see no other sign. He is a gone man surely. His understanding warped and turned backward. To see him blighted the way he is would stir the heart of a stone.

RALPH. He surely got some vision or some warning, or there lit on him a fit or a stroke.

STAFFY. Twice a child and only once a man. He is turned to be innocent with age.

RALPH. It would be a bad thing he to meet with his death unknown to us.

DELIA. It would be worse again he that is gone out of his latitude to be brought away to the asylum.

RALPH. I don't know.

DELIA. But I know. He to die, and to make no will, it is ourselves, by rule and by right, that would lay claim to his wealth.

STAFFY. So we could do that, and he to come to his end in the bad place, God save the mark!

DELIA. Would you say there would be no fear the Government might stretch out and take charge of it, saying him to be outside of his reason?

RALPH. That would be the worst of all. We to be forced to hire an attorney against them, till we would break one another at law.

DELIA. He to be stopping here, and being light in the brain, it is likely some thief travelling the road might break his way in and sweep all.

RALPH. It would be right for us keep some sort of a watch on it.

STAFFY. What way would we be sitting here watching it, the same as a hen on a pebble of flint, through a quarter or it might be three quarters of a year? He might drag for a good while yet, and live and linger into old days.

DELIA. To take some cross turn he might, and to come at us violent and maybe tear the flesh from our bones.

STAFFY. It is best for us do nothing so, but to leave it to the foreknowledge of God.

DELIA. There is but the one thing to do. To bring it away out of this and to lodge it within in my own house. We can settle out a place under the hearth.

STAFFY. We can make a right division of it at such time as the end will come.

RALPH. What way now will we bring away the crock?

DELIA. Let you go outside and be watching the road while Staffy will be bringing out the gold.

STAFFY. Ah, I'm not so limber as what Ralph is. There does be giddiness and delay in my feet. It might fail me to heave it to a hiding place and to bring it away unknownst.

DELIA. Let you go out so and be keeping a watch, and Ralph will put it on the ass-car under sacks.

RALPH. Do it you. I am not of his own kindred and his family. Any person to get a sketch of me bringing it away they might nearly take myself to be a thief.

DELIA. We are doing but what is fair and is right.

RALPH. Maybe so. But any neighbour to be questioning me, it might be hard put a skin on the story.

DELIA. There is no person to do it but the one. (*Calls from the door.*) Come in here from the shed, Simon Niland, if the sluggishness is banished from your eyesight and from your limbs.

SIMON (*at door*). I was thinking to go travel my road.

DELIA. Have you any desire to reach out your hand for to save a mortal life?

SIMON (*coming in*). Whose life is that?

STAFFY. The man of this house that is your uncle and is owner of wealth closed up in a jar. We now being wittier than himself, that has lost his wits, have our mind made up to bring it away.

SIMON. Outside of his knowledge is it?

STAFFY. It will be safe and well minded and lodged in loyal keeping, it being no profit to him that is at this time shook and blighted, but only a danger to his days.

DELIA. The seven senses to be going astray on him, what would ail any tramp or neuk would be passing the road, not to rob him and to lay him stone dead?

STAFFY. Go in now and bring out from the room and to such place as we will command, that gallon jar of gold.

RALPH. It being certain it will be brought away from him, it is best it to be kept in the family, and not to go nourishing lawyers or thieves.

SIMON. Is it to steal it I should?

STAFFY. What way will it be stealing, and the whole of us to be looking on at your deed?

SIMON. Ah, what call have I to do that much and maybe put myself in danger of the judge, for the sake of a man is without sense.

DELIA. Let you do it for my own sake so. You heard me giving out news on yesterday of the white goats are on the bounds of being sold. The neighbours will give me no more credit, where they loaned me the price of a crested side car was auctioned out at a quality sale.

RALPH. Picking the eyes out of my own head they are, to pay the little bills they have against her.

DELIA. I am no way greedy, I would ask neither food or bite, I would not begrudge turning Sunday into Friday if I could but get my heart's desire. Such a thing now as a guinea-hen would be bringing fashion to the door, throwing it a handful of yellow meal, and it in its speckled plumage giving out its foreign call!

SIMON. I have no mind to be brought within the power of the law.

DELIA. You that are near in blood to refuse me so small an asking, what chance would I have sending requests to Heaven that is beyond the height of the clouds! (*Weeps.*)

STAFFY. That's the way with them that are reared poor, they are the hardest after to humour, striving to bring everything to their own way. But there's a class of people in the world wouldn't do a hand's turn, no more than the bird upon the tree.

RALPH. I wonder you not to give in to us, when all the world knows God formed young people for to be giving aid to elder people, and beyond all to them that are near to them in blood.

STAFFY. Look now, Simon, let you be said and led by me. You having no great share of wisdom we are wishful to make a snug man of you and to put you on a right road. Go in now and you will not be kept out of your own profit and your share, and a harbour of plenty beyond all.

SIMON. It might be guarded by a serpent in a tree, or by unnatural things would be in the similitude of cats.

STAFFY. Ah, that class is done away with this good while.

RALPH. There is no person having sense, but would take means, by hook or by crook, to make his pocket stiff and he to be given his fair chance. It is to save you from starvation we are wishful to do, as much as to bring profit to ourselves.

STAFFY. You not to follow our say you will be brought to burn green ferns to boil your victuals, or to devour the berries of the bush.

SIMON. I would not wish a head to follow me and leap up on the table and wrestle me, or to drink against me with its gory mouth.

STAFFY. You that have not the substance of a crane's marrow, to go shrink from so small a bidding, let you go on the shaughraun or to the workhouse, where you would not take our advice.

SIMON. I'll go do your bidding so. I will go bring out the crock.

STAFFY. There is my whiteheaded boy! I'll keep a watch, the way Damer will not steal in on us without warning.

RALPH. He should have the key in some secret place. It is best for you give the lock a blow of your foot.

SIMON. I'll do that. (*He gives door a kick. It opens easily.*)

DELIA. Was I right now saying Damer is turned innocent? Sure the door was not locked at all.

SIMON (*dragging out jar*). Here it is now.

RALPH. So it is and no mistake.

STAFFY. There should be great weight in it.

RALPH. I am in dread it might work a hole down through the timber of the car.

DELIA. Why wouldn't we open it here? It would be handier bringing it away in small divides.

RALPH. The way we would make sure of getting our own share at the last.

DELIA. Let you draw out the cork from it.

RALPH. I don't know can I lift it. (*Stoops and lifts it easily.*) The Lord protect and save us! There is no weight in it at all!

STAFFY (*seizing and shaking it*). Not a one penny in it but clean empty. That beats all.

DELIA. It is with banknotes it is stuffed that are deaf and do be giving out no sound. (*She pokes in a knitting pin.*) Nothing in it at all, but as bare as the canopy of heaven!

RALPH. There being nothing within in it, where now is the gold?

STAFFY. Some person should have made away with it.

DELIA. Some robber or some great rogue. A terrible thing such ruffians to be around in the world! To turn and rob a poor man of all he had spared and had earned.

STAFFY. They have done him a great wrong surely, taking from him all he had of comfort in his life.

RALPH. My grief it is there being no more hangings for thieves, that are worse again than murderers that might do their deed out of heat. It is thieving is the last crime.

STAFFY. We to lay our hand on that vagabond we'll give him cruelty will force him to Christian habits.

RALPH. Take care might he be nearer than what you think! (*He points at Simon. All look at him.*)

STAFFY. Sure enough it is with himself only we found him on the hearth this morning.

DELIA. He hasn't hardly the intellect to be the thief.

SIMON. I tell you I never since the day I was born could be charged with the weight of a brass pin!

STAFFY. It is to Damer, my fine boy, you will have to make out your case.

SIMON. So I will make it out. Where now is Damer?

STAFFY. He is gone down the road, where he brought away Jubair the dog.

SIMON. What are you saying? The dog gone is it? (*Goes to door.*)

RALPH (*taking hold of him*). What makes you go out in such a hurry?

SIMON. What is that to you?

DELIA. What cause has he to be making a run?

SIMON. Let me mind my own business.

STAFFY. It is maybe our own business.

SIMON. To make a search I must in that dog's kennel of straw.

DELIA. Go out, Ralph, till you will bring it in. (*Ralph goes out.*)

STAFFY (*seizing him*). A man to go rush out headlong and money after being stolen, I have no mind to let him make his escape.

DELIA. If you are honest let you stop within and not to put a bad appearance upon yourself making off.

SIMON. Let me out! I tell you I have a thing concealed in the box.

STAFFY. A strange place to go hiding things and a queer story altogether.

DELIA. Do not let go your hold. He to go out into the street, he has the wide world before him.

RALPH (*dragging kennel in*). Here now is the box.

SIMON. (*breaking away and searching it*). Where at all is it vanished?

STAFFY. It is lies he was telling. There is nothing at all within in it only a wisp of barley straw.

SIMON. Where at all is it?

STAFFY. What is it is gone from you?

SIMON. Not a one pound left!

DELIA. Why would you look to find coins of money down in Jubair's bed?

SIMON. It is there I hid it.

STAFFY. What is it you hid?

SIMON. All that was in the crock and that I took from it. Where now is my bag of gold?

STAFFY. Do you hear what he is after saying?

RALPH. A lad of that sort will not be safe but in the gaol. Let us give him into the grip of the law.

DELIA. No, but let the man owned it do that.

STAFFY. So he can task him with it, and he drawing to the door.

DELIA (*going to it*). It is time for you, Patrick, come in.

(*Damer comes in dragging a sack.*)

RALPH. You are after being robbed and left bare.

DELIA. Not a one penny left of all you have cast into its mouth.

RALPH. Herself made a prophecy you would be robbed with the weakening of your wits, and sure enough it has come about.

DELIA. Not a tint of it left. What now do you say, hearing that?

DAMER (*sitting down by the hearth and laying down sack*). If it should go it must go. That was allotted to me in the skies.

DELIA. Is it that you had knowledge ere this of it being swept and lost?

DAMER. If I had not, why would I have been setting my mind upon eternity and striving to bring to mind a few prayers? And to have parted with my wicked dog?

DELIA. Let you turn around till you will see before you the man that is the robber and the thief!

SIMON. Thief yourself! You that had a plan made up to bring it away.

DAMER. Delia, Delia, what was I laying down a while ago? It is the love of riches has twisted your heart and your mind.

DELIA. Is it that you are contented to be made this one's prey?

DAMER. It was foretold for me. I to go stint the body till I near put myself to death without the Lord calling on me, and to lose every whole pound after in one night's card playing.

DELIA. Is it at cards you lost it?

DAMER. With that same pack of cards you laid out under my hand, I lost all I had gathered to that one.

STAFFY. Well, there is nothing so certain in the world as the running of a fool to a fool.

DELIA. Is it taking that lad you are to be a fool? I thinking him to be as simple as you'd see in the world, and he putting bread upon his own butter as we slept!

RALPH. We to have known all then we know now, we need not have wasted on him our advice.

DAMER. Give me, boy, one answer. What in the world wide put venture into you that made you go face the dog?

SIMON. Ah, what venture? And he being as he is without teeth?

DAMER. You know that, what no one in the parish or out of it ever found out till now! You should have put your hand in his jaw to know that much! A right lad you are and a lucky lad. I would nearly wish you of my own blood and of my race.

DELIA. Of your own blood is it?

DAMER. That is what I would wish.

DELIA. Is it that you are taking Simon Niland to be a stranger?

DAMER. What Simon Niland?

DELIA. Your own nephew and only son to your sister Sarah.

DAMER. Do you tell me so! What way did it fail me to recognise that, and he having daring and spirit the same as used to be rising up in myself in my early time?

DELIA. He was born the very year of you coming into possession of this place.

DAMER. The same year my luck turned against me, and every horse I would back would get the staggers on the course, or would fail to rise at the leaps. All the strength of fortune went from me at that time, it is into himself it flowed and ran. The dead spit and image of myself he is. Stop with me here through the winter season and through the summer season! You to be in the house it is not an unlucky house will be in it. The Royalty of England and of Spain cannot touch upon yourself. I am prouder of you than if you wrote the wars of Homer or put down Turgesius of the Danes! You are a lad that can't be beat. It is you are the Lamb of Luck!

STAFFY. What call has he or any of us to be stopping under Damer's roof and he owning but the four walls presently and a poor little valley of land?

RALPH. There is nothing worth while in his keeping, and all he had gathered after being robbed.

DAMER. Is that what you are saying? Well, I am not so easy robbed as you think! (*Takes bag from the sack and shakes it.*) Is that what you call being robbed?

SIMON. That is my treasure and my bag!

STAFFY. I thought it was after being brought away from the two of you.

DAMER. You are out of it! It is Jubair did that much for me. Jubair, my darling, it is tonight I'll bring him back to the house! It is not in the box he will be any more but alongside the warmth of the hearth. The time I went unloosing his chain, didn't he scrape with his paw till he showed me all I had lost hid in under the straw, and it in a spotted bag! (*Opens and pours out money.*)

SIMON. It is as well for you have it back where it stopped so short with myself.

DAMER. Is it that I would keep it from you where it was won fair? It is a rogue of a man would do that. Where would be the use, and I knowing you could win it back from me at your will, and the five trumps coming into your hand? It is to share it we will and share alike, so long as it will not give out!

DELIA. A little handsel to myself would do the both of you no harm at all.

DAMER. Delia, my darling, I'll go as far as that on this day of wonders. I'll handsel you and welcome. I'll bestow on you the empty jar. (*Gives it to her.*)

DELIA. I'll take it. I'll let on it to be weighty and I facing back into Loughtyshassy.

RALPH. The neighbours seeing it and taking you to be his heir you might come to your goats yet.

DELIA. Ah, what's goats and what is guinea-hens? Did ever you see yoked horses in a coach, their skin shining out like shells, rising their steps in tune the same as a patrol of police? There are peacocks on the lawns of Lough Cutra they were telling me, having each of them a hundred eyes. (*Goes to door.*)

SIMON (*putting his hand on the jar*). I don't know. (*To Damer.*) It might be a nice thing for the two of us to start gathering the full of it again.

DAMER. Not a fear of me. Where heaping and hoarding that much has my years withered and blighted up to this, it is not to storing treasure in any vessel at all I will give the latter end of my days, or to working the skin off my bones. Give me here that coat. (*Puts it on.*) If I was tossed and racked a while ago I'll show out good from this out. Come on now, out of this, till we'll face to the races of Loughrea and of Knockbarron. I was miserable and starved long enough. (*Puts on hat.*) I'm thinking as long as I'll be living I'll take my view of the world, for it's long I'll be lying when my eyes are closed and seeing nothing at all!

(*He seizes a handful of gold and puts it in Simon's pocket and another in his own. They turn towards the door.*)

Curtain.

HANRAHAN'S OATH

HANRAHAN'S OATH

Persons

Mary Gillis	*A Lodging-house Keeper.*
Margaret Rooney	*Her Friend.*
Owen Hanrahan	*A Wandering Poet.*
Coey	*A Ragged Man.*
Mrs. Coey	*His Wife.*
Michael Feeney	*A Poteen-maker.*

Time: *Before the Famine.*

Scene: *A wild and rocky place. Door to left of a stone cabin that was once the bed of a Saint.*

Mary Gillis (*coming from right*). Did you get any tidings of him, Margy?

Margaret Rooney. All I heard was he was seen going over the scalp of the hill at daybreak.

Mary Gillis. Bad cess to him! Why wouldn't he stop in the house last night beyond any other night?

Margaret Rooney. You know well it was going to the preaching of that strange friar put disturbance in his mind.

Mary Gillis. Take care is he listening to him yet.

Margaret Rooney. He is not. I went in the archway of the chapel and took a view. The missioner is in it yet, giving out masses and benedictions and rosaries and every whole thing. But as to Owen Hanrahan, there was no sign of him in it at all.

Mary Gillis. It is to the drink houses I went searching for him.

Margaret Rooney. He was never greatly given to drink.

Mary Gillis. If he isn't, he is given to company and he'd talk down all Ireland.

Margaret Rooney. So he is a terror for telling stories, and it is yourself made your own profit by it. It is his gift of talk brought the harvesters that would live and die with him, to your house this five weeks past.

Mary Gillis. Yourself that is begrudging me that, where you want to keep him to yourself.

MARGARET ROONEY. So I would keep him, I to find him. I wouldn't wish him to go travelling. He had his enough of hardship. There is no great stay in him.

MARY GILLIS. There are but the two roads for him to travel from the scalp, over and hither. He to come this way, believe me I'll bring him back to the town.

MARGARET ROONEY. He wouldn't go with you.

MARY GILLIS. I have a word will bring him, never fear.

MARGARET ROONEY. What word is that?

MARY GILLIS. What was it he was giving out to the two of us ere yesterday, the time he came back after having drink taken at the sailor's wake?

MARGARET ROONEY. I don't keep in mind what he said.

MARY GILLIS. You maybe remember the story he gave us of one Feeney that he was with at a mountain still, and that made an assault on a gauger.

MARGARET ROONEY. Feeney was the name, sure enough—, but what signifies that?

MARY GILLIS. I'll make a spancel from that story will bring him into hiding in the Borough.

MARGARET ROONEY. You might not. It's little you know the twists of a poet's mind. He to have the fit of wandering, it is round the wide world he might go.

MARY GILLIS. Hurry on now, let you go the lower road and see will you bring him any better than myself. (*Pushes her.*)—Go on now, he might pass and go on unknownst to you!

MARGARET ROONEY. I'll not be three minutes going down the hill. (*Goes.*)

MARY GILLIS (*sitting down*). That you may! It's the hither road he is coming.

HANRAHAN (*coming in, his head bent down*). Isn't it a terrible place we are living in and terrible the wickedness of the whole world!

MARY GILLIS. What is it ails you, Owen Hanrahan?

HANRAHAN. People to be breaking all the laws of God and giving no heed to the beyond!

MARY GILLIS. It is likely the preaching of the friar put those thoughts athrough your head.

HANRAHAN. Murders and robberies and lust and neglecting the mass!

MARY GILLIS. Ah, come along home with me to the dinner. You are fasting this good while back.

HANRAHAN. What way can people be thinking of gluttony, and the terrors of the grave before them.

MARY GILLIS. Come on now to the little house, and the drop of drink will put such thoughts from your mind.

HANRAHAN. Drink! That was another of them! Seven deadly sins in all!

MARY GILLIS. What call has a poet the like of you to go listening to a missioner stringing talk? You, that is so handy at it yourself.

HANRAHAN. A lovely saint he was! He came from foreign. To let fall a drop of scalding water on your foot would be bad, he said, or to lay your hand on a hot coal on the floor; but to die with any big sin on your soul; it will be burning for ever and ever, and that burning will be worse than any burning upon earth. To say that he did, rising up his hand. The great fear he put on me was of eternity. Oh, he was a darling man!

MARY GILLIS. Ah, that is the way that class to be beckoning flames at the people, or what way would they get their living? Come along now where you will have company and funning.

HANRAHAN. Leave touching me! I have no mind to be put away from my holy thoughts. Three big mastiffs, their red gullets open and burning the same as three wax candles!

MARY GILLIS. Come along, I tell you, to the comforts of the town.

HANRAHAN. Get away, you hag, before I'll lay a hand on you!

MARY GILLIS. After the good treatment I gave you this five weeks past, beyond any lodger was in the house!

HANRAHAN. Be off, or I'll do you some injury!

MARY GILLIS. It's kind for you do an injury on me, the same as you did on the man that was sent before the judge!

HANRAHAN. Who was that?

MARY GILLIS. Feeney that stuck down the gauger.

HANRAHAN. Anyone didn't see who did it—He was brought before no judge!

MARY GILLIS. You didn't know he was taken and charged and brought to the Tuam Assizes?

HANRAHAN. They could have no proof against him. It was a dark cloudy night.

MARY GILLIS. That is what they are saying. It was in no fair way it was made known who did it.

HANRAHAN. Ah what did he do but put up his fist this way . . . and the gauger was standing where you are supposing . . . and there was a naggin in poor Feeney's hand (*stoops for a stone*)—

and there lit a stroke on him (*strikes as if at her*)— It's hard say was it that knocked him or was it the Almighty God.

MARY GILLIS. There is another thing the people are saying.

HANRAHAN. What is that?

MARY GILLIS. They are saying there was another man along with Feeney at the bog-still.

HANRAHAN. What harm if they are saying that?

MARY GILLIS. It will be well for that man not to be rambling the countryside, but to stop here in the shelter of the town where it is not known. It is likely his name is given out through the baronies of Galway and to the merings of County Mayo.

HANRAHAN. Little I care they to know I was in it. What could they lay to my charge?

MARY GILLIS. You had drink taken. You have no recollection what you said in the spree-house in Monivea. It is the name of an informer you have gained in those districts, where you gave out the account of Feeney's deed, in the hearing of spies and of Government men.

HANRAHAN. That cannot be so! An informer! That would be a terrible story!

MARY GILLIS. A poor case they are saying, you to be roaming the country free, and Feeney under chains through your fault.

HANRAHAN. An informer! I'll go give myself up in his place! I'll swear it was I did it! Maybe I did too. I am certain I hit him a kick that loosed the patch on my shoe. (*Holds foot up.*) I'll go set Feeney free.

MARY GILLIS. You cannot do that. He is gone to his punishment, where he was convicted of assault and attempt to kill.

HANRAHAN. In earnest?

MARY GILLIS. It is much he escaped the death of the rope. It is to send him to transportation they did.

HANRAHAN. The Lord save us!

MARY GILLIS. Sent out in the ship with thieves and vagabonds to Australia or Van Dieman's Land, to be yoked in traces along with blacks driving a plough for the over-Government.

HANRAHAN. Transported and judged! It is a bad story for me that judgment is! And it to be brought about through me giving out too much talk!

MARY GILLIS. Ah come along and get a needleful of porter and we'll have a good evening in the town.

HANRAHAN. There will be no good evening or good morrow come

to me for ever! Let me run to take his place in the ship and in the chains.

MARY GILLIS. Sure it sailed away yesterday. It is ploughing his way across the green ocean Michael Feeney should be at this hour.

HANRAHAN. I'll go to judgment all the same! they'll send me out after him and set him free!

MARY GILLIS. Not a fear of them, and they having him in their hand. And it's likely anyway the ship might go down in some storm.

HANRAHAN. To have sent a man to his chastisement through chattering! That is not of the nature of friendship. That is surely one of the seven deadly sins!

MARY GILLIS. Sure there is nothing standing to you only your share of talk.

HANRAHAN. It is that was my ruin! It would be better for me be born without it, the same as a blessed sheep! It is the sin of the tongue is surely the blackest of all! A man that died with drink in him, the missioner was saying, the soul would sooner stop in torment a thousand years than come back to the body that made it so unclean. And surely my soul would think it worse again to be coming under the sway of a tongue that had it steered to the mouth of the burning mountain, that is said to be the door of hell!

MARY GILLIS. Ah, it is your own talk had always pleasantness in it—come on now—the people love to see you travelling through the town.

HANRAHAN. It is the tongue that does be giving out lies and spreading false reports and putting reproach upon a neighbour, till a character that was as white as lime will turn to be black as coal!

MARY GILLIS. No, but good words yourself does be putting out. Whoever you praised was well praised.

HANRAHAN. A cross word in this house, and a quarrel out of it in the next house, and fighting in the streets from that again, till the whole world wide is at war. The man that would make a gad for the tongue would be put far beyond Alexander that laid one around all the kingdoms of the world!

MARY GILLIS. It is the roads would be lonesome without the sound of your own songs.

HANRAHAN. To make silence in the roads for ever would be a better task than was ever done by Orpheus, and he playing harpstrings to the flocks!

MARY GILLIS. It is not yourself could keep silence in the world, without you would be a ghost.

HANRAHAN. My poor Feeney! He that wore out the night making still-whiskey would put courage into armies of men, and the hares of the mountain gathered around him looking on. I could cry down my eyes, he to be at this time in the black hole of a vessel you couldn't hardly go into head and heels, among rats and every class of ravenous thing! Have you ere a knife about you or a sword or a dagger, that you'll give it to me to do my penance, till I'll cut the tongue out from my head and bury it under the hill?

MARY GILLIS. Ah, come along and do your penance the same as any other one, saying a rosary alongside your bed.

HANRAHAN. I'll go no more into the room with lodgers and strangers and dancers and youngsters enjoying music. I will wear out my time in this cabin of a saint, shedding tears unknownst to the world, hearing no word and speaking no word will be putting my repentance astray. There is great safety in silence! It will cut off the world and all of sins at the one stroke.

MARY GILLIS. It is not yourself could keep from the talk without you would be dumb.

HANRAHAN. So I will be dumb and live in dumbness, if I have my mind laid to it! I will make an oath with myself. (*Puts up hands.*) By the red heat of anger and by the hard strength of the wind I will speak no word to any living person through the length of a year and a day! I will earn Feeney's pardon doing that! I'll be praying for him on all my beads!

MARY GILLIS. Ah, before the year is out he will have his escape made, or maybe have done some crime will earn him punishment, whether or no, without any blame upon yourself. It will fail you to stop in this wilderness. You were always fond of life.

HANRAHAN (*sitting down and taking off boots*). Bring away my shoes to some safe place to the end of my penance, that I will not be tempted to break away! Mind them well till the time I will be wanting them again.

MARY GILLIS. It is a big fool you are and a cracked thief and a blockhead and a headstrong ignorant man!

HANRAHAN. I am not in this place for wrastling! It is good back-answers I could give you, if it wasn't that I am dumb!

MARY GILLIS. I'm in no dread of your answers! I'd put curses out of my own mouth as quick as another the time I would be vexed!

HANRAHAN. Get out now of this! The devil himself couldn't do his repentance with the noise and the chat of you! (*Threatens her.*)

MARY GILLIS. Whisper now, one thing only and I'll go.

HANRAHAN. Hurry on so, and say what is it.

MARY GILLIS. What place did you put the keg of still-whiskey you were saying you brought away at the time Feeney ran, the gauger being stretched on the bog?

HANRAHAN. What way can I whisper it, and I under an oath to be dumb!

MARY GILLIS. Is it in the bog you hid it? Or within a ditch or a drain. Let you beckon your hand at me, the time I'll give out the right place, and you'll not break your promise and your oath. Under a dung-heap maybe . . . Let you make now some sign . . .

HANRAHAN (*seizing stick and rushing at her*). Sign is it? Here's signs for you! My grief that I cannot break my oath!

MARY GILLIS (*who has rushed off looking back*). Your oath is it? You may believe me telling you, it will fail you for one day only to keep a gad upon your tongue! (*Goes.*)

(HANRAHAN *shakes fist at her and sits down. Rocks himself and moans.*

A ragged man with a sack of seaweed comes in and looks at him timidly.)

COEY. Fine day! (HANRAHAN *takes no notice.*) Fine day! (*Louder.*) Fine day, the Lord be praised! . . . (HANRAHAN *scowls.*) What is on you? FINE DAY! Is it deaf you are . . . Is it maybe after taking drink you are? To put your head down in the spring well below would maybe serve you. (HANRAHAN *shakes head indignantly.*) Is it that you are after being bet? A puck on the poll is apt to put confusion in the mind. (*Another indignant shake.*) Tell me out now, what is on you or what happened you at all?

(HANRAHAN *gets up. Makes same dumb show as he did to* MARY GILLIS, *stoops, picks up stone, rushes as if to threaten* COEY.)

COEY. The Lord be between us and harm! It is surely a wild man is in it! (*He throws down basket and rushes off right.*)

HANRAHAN. Ah, what is it ails you? That you may never be better this side of Christmas . . . What am I doing? Is it speaking in spite of myself I am? What at all can I do! I to speak, I am breaking my oath; and I not to speak, I have the world terrified. (*Sits down dejectedly, then starts.*) What is that? A thorn that ran into me . . . a whitethorn bush. . . . It is Heaven put it in my way. There is no sin or no harm to be talking with a bush, that is a fashion among poets. Oh, my little bush, it is a saint I am out and out! It is a man without blame I will be from this time! To go through the whole gamut of the heat and of the frost with no person to be annoying me till I get a fit of talk and be letting out wicked words, that is surely the road will reach to Paradise. It is a right plan I made and a right penance I put on myself. As I converse now with yourself, the same as with a living person, so every living person I may hold talk with, and my penance ended, I will think them to be as harmless as a little whitethorn bush. It is a holy life I will follow, and not to be annoyed with the humans of the world that do be prattling and prating, carrying mischief here and there, lavish in tale-bearing and talk! It is a great sin from God Almighty to be ballyragging and drawing scandal on one another, rising quarrels and rows! I declare to honest goodness the coneys and the hares are ahead of most Christians on the road to heaven, where they have not the power to curse and damn, or to do mischief through flatteries and chatterings and coaxings and jestings and jokings and riddles and fables and fancies and vanities, and backbitings and mockeries and mumblings and grumblings and treacheries and false reports! It is free I am now from the screechings and vain jabberings of the world, in this holy quiet place that is all one nearly with the blessed silence of heaven! (*He takes up his beads.*)

(COEY *and* MRS. COEY *come on and look at him from behind.*)

COEY. A wild man I tell you he is, wild and shy.

MRS. COEY. Wording a prayer he would seem to be, letting deep sighs out of himself. A wild man would be apt to be a pagan or an unbeliever.

COEY. I tell you he rose up and made a plunge at me and rose a stone over my poll. If it wasn't for getting the bag I left after me, I wouldn't go anear him. It's a good thought I had taking out of it the two shillings I got for the winkles I sold from the strand, and giving them into your own charge. . . . Take care would he turn and make a run at me!

MRS. COEY. He is no wild man, but a spoiled priest or a crazed saint or some thing of the sort.

COEY. Striving to put curses on me he was, but it failed him to bring them out. It might be that he was born a dummy into the world, and drivelling from his birth out.

(HANRAHAN *listens.*)

MRS. COEY. Would you say now would he be Cassidy Baun, the troubled Friar, that the love of a woman put astray in his wits?

COEY. A half-fool I would say him to be. But it might be that he has a pain in the jaw or a tooth that would want to be drawn. Or is it that the tongue was cut from him by some person had a cause against him.

168

(HANRAHAN *turns indignantly and puts tongue out.*)

MRS. COEY. He is not maimed or ailing. It is long I was coveting to see such a one that would have power to show miracles and wonders, or to do cures with a gospel, or put away the wildfire with herbs.

COEY. Let him show a miracle or do something out of the way, and I'll believe it.

MRS. COEY. If he does, it is to myself he will show it. I am the most one is worthy.

COEY. Have a care. He is about to turn around.

MRS. COEY (*sitting down*). Let me put a decent appearance on myself before he will take notice of me. (*Begins putting on the pair of boots* HANRAHAN *had given to* MARY GILLIS' *charge, and which she takes from under her shawl.*)

COEY. A pair of shoes! What way did they come into your hand?

MRS. COEY. It is that I found them on the road. . . .

COEY. They are belonging so to some person will come looking for them.

MRS. COEY. They are not but to myself they belong . . . it is that they were sent to me by messenger.

COEY. And who would bestow you shoes, you that never put a shoe or a boot on you and the snow three feet on the ground, and you after going barefoot through the frost of two score of years!

MRS. COEY. There's plenty to bestow them to me. Haven't I a first cousin went harvesting out in England where there is maybe shovels full of gold.

(HANRAHAN *comes across quickly, seizes boots angrily and takes them away, shaking his fists at her.*)

COEY (*retreating*). There is coming on him a fit of frenzy! Run now. Let you run!

(HANRAHAN *seizes and shakes her.*)

MRS. COEY (*on her knees*). Oh leave your hand off of me, blessed father! I'll confess all! Oh it is a miracle is after being worked on me! (*Another shake.*) A miracle to put shame on me where I told a lie, may God forgive me! on the head of the boots!

COEY. I was thinking it was lying you were.

MRS. COEY. How well he knew it, the dear and the holy man! He that can read the hidden thoughts of my heart the same as if written on my brow!

COEY. Is it to steal them you did?

MRS. COEY (*to* HANRAHAN). Do not look at me so terrible wicked, and I'll make my confession the same as if it was the Bishop was in it!

COEY. Is it that I am wedded with a thief and a robber!

MRS. COEY. I am not a thief, but to tell a lie I did, laying down that I got them from my first cousin, where I bought them from a woman going the road.

COEY. That's another lie, where would you get the money?

MRS. COEY. Your own two shillings I gave for them that you put in my care a while ago. Take the shoes, holy saint, for I'll lay no hand on them any more. There never was the like of it of a start ever taken out of me.

COEY. You asked a miracle and you got a miracle you'll not forget from this day. (*Takes off hat.*) I'll never go against such things from this out. A good saint he is, by hell!

(MARGARET ROONEY *comes on,* HANRAHAN *catching sight of her flings down boots and crouches behind bush.*)

MARGARET ROONEY. Did you see anyone passing this side?

COEY. Not a one.

MARGARET ROONEY. I am in search of a friend I have, that is gone travelling the road.

MRS. COEY. There is not a one in this place but the blessed saint is saying out prayers abroad under the bush.

MARGARET ROONEY. I knew no saint in this place. What sort is he?

COEY. You would say him to be a man that has not a great deal of talk.

MRS. COEY. He is a great saint; he is so saintly as that there couldn't be saintlier than what he is. He is living in the wilderness on nuts and the berries of the bush, and his two jaws being bloomy all the time.

COEY. He to be known, the people will come drawing from this to Dublin till he will have them around him in throngs.

MARGARET ROONEY (*seizing boots*). What way did you get those shoes?

COEY. It was the saint threw them there in that place.

MARGARET ROONEY. What happened the man that owned them?

MRS. COEY (*pointing to bush*). Sorra one of me knows. Go crave to the saint under the bush to give out knowledge of that. It's himself should be well able to do it. He beckoned the hand at me a while ago and told me all that ever I did.

MARGARET ROONEY (*goes to back of bush but* HANRAHAN *moves round from her*). I ask your pardon father, but will you tell me

what happened the man I am in search of and what way did his
shoes come to this place? I am certain he would not part them
unless he would be plundered and robbed. Tell me where can I
find him.

MRS. COEY. Do not be annoying him now. It is likely he is
holding talk with heaven.

MARGARET ROONEY (*to* COEY). It is maybe you yourself took
the shoes.

COEY. Let you stop putting a stain on my character. I that never
put a farthing astray on anyone!

MARGARET ROONEY. What at all can I do to know is he living or
dead. Or is he gone walking the round world barefoot!

MRS. COEY. Hurry on and get news from that man is under the
bush, before there might angels come would give him a horn and
rise him through the sky!

MARGARET ROONEY. Saint or no saint, I'll drag an answer out
of him!

(*She goes to him, he moves away from her round bush. She
takes hold of his shoulders.*)

COEY. Ah, there will thunder fall on her!

(HANRAHAN *tries to escape but* MARGARET ROONEY *holds him
and looks at his face.*)

MARGARET ROONEY. Is it you, Owen, is in it! Oh what is it
happened at all!

COEY. Will you hearken to her speaking to him as if he was some
common man.

MARGARET ROONEY. Tell me now what parted you from your
shoes and are you sound and well? . . . Answer me now. . . . I think
you very dark not speaking to me. It would be no great load on
you to say, "God bless you"! (*He keeps moving on, she holding
and following him.*) Is it your spirit I am looking on, or your ghost?

MRS. COEY. Look at how he will not let his eye rest upon a
woman, the holy man!

MARGARET ROONEY. Get him to speak one word to me and you
will earn my blessing! . . . Do you not recognise me, Owen, and I
standing in the pure daylight! . . . Don't now be making strange,
but stretch over to the road to be chatting and talking like you
used. . . .

COEY. He has lost the talk, I am telling you. It is but by signs
he makes things known.

MRS. COEY. It is that the people of this district are not worthy
to hear his voice.

MARGARET ROONEY. Is it that you went wild and mad, finding the place so lonesome? What at all but that would cause you to go dumb?

MRS. COEY. Have some shame on you. Can't you see he is not acquainted with you at all?

MARGARET ROONEY. Did there some disease fall upon you, or some sickness? Why wouldn't you come back with me, and I would tend you and find you a cure? . . . Let you answer me back, if it is but to spit at me! Is it that I vexed you in any way, and the stocking I mended with kind worsted covering your foot yet? . . . (*He draws it back.*) Is it to break my heart you will? . . . Is it to put ridicule on me, and to be making a mockery of me you are? Letting on to be dumb! (*He weeps.*) I had great love for him and I thought he had love for me. (*She turns away. He is stretching out his arms' to her when* MARY GILLIS *comes on.* HANRAHAN *breaks away, making a grab at boots, he sits down to put them on, making a face at her.*) Is that yourself, Mary Gillis? It is in the nick of time you are come.

MRS. COEY (*to* MARY GILLIS). Give me back now the two shillings I paid you for that pair of shoes.

MARGARET ROONEY. Will you draw down on these fools of the world that this is no saint, but Owen Hanrahan?

MRS. COEY. No, but she is under delusions! A man from God he is! Miracles he can do, and he living, and at the time he'll be dead there is apt to be great virtue in his bones.

MARGARET ROONEY. Tell them, can't you, that he is Owen Hanrahan?

MARY GILLIS (*puts arms akimbo*). And what is it makes you say this to be Owen Hanrahan?

MARGARET ROONEY. Are you gone cracked along with them?

COEY AND MRS. COEY. That's the chat! That's the chat!

MARY GILLIS. There will a judgment come on you, Margy Rooney, for putting on a holy Christian, is dwelling in the blessed bed of a saint, the name of a vagabond heathen poet does be filling the long roads with his follies and his lies!

(HANRAHAN *scowls at her.*)

COEY. That's right! That's right! A great shame the name of this holy friar to be mixed with any sinful person at all.

MARGARET ROONEY. Is it the whole world has gone raging wild?

MARY GILLIS. Hanrahan the poet is it? God bless your health! That is a man should not be spoken of in this saintly place. He is the greatest schemer ever God created! There is no beat to him!

Putting lies on his own father and mother in Cappaghtagle! Letting his father be buried from the poorhouse that was gaoled for sheep-stealing! Sure that one would hang the Pope!

> (HANRAHAN *makes faces at her again.*)

MARGARET ROONEY. Give over now cutting him down! (*Tries to put hand over her mouth.*)

MARY GILLIS (*freeing herself*). It is not dumb I am myself, the Lord be praised, the same as this holy man. And I say, if you must put a name on him, let it be the name of some poet worth while, such as Carolan or Virgil or Sweeney from Connemara. It is Sweeney that is great! (MARGARET ROONEY *tries to stop her, but she backs and goes on.*) It is himself can string words through the night-time. But as to poor Owen Hanrahan, it is inhuman songs he makes. Unnatural they are, without mirth or loveliness or joy or delight.

> (HANRAHAN *writhes with anguish and makes threatening signs.*)

You'd laugh your life out, listening to the way he was put down one time by Sweeney, the Connemara boy!

> (HANRAHAN *throws himself down and bites the grass.*)

MARGARET ROONEY. If you are Hanrahan, let you put her down under a poet's curse. And if you are a saint, let you make a grass-hopper of her with the power of a saint!

MARY GILLIS. It is bawneen flannel and clean, that dumb friar is wearing; but as to Owen Hanrahan, it is a stirabout poet he is, and greasy his coat is, with all the leavings he brings away from him and he begging his dinner from door to door.

> (HANRAHAN *gets up and rushes at her. She shrieks and runs right. She knocks against* FEENEY *who is coming on.* HANRAHAN *stops short and goes quickly into cabin.*)

FEENEY. Mind yourself, woman! You all to had me knocked, barging and fighting and raising rings around you! I'll make you ask my pardon so sure as my name is Feeney!

MARY GILLIS. Michael Feeney is it? (*He nods.*)

MARGARET ROONEY. What is it brings you here?

FEENEY. This is a place if you'd go astray, you'd go astray very quick in it. Crosscutting over the mountain I was, till I'd face back to my own place near Tuam. And I got word there is a friar from foreign here in some place, giving out preachings and absolutions.

MRS. COEY. No, but a holy man that is in the cabin beyond. A great saint he is, out and out!

FEENEY. That'll serve me as well, where I missed attending

COLLECTED PLAYS: COMEDIES

mass this fortnight back, where I was . . . travelling . . . In very backward places, I was. It is home I am facing now, and I'd sooner give out my confession to a stranger than to our own priest, might be questioning me where is my little mountain still, he being a Father Matthew man, that wouldn't so much as drink water out of a glass but from a teacup.

COEY. You did well coming to himself that can put no question to you at all.

MRS. COEY. My grief that he cannot word out a rosary or give us newses of the fallen angels, being dumb and bereft of speech.

FEENEY. That will suit me well, so long as his ears are not closed, and that he can get me free from going to confession for another quarter of a year on this side of St. Martin's Day.

(*He kneels at door.*)

MARGARET ROONEY (*trying to move him away*). Do not be pushing on him where he might be in a sleep or a slumber.

MRS. COEY (*awed*). It is maybe away in a trance he might be, and the angels coming around him. It is in that way his miracles and wonders come to him.

COEY (*getting behind him*). Mind yourself. He might likely burst demented out from his trance and destroy the world with one twist of the hand.

MRS. COEY. He is bended now, holy father. Be so liberal as to reach your hand for the good of his soul.

MARY GILLIS. It would maybe be right, the whole of us to go in and see is there a weakness come upon him with his fast.

(*A hand is hurriedly stretched out.*)

FEENEY (*having knelt a moment shouts*). What is that I see! I recognise that yellow patch! Owen Hanrahan's boots! (*Jumps up and drags.*) Come out now, out of that!

MARGARET ROONEY. Let you leave dragging him! (*Tries to stop him.*)

FEENEY (*dragging him out with a loud laugh*). Is it yourself, Owen Hanrahan, is setting up to be no less than a saint? Is it for sport or for gain you are working miracles and giving out benedictions?

HANRAHAN. Is it not transported you are!

FEENEY. Why should I be transported, without you would be wishful of it?

HANRAHAN. Taken and judged and sent out to Van Dieman's Land!

FEENEY. It is seemingly well pleased you would be, I to be there, and my neck in the hemp along with it.

HANRAHAN. Is that the thanks you are giving me, for doing penance under dumbness, on the head of you being gaoled in a ship!

FEENEY. Little you'd care, I to linger my life out on a treadmill or withering in a cell!

HANRAHAN. Don't I tell you I am working out my repentance with the dint of my grief, where it was through my talk you were made a prisoner, and brought to the Court, and led away under chains, and blacks maybe beating you with whips.

FEENEY. What are you raving about, making me out a rogue and putting that stain on my name, I that never stood in a court, or a dock, or was brought away in a ship, or ever rattled a chain, or put my head upon a block!

HANRAHAN. Having the name of an informer put on me for your sake!

FEENEY. Is it that you are after being an informer? Giving out to the world the hidden bog-hole where I have my still!

HANRAHAN. I did not!

FEENEY. And you lurking in a cleft and letting on to be wording your beads! But I'll knock satisfaction out of you. I'll have you baulked!

HANRAHAN. It is likely the gauger gave it out!

FEENEY. He wouldn't put the people against him saying that. A neighbour made me out and told me he swore he disremembered all that happened. Death and destruction on me, but he's a more honourable man than yourself!

MARGARET ROONEY. What have you against one another so?

FEENEY. Blessed if I know.

HANRAHAN. If I haven't anything against him, there are others I have it against. (*To* MARY GILLIS) Let you be ashamed and under grief, for the way you have us made fools of. It is up here in this cabin yourself has a right to stop for the centuries earning my forgiveness to the end of your life, sleeping in your pelt and scraping your bare feet on the rock, like myself was doing, and speechless, and without defence, the same as I was myself, through the story you made up and the lies!

MARGARET ROONEY. That's the chat, Owen! That is yourself is come back to us!

MRS. COEY. Well now, for a saint of silence hasn't he a terrible deal of talk?

MARY GILLIS. As savage as a wasp out of a bottle he is! His talk is seven times sharper than before, and a holy terror to the whole world. I'll go call to the true friar at the Chapel to say are you not bound to silence for a year and a day by your oath!

HANRAHAN (*putting arm round* MARGARET ROONEY *and shaking fist at* MARY GILLIS *as he takes up his coat*). You will, will you? Well I am not bound! How would I know, the time I took the oath in my lone, there would be schemers coming around me challenging and annoying me? It is yourself that broke the bond, following after me! And you have a great wrong done to me. The next time I will take an oath of silence it is in the market square I will take it, the night before the spring fair, and the pigs squealing from every paling and every car, and hawkers bawling, sooner than to be narrowed up on a crag where I cannot make my escape from the tongue of a woman that is more lasting than the sole of my shoe! It's bad behaviour you showed, with your lies, and a great shame for you, and you being a widow and advanced out a while. It's a great wonder the Lord to stand the villainy is in you! I'll make you go easy! The time you rose me out of my senses, tearing away my character, and I being dumb, I had myself promised I would make a world's wonder of you in the bye and bye, and my year and a day being passed! You disgrace, you! The curse of my heart on you! Go on now, you withered sloe bush, you cranky crab fish, you hag, you rap, you vagabond! May your day not thrive with you, and that you may be seven hundred times crosser this time next year, and it is good curses I'll be making, and the first I'll put on you is the curse of dumbness, for that is the last curse of all!

Curtain.

THE WRENS

THE WRENS

PERSONS
> THE PORTER.
> KIRWAN'S SERVANT.
> CASTLEREAGH'S SERVANT.
> WILLIAM HEVENOR ⎱ *Strolling Singers.*
> MARGY HEVENOR ⎰

TIME. *January 22nd, 1799.*

SCENE. *Outside House of Commons, Dublin.* PORTER *at top of steps.* KIRWAN'S SERVANT *arriving.*

KIRWAN'S SERVANT. Fine morning.

PORTER. Middling; for January.

KIRWAN'S SERVANT. Are they making speeches yet?

PORTER. They are. Arguing and debating, Lords and Commons, through night and through dawn, till they have the world talked upside down.

KIRWAN'S SERVANT. I suppose nearly the most of them is in it?

PORTER. What there isn't of them you wouldn't miss out of it, unless it might be your own master, Mr. Kirwan.

KIRWAN'S SERVANT. He quitted the House after his big speech. He laid down to them a good line of talk.

PORTER. He got over all his enemies in that speech.

KIRWAN'S SERVANT. He did, and the enemies of Ireland. They are as good as put down altogether. He'll be coming back in a while's time.

PORTER. Why wouldn't he, and the vote to be taken yet? He's a man that has no mix in him.

KIRWAN'S SERVANT. Around in the attorney's office he is, writing out documents to go by messengers to England so soon as the bill will be thrown out. He bade me to go call him at the time the vote will be coming on.

PORTER. It will not be long till that time. The speeches should be at their last goal.

KIRWAN'S SERVANT (*going to door*). I'll take my station here.

So soon as they'll start to clap the bell I'll go warn him. Though it's likely his one vote won't be hardly needed, with all that will be against the bill.

PORTER. Maybe so. It's hard say. It being to be it will be.

KIRWAN'S SERVANT. There is no man is honest and is straight but will give his voice against it.

PORTER. It's hard know what might happen from when we get up in the morning to when we go to bed at night; or half that time.

KIRWAN'S SERVANT. Here is Lord Castlereagh's servant coming to gather news for his master—my black curse on him—that is one of the old boy's comrades!

CASTLEREAGH'S SERVANT (*coming in*). Fine day!

KIRWAN'S SERVANT. It will be a better day inside an hour's space, when the bill for the Union with England will be defeated and thrown out. My joy go with it in a bottle of moss! If it never comes back it is no great loss!

CASTLEREAGH'S SERVANT. If it is it will be because there's more fools than wise men within the walls of that house.

KIRWAN'S SERVANT. It is what you're thinking that your master has the whole county bought. But let me tell you that he has not. It would take a holy lot to do that!

CASTLEREAGH'S SERVANT. There is no person having sense but would wish to be within the Empire of England.

KIRWAN'S SERVANT. He would not, unless he would come of a bad tribe and a bad family, and would be looking for a pension for his vote.

PORTER. It might be so. Money does everything in the worst possible way.

CASTLEREAGH'S SERVANT (*to* PORTER). You'll be apt to lose your own job of standing on the thrassel of that door, and the Parliament to be housed over in London. It would be best for you while you have time shift over to our side. (*Shows him a purse and shakes it.*)

PORTER. I don't know. Someway foreign money doesn't go far.

KIRWAN'S SERVANT (*sarcastically*). What will he divide on you so? Why wouldn't you wish to be made a Lord? Or ask a County Court judgeship, and your wife to be flying hats and feathers. Have you any knowledge of the law?

PORTER. More than the most of them! I am well able to administer an oath.

CASTLEREAGH'S SERVANT (*to* KIRWAN'S). There is no one

against the bill but some that are like yourselves not having learning and that don't travel.

KIRWAN'S SERVANT. There are, and noble and high-blooded people are against it! Languaged people that can turn history to their own hand!

PORTER. They might not. To be supple with the tongue is not all.

KIRWAN'S SERVANT. I tell you the most thing in the mighty world could not save that bill from being thrown out and refused!

PORTER. It's hard say. There was no great strength in the wrens that destroyed Ireland the time they went picking crumbs on a drum, and wakened up the army of the Danes.

KIRWAN'S SERVANT. And what sort is it you are thinking will destroy the liberties of Ireland this day? Is it that couple of raggedy strollers are disputing along the side path of the Green?

(*Enter* HEVENOR *and* MARGY, *disputing.*)

MARGY (*pushing* HEVENOR). Bad cess to you bringing me foraging around, running and wandering, by roads and cross roads, by hedges and by walls, the cold and the slashing rain upon me! There's no stay in you but as if you were a wild duck. From country to country it goes.

HEVENOR. Well for me if I had its wings! To stop in the one place with your talk at me and your prating, I'd as soon be in the body of a gaol!

MARGY. I to have nothing of my own, or a skirt that would bring me to the church, no more than a dog or a sow!

HEVENOR. That is lies you are telling and you owning by marriage a good man that is myself!

MARGY. I could have had great marriages if I didn't choose you, and many wondered at me!

HEVENOR. Be easy now! It's too much you have to say. It would take twenty to keep you in chat!

MARGY. And I dreaming the day I wed with you of little houses as white as snow, and a bunch of keys in my hand!

HEVENOR. Ah, you're entirely too lavish in talk.

MARGY. My old fathers that had stock and land, and the bacon over their head. And what am I myself but a holy show by the side of the road? To bring me singing through the streets, that is the last thing of all. God help the poor! The rich can rob around.

HEVENOR. Hold your whisht, can't you? There is grand people up at that door.

MARGY. English they should be by the rich clothes of them. They are your business. Let you word out a Government song.

HEVENOR (*sings*)

> A song for Britain and her sons,
> A song of harmony,
> And now and ever let it breathe
> Of truth and loyalty.
> Its theme the same where'er we be,
> Her palace isle we'll sing,
> The laurels and the victory
> Of Britain and the King!

CASTLEREAGH'S SERVANT. That's very good! The whole country is turning to join with Britain, the hungry as well as the high up.

KIRWAN'S SERVANT (*threatening* HEVENOR). Get out of this with your bawling, if it fails you to sing straight and sing honest!

HEVENOR. I am singing honest.

KIRWAN'S SERVANT. You are not, but for profit and gain.

HEVENOR. Amn't I a Catholic? Why wouldn't I go with the Bishops and the Clergy?

CASTLEREAGH'S SERVANT. They have sense, coming to our side.

HEVENOR. Sure the Government has them promised that the Parliament to change over to London, there'll be Catholic Emancipation on the minute!

KIRWAN'S SERVANT. I never could believe in lies!

HEVENOR. That's my hearing of the thing.

KIRWAN'S SERVANT. I wouldn't believe it from the Pope!

MARGY. That's what I do be telling him myself—England is all promise and no pay.

HEVENOR. What did my own Bishop put out down in Mayo? "Let us join," says he, "with the British,'" says he, "that are the wisest, the freest and the happiest people on the whole face of the earth! "

MARGY. Ah, he is but in dread of corner boys like yourself joining strikes and setting themselves up against the Pope the same as those lads out in France.

HEVENOR. "For self and clergy," says he, "we will stand and fall with the British."

MARGY. What will stand will be on the other side, and what will fall will be on this side! It is England will get the cream and leave us the broken milk.

HEVENOR. No, but we being paired and wedded with the Sassenach, we'll be full and easy like themselves.

MARGY. To be banishing away reared people to be playing

skittle-alley out in London! That will give the country no fair play.

HEVENOR. Showing kindness and sharing wealth the same as the children of one house!

MARGY. What a fool I am! Doesn't the world know the English to be hard and wicked and the Irish fair and easy? It is to turn Dublin you would to be but a little village of houses?

HEVENOR. Women have no intellect to give out such things; great voice and little head!

MARGY. I would not to gain the big world entirely give leave to the Parliament to shift over out of this so much as nine lengths of a cow's tail! London is entirely too thronged. As many people as you'd see wheat in a field. How would we get our own handling and our way?

HEVENOR. It's a bad way we are getting up to this!

MARGY. A great wonder the Lord to stand the villainy is in it! The English are the worst people under the rising sun. With what sort is it you are wishful to mingle and join, after God Himself putting out His hand to banish snakes and serpents out of Ireland?

HEVENOR. There is plenty of that class in it yet ready to ate one another.

MARGY. We might ate one another at some times, but they'd ate the whole of us!

HEVENOR. Too much of quarrelling and slandering. It is time for us live in peace.

MARGY. Ah, for ten thousand years Ireland was fighting and what would ail her to stop at this time?

HEVENOR. It is the power of England will put down your pride, and the law of the Union passed.

MARGY. If they do pass it no one would be forced to obey it. It is a good man said that.

HEVENOR. Them that said it will be put down as rebels.

MARGY. It is rebels in good clothes will be put down that time in place of rebels in frieze. It is all rebels we'll be together, the Lord be praised! I tell you I to suckle 20,000 sons, I'd rear them the same as Hannibal!

KIRWAN'S SERVANT. Good woman! That is right talk!

HEVENOR (to CASTLEREAGH'S SERVANT). It is emancipation she begrudges us, and we to be equal with the Protestants.

MARGY (to KIRWAN'S SERVANT). All the laws of England would not make you the equal of myself! I never will give in to be reduced to a Catholic!

HEVENOR (*to* CASTLEREAGH'S SERVANT). Isn't she the great Protestant with her high notions?

MARGY. If I am, it's in the shadow of a Protestant house I was reared, and a good house. Wasn't my grandmother hen-woman to the Duke of Leinster? God be with my poor Lord Edward, the best that ever ate the world's bread! It's often she roasted an egg in the ashes for him and he in his young age. It is for himself she's wearing a black ribbon on this day, tied around the frill of her cap. It's myself will sing him through the three parishes.

(*Sings*)

We'll arm ourselves for God is good and blesses them who lean
On their brave hearts and not upon an earthly king or queen;
And freely as we lift our hands we vow our blood to shed
Till in some day to come the green will flutter o'er the red!

KIRWAN'S SERVANT. More power to you, Ma'am! That every day may thrive with you! (*Gives money.*)

HEVENOR (*to* CASTLEREAGH'S SERVANT). Give myself some little coin into my hand, your honour, and I'll give out a good verse for the Union.

(*Sings*)

The laurels and the victories
Of Britain and the King.

CASTLEREAGH'S SERVANT. I'll do that much for you.

(*Puts hand in pocket and takes out money.*)

MARGY (*pushing back his hand*). Do not give it to himself but to me! Everything he will handle he will drink it.

HEVENOR. I'm no good when I'm in my sense and in my mind. But when I have a drop taken, it's then I will bring out the songs.

MARGY. He had enough taken yesterday to last him to the world's end! Going to public houses in company does not answer him. The drink does but drive out his wits.

HEVENOR. It's to put a good mouth on herself she says that. She pretends to be proud, and reflects on me.

MARGY. When they get themselves into a habit it is hard for them get out of it after!

HEVENOR. That you may never have the price of your shroud! That one would begrudge so much as bog water out of a tea-cup.

MARGY. Whatever class of drink he took last night, what way did he get the price of it but to bring away and to put in pawn my stuffed pincushion. When I cast it up to him after he was breaking his heart laughing.

HEVENOR. I did but lighten her travelling load!

MARGY. My pincushion I got from the minister's wife and I a child rising up. The first little stick of furniture ever I had, and I bringing it from road to road till such time as I'll get a little table to put it on, and a room would hold the table, and the bed; and a little kitchen along with it, the way I'd be in Heaven having a little place of my own.

HEVENOR. You'll never be in Heaven or within fifteen mile of it!

MARGY. So much as the image of a farthing he never leaves it in my hand. Give him the pledge against drink. That's the only best thing to do. He is a young fellow that has no understanding.

HEVENOR. That the Almighty may make you a worthy woman!

MARGY. So wild and arch as he is he's no good for the world only drinking. You to give him a pint he'd ask to go inside in the barrel.

HEVENOR. So stubborn as you are! Would you downface me!

(HEVENOR *sheltering behind* CASTLEREAGH'S SERVANT, MARGY *trying to get at him.*)

MARGY. To make a trade of it he does. He'll drink the devil into him.

HEVENOR. She is such a terrible barge you couldn't stand against her. (*To* CASTLEREAGH'S SERVANT) Give me the bit of silver in my hand and I'll go.

MARGY. Do not till such time as he will have the pledge taken!

CASTLEREAGH'S SERVANT. Will you take it so?

HEVENOR. I'm too well pledged before this, being pledged to herself!

CASTLEREAGH'S SERVANT. Take it now. I'll get you good custom for your songs. You'll be of use to me, coaxing and turning rebels to the side of my master.

KIRWAN'S SERVANT. Don't mind doing that, but take the oath against drink and live peaceful with the good woman at your side.

HEVENOR. It is likely it would fail me to hold to it.

CASTLEREAGH'S SERVANT. Take it to St. Bridget's Day, that is but nine days from this.

HEVENOR. I would feel that much time too long in passing.

KIRWAN'S SERVANT (*sneeringly*). Take it so till the Union bill will be thrown out, and that will be inside of a few hours.

MARGY. That's no use! That much is not worth while.

HEVENOR. It will be worth while if I think it to be worth while.

MARGY. I'd as lief he not to take it at all.

HEVENOR. In troth I'll take it if I have a mind to take it.

CASTLEREAGH'S SERVANT (*to* PORTER). Give him the oath as you are able, and make an end of it.

PORTER. Wait till I'll get the book.(*Goes in at door.*)

HEVENOR. I don't know. I never took a book in my hand to swear this or that.

MARGY. It's best for you wait till such time as you'll get a fright, or a vision of the bones of death, and take the oath in earnest.

PORTER (*coming out*). Kiss the book.

HEVENOR. Give it here to me! (*Snatches and kisses it.*)

PORTER. Word this now after me. (HEVENOR *repeats it after him.*) "I will touch no drop of drink, or anything you'd call drink, until such time as the Union bill now within in that house will be thrown out and rejected and beat! So help me God!" (*Takes book back into house.*)

HEVENOR. I took it now in spite of you. Any man to offer me a glass of whiskey I'd sooner he to give me a clout on the head!

CASTLEREAGH'S SERVANT. Where now is the song?

HEVENOR (*sings*)

> United with Britain may Erin for ever
>> In commerce, in arts, and in science advance;
> United with Britain may Ireland for ever
>> Live mighty and free, independent of France!

MARGY (*to* KIRWAN'S SERVANT). It's much that he does not pull down that green flag, and it having King David's harp on it and the picture of an angel on its front!

HEVENOR. Give me the bit of silver in my hand now, your honour, where I have it well earned.

CASTLEREAGH'S SERVANT. There it is for you.

HEVENOR. That's a valiant lot of money! That you may reign long!

CASTLEREAGH'S SERVANT. Follow on now with that song.

HEVENOR (*tries and clears throat*). Checking that one and her arguments has put a sort of a foggy mist in my throat. I must go banish it with a small drop of porter.

MARGY. Porter! You have no leave to touch that, and you having the pledge taken.

HEVENOR. Ah, won't the bill be cast out before I will get to the drink house?

CASTLEREAGH'S SERVANT. It might not.

HEVENOR (*pointing to* KIRWAN'S SERVANT). That one has it promised me it will.

CASTLEREAGH'S SERVANT. Little he knows. It might never be thrown out at all.

KIRWAN'S SERVANT. I tell you it will be!

CASTLEREAGH'S SERVANT. There is bets on it going through.

KIRWAN'S SERVANT. Wait till you'll see! I'll bet you a golden guinea it is out it will go!

HEVENOR. And must I keep from the drink that not to happen?

CASTLEREAGH'S SERVANT. You took that oath, sure enough. You cannot rise out of it now.

HEVENOR. So I did, God forgive me. (*Turns to* MARGY.) You are the worst head to a man ever I saw, giving me leave to do that!

MARGY. You have the money in your hand to lay out in some better way.

HEVENOR. I wouldn't handle a halfpenny belonging to him, and I as wise then as I am now! Where is the use of it and it not bringing me my heart's desire?

MARGY. It will maybe not rise you out of your senses this time!

HEVENOR. I to be bare empty I would say nothing, but wealth to be in my hand and there to be no frolic or pleasure in it, it is that is killing me entirely.

CASTLEREAGH'S SERVANT. It's an enemy to himself that will turn back to drink that is the misfortune of all.

HEVENOR. Silver crowns in my hand, and I maybe to lay myself down this night as innocent and as timid as a coney of the rocks, never felt the power of still-whiskey!

MARGY. He'll be turning to it again, and the pledge loosened, as sure as there's folly in a fool.

HEVENOR. If I had but thought to take my fill before they knocked a promise out of me. Music that would be going a-through me, and a poet's wreath around my head! Kindness in my heart that I would forgive the whole world, and it after thrusting me from its door!

MARGY. It is fighting it would be more apt to leave you.

HEVENOR. It might—the drink is very lively. Attacking colour sergeants and officers and generals! And I having but a little wattle of a stick and they with all the guns of Buonaparty! It is to hold the gap of battle I would the same as Brian Boru! (*Sings.*)

On Clontarf he like a lion fell, thousands plunged in their
    own gore;
I to be such a hero now I'd ask for nothing more.

KIRWAN'S SERVANT. Ah, what are you making such lamentations over. You have but to hold to your promise till the Bill is cast out and that time will be short.

HEVENOR. That it may be so!

CASTLEREAGH'S SERVANT. What's that you're saying? Sure you're on the side of the Union.

HEVENOR. I was, but I am not. I made another thought.

CASTLEREAGH'S SERVANT. Is it that you are forgetting about Emancipation?

HEVENOR. I am not. It is of my own emancipation I am thinking.

CASTLEREAGH'S SERVANT. Is it a turncoat you are?

HEVENOR. I amn't condemning anyone down, but I wouldn't give an inch of your toe for the man would let anything interfere with his own liberty.

CASTLEREAGH'S SERVANT. You rap! You common rascal!

HEVENOR. Haven't I myself to mind as well as another? As for Lords and Commons, before I will give in to neglect myself, they may die on the side of the road.

MARGY. Ah, you tricker, to turn around for good or bad as quick as that! It is I myself would not do a thing of the sort. To walk honest and walk pure is my way! (*Sings*.)

> I have a leg for a stocking,
>   I have a foot for a shoe,
> I have a *kick* for a croppy,
>   And down with the orange and blue!
> Out with Castlereagh and Pitt and the Union!

CASTLEREAGH'S SERVANT. You fool of a woman! Don't you know the English bill to be cast out your man's pledge is swept along with it.

MARGY. I was forgetting that.

CASTLEREAGH'S SERVANT. Pitt and the Government to get their way on this day, he is bound and tied to temperance and has the life pledge taken.

MARGY. In earnest?

CASTLEREAGH'S SERVANT. A sober man and a quiet man at your side.

MARGY. And the little house I'd have? And the pincushion?

CASTLEREAGH'S SERVANT. What's to hinder you?

MARGY (*sings*).

I have a foot for a stocking,
    I have a leg for a shoe,
I have a *kick* for a croppy,
    And *up* with the orange and blue!

(*A bell rings inside door, but none hear it.*)

KIRWAN'S SERVANT (*shaking her*). That my curse may follow you? Shut your traitor mouth! A disgrace you are to the world!

MARGY. Leave go of me! I have my own business to mind.

KIRWAN'S SERVANT. You to renage that was calling out this very minute on our side!

MARGY. At that time I had not understanding.

KIRWAN'S SERVANT. To go join with them that would send Ireland to the slaughter!

MARGY. It is not Ireland I have in charge. It is William Hevenor I have in charge.

KIRWAN'S SERVANT. To go bring such a great stain on your name and you turning against the country's friends!

MARGY. By my faith it's my own friend I have to think of, and not of the other breed!

KIRWAN'S SERVANT. Can't you be loyal to Ireland that is your own country and your island?

MARGY. So I am loyal—to my man. Everything should be done beyond measure to mind him and to change him for the best. If I wouldn't be thanked by the world I might be thanked by God.

KIRWAN'S SERVANT. A great wonder it is, Judas not to have been a woman!

MARGY. If you had a hundred in family a husband is the nearest. Isn't it better to me Parliaments to go to wrack in the clouds than my man to go live blazing drunk! (*Sings.*)

"Then bumper your glasses, to George drink a health
And give him peace, happiness, honour, and wealth!"

HEVENOR. What's that! Let you quit sounding out that song! Is it that you are singing against myself?

MARGY. If I am it's for your good.

HEVENOR. It's I can sing against yourself so. (*Sings.*)

"Oh the French are on the Sea,"
    Says the Shan Van Vocht!
"Oh the French are on the Sea,"
    Says the Shan Van Vocht!
"Oh the French are in the Bay,

They'll be here without delay,
And the orange will decay,"
        Says the Shan Van Vocht!
MARGY (*putting hand on his mouth*). No, but hearken! (*Sings.*)

United with Britain may Erin for ever
    In commerce, in arts, and in science advance;
United with Britain may Erin for ever
    Live mighty and free, independent of France!

HEVENOR (*breaking free and closing her mouth, sings*).

"And their camp it shall be where,"
        Says the Shan Van Vocht.
"Their camp it shall be where,"
        Says the Shan Van Vocht.
"On the Curragh of Kildare,
The boys they will be there
With their pikes in good repair,"
        Says the Shan Van Vocht!"

(*She throws her shawl over his mouth. They struggle with one another.*)
CASTLEREAGH'S SERVANT. I bet two to one on the woman!
KIRWAN'S SERVANT. I will put all I have on the man.
    (*A great cheering inside House. PORTER comes out and they turn and see him.*)
Come over here. Where were you? If ever you lost sport you lost it today!
PORTER. Do you hear that shouting within in the House?
KIRWAN'S SERVANT. What is it? What happened? Is it time for the vote?
PORTER. The vote is after being taken. Where was your master?
KIRWAN'S SERVANT. I disremembered. I didn't call to him. Listening to these vagabonds—the curse of the country on them. I didn't feel the time passing. It cannot be the bill is thrown out?
PORTER. It is gone through.
KIRWAN'S SERVANT. Gone through! That was a holy crime. I thought it would never come to pass!
PORTER. Your master, Kirwan, would have saved it. It was but got through by one vote.
KIRWAN'S SERVANT (*sitting down on step*). I have a great wrong done him, and all his sweat lost! His heart will be thrashed with this.

PORTER. It's no blame on you to be downcast. It's this House will be lonesome with nothing but its own pure walls. A pity it to be brought to an end when its hour was not spent.

CASTLEREAGH'S SERVANT. And yourself to be left bird alone!

("*Rule, Britannia,*" *is played off. He takes down Green Flag and puts up Union Jack. More cheers inside; and groans from the street.*)

MARGY (*to* HEVENOR). Come on now out of this.

HEVENOR. I never enjoyed a worse day. There was nothing in it but it was wrong.

MARGY. No, but the best day ever came before you. We'll have great comfort in the bye-and-bye and a roof to put over the child. You'll be running down drink from this out, the same as the fox and the cherries. Give me now that money where you will not put it astray on me this time. We'll go get the little pincushion out of pawn!

Curtain.

ON THE RACECOURSE

ON THE RACECOURSE

PERSONS:

MICHELIN, *a good-looking and good-humoured young fellow in poor fisherman's clothes.*

JULIA, *his wife, young and comely, but with discontented expression. Poorly dressed.*

STEVE ROLAND, *young, red-haired, not very robust, tidily dressed in cheap readymade town clothes.*

A few people pass in and off, now and then.

SCENE: *Edge of a field, a little wall or hedge at back.*

MICHELIN *and* JULIA *come on. They are carrying canvas, a tambourine, a stool, some boards and trestles.* JULIA *sits down on the ground.* MICHELIN *begins setting up a little table with the boards, whistling as he does so.*

MICHELIN (*putting up a screen of canvas at the side of his table*). Here now is a little place is fit to shelter the Queens of Germany and of Spain through the whole gamut of the year!

JULIA. There'd have been as good shelter under any old gallows of the far-away times, would be standing up against the sky on the blare blasted side of a hill.

MICHELIN. The sun will be apt to be beaming out ere noon, and putting the chill of the mists to the rout.

JULIA. Ah, the sun has Ireland forgot this good while. There's a winterish appearance on the grass. As the Scripture says, you hardly know the summer to be in it, unless by the leaves of the tree.

MICHELIN. To gather up fire and sticks, and to kindle them at the fall of night, we'll have all the comforts of the world.

JULIA. Sure, there's nothing to boil for the supper unless a pot of green nettles the young turkeys would run from, it not having a tint of meal to thicken it, and they to be dancing with the hunger.

MICHELIN. Here now is a small bit of a loaf was hid and concealed in the sack since the day of the sports at Moycullen.

JULIA. Green mould growing out from it, like you'd see upon a graveyard wall (*throws it away*). My grief not to have waited on my

195

luck when I got the chance of it, and famine and starvation would not have come anear me.

MICHELIN. It is on Steven Roland your mind is dwelling. If I never seen him itself, I'll not give in he to be a better man than what I am.

JULIA. That's a friend I lost in earnest. It was bred in him by good blood to think more of me than what you do, and to have more love for me as well.

MICHELIN. It is to himself I suppose you wish to be giving the treasure from the wild bird's nest that is in your song (*sings*).

> "Oh, I will climb a high, high tree,
>   And rob a wild bird's nest,
>   And back I'll bring whatever I do find
>   To the arms that I love best," she said,
> "To the arms that I love best!"

JULIA. It is in my own arms I'll keep anything I'll find, never fear.

MICHELIN. The duck to learn you its swim, you might chance to reach to him yet, and you wishful to give me back my brass ring.

JULIA. If it was but a ring of rushes I have respect for the marriage rite. I am no tinker's woman to be marketed from hand to hand, if it was for all the treasures of the Eastern world.

MICHELIN. I suppose he should have a valiant lot of money by this.

JULIA. Why wouldn't he, and he these three years or more out in England.

MICHELIN. Hundreds of pounds?

JULIA. Maybe so. Or thousands.

MICHELIN. He could build a house with that much to the stars till he'd be giving out newses of Heaven.

JULIA. If we had but a little ass to go carrying our lumber along from place to place, and a basket with tapes and needles and pins and hair-oil, to traffic and to make our living! (*She takes a little mirror from her dress and arranges her hair.*)

MICHELIN. It is carring along branchy avenues with white Arabians you should be, and a golden crownet on your head.

JULIA. Ah, be quiet. The time we are fasting is no time to go funning, and the time we are left bare naked.

MICHELIN. If the boat was drownded, and the nets were swept, I have skill in my hands and in my wits will bring in a fortune yet.

I am not without a thought there will some good thing turn to me upon the wind this day.

JULIA. It is the wind is all our estate indeed, and our farm the Shuler's road.

MICHELIN (*still arranging cards and roulette board, etc., on his table*). To knock knowledge out of cards, or to set out a thimble on this board is under my hand, there is no better man in Ireland. Wait now till you see. (*He puts a shade over one eye, and on his head an old-fashioned hat with grey locks of hair hanging from inside it*). The lads will think to best me now, but I'll show them the old one-eyed man is a tradesman cannot be bet! (*He sings*).

> O list to the strains of a poor Irish harper,
> And scorn not the strings of his old withered hand!
> Remember his fingers could once move more sharper
> To raise up the strains of his dear native land!

Now, Julia, let you put up your hair, and the comb in it, the way you will shine out good.

JULIA. Why would I go shine out good? What at all will any person think of me, being mixed and mingled with the like of *that* of an old warrior?

MICHELIN. Aged and youthful—that's the way we'll suit all sides. Sound out now a ballad, woman, till it will bring some lads to this corner of the course.

JULIA. Ah, where's the use. It is far we are from the people and from the throng.

MICHELIN. Go on to the brink of them so, where you might gather some little profit. (*She takes up her little tambourine, and goes off.*) I'll rise a verse myself to entice them. The Lord send a fool in my way, and I'll be a whole gentleman! (*Looks out at the side, then sits down and sings:*)

> Oh, who is this poor foreigner that's lately come to town?
> And like a ghost that cannot rest still wanders up and down;
> A poor unhappy Sassenach, if more you wish to know,
> His heart is breaking all for love of Irish Molly O!

(*Steve Roland comes in.*)

MICHELIN (*rattling his dice*). Come on my noble sportsman, speculation is the life of trade! As low as a penny as high as a pound! No deception whatsoever, a fair game and a fair amusement. Steeplechasing and horse racing without the aid of whip or spur!

STEVE. Ah, I'm in no humour for games or gambling.

MICHELIN. What is it ails you?

STEVE (*sitting down and beginning to unlace his boots, sings.*)

> There is a rose in Ireland, I thought it would be mine,
> But now that she is lost to me I must for ever pine.
> Till death it comes to comfort me, for to the grave I'll go,
> And all for loving of my dear, my Irish colleen, O!

MICHELIN. Indeed, there would seem to be trouble on you.

STEVE. To go looking for treasure out in England I did, and to come back looking for treasure.

MICHELIN. It is likely you gained it out in England?

STEVE. A share, a small share. But to earn it in that place, you earn trouble along with it.

MICHELIN. Is that so, now?

STEVE. The smoke didn't look so black, or the streets show out so ugly or so hard till I felt the sods under my feet to-day, and the salt of the bay in my mouth. (*He shakes dust from his boots, and rubs them.*)

MICHELIN. It is likely it is beef and mutton you do be getting the fill of your mouth of in those parts.

STEVE. Hard work, terrible hard work. Take it or leave it, sick or sorry. No holy days and no relief. (*He begins putting on his boots again.*)

MICHELIN. To keep a roof over your head you have means to do, would be a fitting place to shelter a wife?

STEVE. It is that kept me in the factories. That thought was a candle through the years, that never wasted or was spent.

MICHELIN. Fashions and boots and inside wear, and to be dressed out like citizens. That is the most thing a woman does be coveting after.

STEVE. That might be so with some.

MICHELIN. It is the one way with the whole of them.

STEVE. It was not so with her I went working for, and that I came back looking for.

MICHELIN. Is that so?

STEVE. That is a woman would be merry in the heart, being nourished with cresses from the stream, and having no home through the storms of the year but the sheltery side of a bush.

MICHELIN. She should be a world's wonder.

STEVE. Singing the same as a singing bird she would be, and the mountains to be falling on her head.

MICHELIN. I have a wife myself can gather the people around her in flocks and in droves.

STEVE. There is no person but would stand without shoes, in three feet of frost and of snow, to listen to the clear sweet voice of her.

MICHELIN. My own woman that has a voice as strong as a counsellor! The wind to be set in the right quarter you hear her as far as Belmullet.

STEVE. It is often the salmon in the stream at Kilcolgan would gather for to listen to her song.

MICHELIN. At Kilcolgan?

STEVE. That is where she had her dwelling.

MICHELIN. And in what place is she now?

STEVE. The deer knows more than I know. Some other man has her in his keeeping.

MICHELIN. And is it to come back looking for her you did?

STEVE. I did so. I went up the little path, thinking to see her sitting on the bank, reading her little Rosary book and dandelions having roses on them around her feet.

MICHELIN. And she wasn't in it?

STEVE. To wed with some man having a boat she did, and nets. Some man from Barna or from Ballinderreen. Better means he has than myself, that has but seven sovereigns in my bag. (*Takes a little bag from his pocket and shows it.*) That was to bring her back along with me to the town of Manchester.

MICHELIN. Boats and nets are slippery unsteady estate.

STEVE. It was a great deception. It did a great wrong on me bringing me ploughing back across land and sea.

MICHELIN. So you will be going back without her?

STEVE. I don't know. The smell of the sea and the sounds of the racecourse. . . . It is likely you yourself has a better life than mine.

MICHELIN. Ah, it is but a hungry way of living.

STEVE. I nearly think I'd have more comfort in mind to join a rambling gang, and to go rambling wild than to have a fixed home or a trade. Look now, look at the youth on your own brow. There is no one rightly young only those that will travel.

MICHELIN (*standing up straight and taking off shade and hat*). Sure, this is but the appearance I put on myself for fair days and the like at the time I am following my trade. (*Puts them on hastily again.*) Whisht, now—here is Herself is coming.

STEVE. (*looking out where he points, and then turning back to the other side of the booth*). Herself—herself. Is it *your* wife she is?

JULIA (*coming on*). Did you gain nothing yet?

MICHELIN. Sure the day didn't hardly begin up to this. Wait a while and I'll have silver will fill out the creases of your skirt!

JULIA. If all the promises you give would but hold, I'd be wed with a shipful of money in place of a mountain of misery.

MICHELIN. Can't you speak graceful, and there being in the place a high-up man out of England.

STEVE (*keeping a little apart and speaking with a disguised voice*). It's a fine day for the races.

JULIA. It is fine for everyone but ourselves.

STEVE. Indeed, it's not everyone the sun does be shining on.

> (*Julia looks at him closely, recognises him, starting, turns away.*)

MICHELIN. There is a knot of people near. Sound out now a ballad till we'll bring them hither that they may take their chance in the game. Let you give them the Wild Bird's Nest. (*Stands up and calls out.*) Come now, lords and ladies, put the ball where you like, where you fancy. You play and I pay. The feather wins and badly backed!

> (*Three or four people come on and play while* JULIA *sings, looking outwards.*)

JULIA.

> "Oh, I'll not sit on the grass," she said,
> "Nor be a love of thine,
> For I hear you love a Connacht maid,
> And your heart is no longer mine," she said,
> "And your heart is no longer mine! "

> "Oh, I'll not heed what an old man says,
> Whose days are nearly done,
> And I'll not heed what a young man says,
> For he's fair for many a one," she said,
> "For he's fair for many a one! "

> "Oh, I will climb a high, high tree,
> And rob a wild bird's nest
> And back I'll bring whatever I do find
> To the arms that I love best," she said,
> "To the arms that I love best! "

(*She flings out her arms and clasps them to herself as if hold-ing something. As she finishes the gamesters hear the bell and cries, and run off shouting.*)

MICHELIN. Nothing won from that crowd only a handful of coppers (*counts them*).

STEVE. It is a kind woman you are, ma'am, of a young woman to have wed with so ancient a man.

JULIA. Ancient is it?

MICHELIN. Eighty-three years the St. Martin's that's coming! I remember the time the herrings went out of the bay, and clouds of misfortune came upon Ireland.

STEVE. Four legs, two legs, three legs. Crippled and beat as he is, I suppose it is hardly he can walk with a crutch.

JULIA. Not at all, not at all.

MICHELIN. No, but two crutches. Bet up entirely in the bones.

STEVE. It should be a lonesome thing for a comely woman to be going with a blind man.

JULIA. Are you taking him to be blind?

MICHELIN. From my birth up; from my birth up. Mostly dark I am and defeated in the sight.

STEVE. Old people do be contrairy in the hours of the day, and snoring the same as a herd of pigs through the night time.

MICHELIN. Indeed there's not much thought of old people by a good deal of youngsters.

JULIA. No one ever saw *me* would think I would wed with any but a straight upstanding man.

MICHELIN. On and on sickly I do be. I am at some times as deaf as a drum.

JULIA. Stop lying now! (*She tries to take off his hat, but he shields himself with his arm.*)

MICHELIN. It is herself is the kind woman, indeed. She could have joined with a handsome lad, having on him a head of yellow hair.

STEVE. Is that so? Yellow hair. (*Puts his hand uncertainly to his head.*)

MICHELIN. You wouldn't be tired listening to her telling out about him. As straight as in the line army! A true fowler with his gun! He never saw the snipe rising, but he'd knock it.

JULIA. Stop your talk!

MICHELIN. The way she has him pictured out you'd say him to be the son of a King, by a Queen.

STEVE. Where at all did she meet with such a one?

JULIA. Stop your humbugging talk Michelin; You're entirely too supple with the tongue.

MICHELIN. And the riches he made out in England! There isn't hardly figures enough to count them in arithmetic.

STEVE. I never heard of such a one at all.

MICHELIN. Steve, I believe, is the name he had. Steve Roland.

STEVE. Roland! And she made him out so wealthy?

MICHELIN. A room full of gold in his house. Two labourers stripped of their clothes turning it over with forks.

STEVE. She said him to have gold and means?

MICHELIN. She could have had square diamonds on her hands, and a lady's way of life. Starvation and misery with myself she chose, and he having full bags of coin.

JULIA. You have too much chat!

MICHELIN. Let you go sing again, Julia. Draw down on them some of the old troubles of Ireland, that might make them turn to the cards or the dice.

(*Julia goes to the side again and looks through her sheaf of ballads.*)

STEVE (*to* MICHELIN). Rich she said. To have gold she said? Well, she to have said so, it is so. I didn't tell you that I am a rich man myself!

(*He takes out his little bag, as* JULIA *prepares to sing.*)

MICHELIN. Come on, so sir, take a turn at the board! (*Calls out.*) Sing out strong, Julia, we have the half of the day wasted! . . . Nominate your colour, sir, while the ball is rolling! Thank you, sir, and the black wins again. The lucky black—one down, two down, any more or any other! Off she goes again! (*They go on playing while* JULIA *sings at the side with her back to them*).

JULIA.

Righ Shamus he has gone to France, and left his crown behind,
Bad luck be theirs both night and day put running in his mind.
Lord Lucan followed after him with his slashers brave and
    true,
And now the doleful keen goes up, What will poor Ireland do?
What will poor Ireland do? What can poor Ireland do?
Our luck, they say, has gone to France, then what can Ireland
    do?

Oh, black's your heart, Clan Oliver, and colder than the clay,
Oh, high's your heart Clan Sassenach, since Sarsfield's gone
    away!

It's little love you bear to us for sake of long ago,
But hold your hand, for Ireland still can strike a deadly blow,
Can strike a deadly blow,
Och! Heaven help! It's she that still could strike the deadly
    blow!

(*Steve has put down his last sovereign. He throws the empty
    bag to* MICHELIN, *who puts the money into it quickly.*)

MICHELIN (*loudly*). Come on again, sir! The luck will come to
you yet! For one time it will go for me there will maybe six times
turn against me!

(*The bell rings, and people are heard shouting, and running
    towards it.*)

STEVE (*turning to* JULIA, *who has come back to them*). That is a
good song. I am a long time without hearing it or the like of it.

JULIA. What a hurry they were in going, and in no hurry at all to
part with their ha-pence. (*She holds up her empty tambourine.*)
That's all I'll do of singing. I'm near dead with the hunger.

MICHELIN. There was better luck came to myself, and I sitting
at the board. (*He holds up the little bag and shakes it.*) That's
what's better than ha'pence.

JULIA. What way did you get it? (*To* STEVE.) I'd be sorry if it
was on yourself he lessened that much.

STEVE. Is it belittling myself and my means you would be,
ma'am? I tell you my wealth is all one with the wealth of Steve
Roland! (*Takes up his bundle.*) I'll go now put a few sovereigns on
a horse having two red ears. There was a mermaid foretelling him
to win, and she racking her hair in the waves. Well, it is great sport
I had to-day! I'll be talking of it maybe in the far countries of the
world! (*He goes off singing.*)

Oh, never fear for Ireland, for she has soldiers still,
For Rory's boys are in the wood and Remy's on the hill,
And never had poor Ireland more loyal hearts than these,
May God be kind and good to them, the faithful Rapparees,
The fearless Rapparees,
The men that rode at Sarsfield's side, the roving Rapparees!

MICHELIN. There now, we can pitch out that bit of a green loaf!
It is crackers we will buy at the booths! (*He pours the money
from the bag.*) Seven golden sovereigns won in the snap of a finger!
That lad went random altogether!

JULIA. Gold! Is it gold it is! (*Takes it in her hand.*) I never felt that weight of it in my hand, nor the half of it. You knocked a bad turn out of him taking it.

MICHELIN. He made a snug man of me anyway. I can leave this old rubbish of a board to go rot (*Kicks it.*) He came like a seagull to our relief!

JULIA. You have a right to go after him and give it back to him, where he earned it with hands and sweat!

MICHELIN. Sure he gave himself out to be as rich as Steve Roland.

JULIA. He is not. It is much if you left him enough to bury him.

MICHELIN. Ah, he to die, it is likely the police won't leave him overhead. Well, I to have that weight of gold in my hand I'll throw up a ladder of luck will reach to the treasuries of the moon!

JULIA. You will not keep it or spend it. You will go hurry after him with it. I now will tell you a thing will make you do that of your own will. That lad was Steve Roland that I gave my promise to, and that came back seeking for me to be his wife.

MICHELIN. I partly guessed that.

JULIA. You thought that?

MICHELIN. I did, and it was grafted in my mind.

JULIA. You took his money knowing that?

MICHELIN. Won it, my darling, won it.

JULIA. No, but tricking you did it. You are a tricker and a rogue of the gallows. I tell you it is to cheat you did. You maybe lost God doing that.

MICHELIN. So I was thinking myself. Which of us lost the most? If he parted with his earthly store, it is likely I may have parted with heaven.

JULIA. Why did you win it so?

MICHELIN. For the same reason he lost it. To fill your little mouth with bees' honey and with bread.

JULIA (*looks in her little glass*). The both of you did that for me? (*Smiles.*) Well, men are a comical class!

Curtain.

MICHELIN

MICHELIN

PERSONS
    MICHELIN. *An old wandering Beggar*
    HONOR COSTELLO. *A young girl*
    LARRY MONAHAN. *A young man.*

A large rock by the wayside. MICHELIN *comes in, as if from a journey. Sits down beside it. Sings.*

> I to be on the mountain
> My hundred times loved one with me
> We'd nestle together as quiet
> As birds on the bough of a tree.

> It's well for the birds in wild weather
> To rise up so high in the air
> To rest on the one bough together
> Without trouble or sorrow or care!

(HONOR *has come with a pail in her hand and stands at the back listening. She wipes her eyes with the back of her hand.*)

MICHELIN. Is that yourself Honor Costello? I was thinking you might be coming to the well. I stopped on my road purposely. Singing that little song I was to pass the time.

HONOR. It made me cry Michelin. (*Wipes her eyes*).

MICHELIN. Why now is that? Believe me, if it is but the poorest cabin, it should be the greatest blessing from Heaven down to own a little place and a shelter of your own.

HONOR. I'd be well pleased to be like the bird that can make its own choice of a nesting place.

MICHELIN. Sure you have your choice made of a comrade this long time. Wait a minute. (*Puts hand in his pocket and takes out a letter wrapped in a piece of rag.*)

HONOR. Oh, Michelin, the way it is now, I'd sooner be put sitting by the roadside!

MICHELIN. What are you talking about?

HONOR. They have a match made out for me—in the upper part of the parish.

MICHELIN. The upper part of the parish. Then it's not Larry Monahan? Who is it now?

HONOR. You should know him—in the slated house at the cross road.

MICHELIN. The licensed house! (*Puts letter back in his pocket.*) That's a snug place. All the luck of the world to you. That you may reign long in it. You won't forget poor Michelin?

HONOR. I'd sooner be without it than within.

MICHELIN. That man is turning over riches. He has a strong shop.

HONOR. I wouldn't like him if he owned the world.

MICHELIN. Ah, the marriage does a great change in people.

HONOR. A widower man. As deaf as a beetle.

MICHELIN. A fine settled down man.

HONOR. As grey as any badger ever was known.

MICHELIN. It's likely he'll give you the handling of his money.

HONOR. He gave a long time to the world. He's as cross as a bag of weasels.

MICHELIN. Believe me a woman is better able to barge than an old man under the roof. You'll master him.

HONOR. Let him wed with some century woman.

MICHELIN. By cripes, if I got his place I'd knock a good turn out of it.

HONOR. I would never content my mind to go in it if it was as fine and as big as the world.

MICHELIN. That is foolishness. It is that you have your mind set yet on that youth of a young man, Larry Monahan, that hasn't lodging for a hen?

HONOR. If I have it's little it serves me.

MICHELIN. What is he but a wild lad that has no provision, beyond maybe a tin can and a cat.

HONOR. He's a lovely boy and a decent boy, and a boy that was never handled by the police. That didn't deserve trouble from God or man!

MICHELIN. And can you tell me now where is he?

HONOR (*sitting down and wiping eyes with her hand*). Oh Michelin, to vanish away he did, and not a goodbye in the world wide. I'm thinking something happened him down entirely in the far end of the province.

MICHELIN. Ah, it's best quit thinking of him, and he a rambler going east and west. The fret will put you in your grave. It's the terriblest thing known.

HONOR. He is lying in my heart always for fear anything would happen him.

MICHELIN. It's likely he quitted this lonesome parish for some place where he'd see sports and pleasures. New York maybe—or Philadelphia.

HONOR. He did not. I am sure and certain wherever he is he is striving to make out a living. We cannot earn money sitting down. He's well able to take the scythe, take the spade—take the slob for the turf.

MICHELIN. It's natural a lad to let what's behind him slip from his mind with all the music and funning in the dance house and in the towns.

HONOR. You are out! He is not that sort. It is not kind for him to be a rogue.

MICHELIN. Singing and fooling and following after sport and terriers and horses.

HONOR. I would not believe it from the Pope.

MICHELIN. It's only foolishness to give up means and wealth for a rambling lad will be lighting his pipe with his fingers yet.

HONOR. I wouldn't feel the day long with him if it was the longest day of the year.

MICHELIN. To come back itself what would he give you but maybe an old straw bed and the rats cutting it. It's best take my advice. I never preached poverty to anyone. I'm too brave and too gay to do that.

HONOR. There is a league between us will never be broken. Not a night or morning but I put him under my prayers.

MICHELIN. A fine slated house where you'd see the neighbours coming to the door.

HONOR. I wouldn't care if it went into the clouds.

MICHELIN. Every day Christmas with company and all around you.

HONOR. I'd sooner live with him quiet and unknown to the world, if it was the grandest from this to Dublin.

MICHELIN (*he has got up and turned and looked down the road*). Well, it's best quit thinking of him—A drifty lad going east and west—(*takes her shoulders and turns her.*) Look now there's people coming up the road—It's best for you hurry around the turn. You would not wish the neighbours to see you with the tracks of tears down your face. (*He takes her shoulders and gently pushes her out of sight.*)

    (*Sits down and rubs his boots with a bunch of grass humming an air.*)

VOICE OF LARRY *heard singing*:

> There grows a tree in the garden
> With blossoms that tremble and shake
> I'll lay my hand on the bark now
> And I think that my heart must break.
>
> I thought O my life!
> That one house between us, love, would be!
> And I thought I would find
> You coaxing my child on your knee!

MICHELIN (*as* LARRY *enters*). That's a gloomy sort of a song to be singing.

LARRY. If it is it's because I am gloomy in the mind.

MICHELIN. The sun shining as if St. Patrick has turned the stone for fine weather.

LARRY. I'd sooner the sky to be pouring wet from Heaven down!

MICHELIN. It would be a bad story the crops to fail away.

LARRY. Let the clouds make a wheel and cover them.

MICHELIN. The white dew of May upon the grass.

LARRY. That it may turn as black as a smith's coal.

MICHELIN What at all ails you?

LARRY. It is a great wonder the Lord to stand the villainy is in the world.

MICHELIN. Tell me out now your trouble.

LARRY (*throwing himself down*). My heavy curse upon all the women on this side of the ocean.

MICHELIN. What at all ails you?

LARRY. I'm done with their fibs and flatteries, their grins and grimaces.

MICHELIN. Some giddy young girl has your mind tossed here and there?

LARRY. I will not curse her but leave her to the Almighty!

MICHELIN. She has you made a fool of?

LARRY. I that thought her heart as sound as the heart of the soundest tree. I have the curse of misfortune upon me this day.

MICHELIN. Ah, you'll be apt to find some other one.

LARRY. I wouldn't take another if she brought half Ireland, and all Boston along with it. Tempted with ribbons and feathers and hats and the world of vanities around her. I would not take her now if she was covered with all the jewelleries of the world.

MICHELIN. Good lad. That's the way to meet troubles. A pity to give in to fret through any treachery of a woman.

LARRY. Maybe there might have been force put upon her.

MICHELIN. Not a force in the world. Why would there be force?

LARRY. What do you know about it?

MICHELIN. Sure she was talking with myself for a while yesterday.

LARRY (*getting up*). Talking with yourself? What did she say? Did she make any excuse?

MICHELIN. Not an excuse in the world wide. What call had she to make excuses. The praises of the seven parishes will be upon her. A girl that has done a great match.

LARRY. Is it truth you are speaking?

MICHELIN. A warm house they were telling me, wine upon the table, bacon from the rafters. And herself the mistress of it all.

LARRY. And you wouldn't tell her she was breaking her promises and her word?

MICHELIN. Is it that I would come between herself and her luck? And I am kindhearted as I am. Sure she sat down with me till we settled the world. She made a smile of a laugh going away.

LARRY. You have great impudence praising yourself.

MICHELIN. So I am praising myself. And so would the world be praising me, my case to come up before it.

LARRY. That's the talk I had a right to expect from a vagabone beggar.

MICHELIN. If I am, I am asked nothing of yourself. When I do go beg I go to the highest quality.

LARRY. You wouldn't have long to live if I had a shovel in my fist. I have a mind to wring your neck.

MICHELIN. I did well giving her an advice against you. A beauty woman. She never can put her curse upon me. She got sense turning her back on a vagabone like you that hasn't got lodging for a hen, and giving her promise to a settled man with means and a good way of living.

LARRY. Let her go now and let her get what she has earned—— (*Puts his hand over his eyes.*) But O! my grief! When I think of the little smile and the laugh of her, my heart turns to the blackness of a black coal. (*He sobs.*)

HONOR (*coming from behind the rock*). Larry.

LARRY. Who is that speaking?

HONOR. Wouldn't you know my voice where I know your voice?

LARRY. If I know it I will go where I will never hear the sound of it.

HONOR. Is it that I have your love lost? That is the breaking of my heart to me.

LARRY. I will never keep love for a woman that belongs to another man.

HONOR. Oh! What are you saying!

LARRY. I'd be only a fool to her, loyal to her and she not loyal to me.

HONOR. I belong to no one in the wide world but yourself.

LARRY. Go back to your ribbons and your feathers and your necklaces.

HONOR. I own nothing but this poor gown.

LARRY. To your turkey cocks and ducks and fowl and the world and all around you.

HONOR. I thought I had your love, and that gone there is nothing left for me.

LARRY. Is it that they lied saying you are wed?

HONOR. My grief that you gave in to a lie. I will go now and turn it to a truth.

LARRY (*holding her*). Stop with me I say.

HONOR. I would sooner go swimming in the surges and drown myself in the salt tide.

LARRY. I that would plough the ocean for you. There is nothing worth while in the whole of the universe but only your four bones.

HONOR. There is no back way. It is best for me to take leave of my life.

LARRY. Then it's best for myself never to go back to the little limewhite house I had made ready for you.

HONOR. I am asking no house.

LARRY. A good thatch to it. And a kitchen with a dresser of plates.

HONOR. I was content to go to any poor place at all.

LARRY. And the little farm of land was willed to me by my first cousin that died. I told you all that in my letter.

HONOR. I got no letter.

LARRY. I gave it to a neighbour where I was—he said he had trusted it to a travelling man he knew that was coming this road and that gave his promise to bring it safe. (MICHELIN *is slipping away.*)

HONOR. Oh! What happened it.

LARRY (*seizing* MICHELIN). I'll engage it was yourself! Give me out the letter—— (*Turns out his pocket.*) There it is. And a promise in it you would give him a silver shilling the time he would put it into your hand.

HONOR. Oh, Michelin. That was a bad way you treated me.

MICHELIN. Sure I thought I was doing better again for you when I heard of the great match in your own parish. I never knew this lad had means come to him. All I knew was the promise I'd get a shilling. It was for your own benefit I gave up that reward.

LARRY. It's a thrashing you're likely to get and all the trouble you are after bringing on me. I have a mind to strike a fist on you. (HONOR *takes and holds his hand.*) Come on now my heart's love, till we all bring our case to the priest.

HONOR. You'll have luck yet Michelin and the sun shining as it is this day. Come to the Chapel and you won't be without a hansel. (*They go off hand in hand.*)

MICHELIN. It's hard a thing will turn around and hit you, and you but striving to do good in the world. I'd best take the road to the drink house at the cross before this news will reach to it—I might chance a bite or a sup. It's as good for me stop meddling. The world is with the young, with the young. (*Sings as he goes*)

> There's no place for the withered rush
> The time it is broken and old
> The leaves to have gone from the bush
> What shelter is it from the cold?
>
> But back at the Tuam races
> Jockeys jostling to hear me sing
> It's then we'd have changed our places—
> It's myself would put on the ring! (*Goes off.*)

Curtain.

THE MEADOW GATE

"Conal"

THE MEADOW GATE

PERSONS
  CONAL.
  SEUMAS.
  ELLIE.
SCENE. *A Gate.* CONAL *leaning over it, a hayfork in his hands.
He looks over the gate. Sits down and sings.*

CONAL (*sings*).

I wish my love was a red, red rose, to bloom in yon garden fair
And I to be the gardener, that rose should be my care;
I'd tend the pretty flowers around, sweetwilliam, pink and rue,
Primrose and thyme, but, most of all, sweet rose I'd cherish
  you.

(*A voice heard singing right.*)

I wish I was a butterfly, I'd light on my love's breast:
I wish I was a nightingale to sing my love to rest.
I'd sing at noon, I'd sing at eve a love song sweet and slow.
And year by year I will love my dear, let the wind blow high
  or low.

(SEUMAS *comes on singing. He wears bawneens, has coat over
  his arm; hayfork in hand.*)
CONAL. You are in a great hurry so early in the day. By the look
of you, you are a stranger.
SEUMAS. To the big meadows I am come, thinking I might get a
chance to turn over a bleach of hay.
CONAL. That is where I'll be going myself in a while's time.
SEUMAS. I'm on the right road so.
CONAL. It is likely it is from some far place you are come?
SEUMAS (*sitting down and taking off shoes flicks dust from
them*). By the dust on me you'd say I walked through the seven
parishes.
CONAL. It is the sign of the red clay is on you. You should be a
mountainy man.

217

SEUMAS. From the south I came, crossing over the hills.

CONAL. Making your escape from some trouble maybe?

SEUMAS. No, but coming to look for what would lift all trouble off me, now and for ever.

CONAL. It would be hard find that unless in the high heaven. What now is your quest?

SEUMAS. The best in the world would tell a lie sometimes, but I never will tell one to you. It is a right girl I came following, that would turn the hardest road of stones to a flowery path of paradise.

CONAL. Who is she, now?

SEUMAS. She came visiting a neighbour, and then she was gone —and never knew she brought with her my heart's love.

CONAL. She must be a great sort.

SEUMAS. In face and form and manners she is beyond anything seen in any woman at all.

CONAL. That you may be happy. But I'm sure and certain sure she is in no way better looking than my own young girl that I am come to this place to meet.

SEUMAS. There is no one can compare with her in all the seven parishes.

CONAL. My girl that is given in to be the best at every hurling and every country meeting.

SEUMAS. Mine is the star woman of this side of the ocean.

CONAL. The sun itself would begrudge the light that is in my one's eyes.

SEUMAS. The world and all is thought of mine by all that ever laid an eye on her.

CONAL. A real lady. As neat as an egg.

SEUMAS. She wouldn't look after or believe anything unless she'd see it and hear it herself.

CONAL. That grand you wouldn't think the day long with her.

SEUMAS. Not flighty in her dress.

CONAL. Spinning wool and flax and tow.

SEUMAS. Knitting stockings—going through barley and oats.

CONAL. The worst winter that ever crossed us she'd turn it to a summer day.

SEUMAS. To be talking seven year I could not tell you all the good of mine.

CONAL. It's given in to her by gentle and simple, the poor and the high up.

SEUMAS. Her name is sung through the seven parishes.

CONAL. A real beauty and a good dancer.

SEUMAS. As kind a woman as ever gave her word to a man. A little saint, and a loughy woman besides.

CONAL. The grandest from this to Dublin. You'd love to see her travel through the town.

SEUMAS. The very beauty of all beauties.

CONAL. The finest girl that the sun could shine on her.

SEUMAS. Running and laughing and singing—You could not find her equal in all Ireland.

CONAL. It's easy talking. There's no such girl on this side of the world unless my own.

SEUMAS. Easy yourself.

CONAL. Keep your tongue off me.

SEUMAS. She to be run down I'd give out challenges to the whole world.

CONAL. I wouldn't give the point of a rush for anyone that would look at yourself.

SEUMAS. Any woman in Ireland that would rear your son would be sorry.

CONAL. Stop your chat, you mean little tinker.

SEUMAS. Some fierce Trojan of a woman a charitable neighbour made out for you.

CONAL. A woman worth while would cock up her nose at *you*.

SEUMAS. She would be a hasty cranky one or she would not match with yourself.

CONAL. No person would wed with you unless she'd be as deaf as a beetle.

SEUMAS. Any one to wed with you wouldn't have the sense of a child.

CONAL. And you'll get no one only a prattler that you never could bridle her.

SEUMAS. Come on now till I'll make splits of you.

CONAL. You may set your coffin making for I'll bear you to the ground.

(*They throw down hayforks and are about to make at one another. A sound of people and carts. A girl,* ELLIE, *rushes on.*)

ELLIE. Let you stop fighting till we'll pass the road.

SEUMAS. Wrastle your best. Come on.

CONAL (*as girl seizes him*). Let you not be striving to drag us asunder.

ELLIE. Conal. Is it yourself at all.

SEUMAS. Let me at him.

ELLIE (*seizing his arm*). Hold your hand. Oh. It is Seumas.

SEUMAS. I'll silence him. He was after running you down.

CONAL. No, but he himself that was running you down. (*Hits at* SEUMAS.)

ELLIE. Is it that the two of you were running me down? (*She goes between them.*) It's a bad story for me you to have done this.

CONAL. It is time for you to come and hear what this ruffian is saying about you.

ELLIE. Seumas is it? He that was so gentle and so kind on the south side of the mountain.

SEUMAS. This lad that drove me wild—miscalling you—a red enemy to you.

CONAL. A fierce Trojan, he said you were, some charitable neighbour had made out for me.

SEUMAS. No, but himself said he wouldn't give the point of a rush for you.

CONAL. A hasty, cranky woman, he said. That any man to wed with yourself wouldn't have the sense of a child.

SEUMAS. A prattler that no one could bridle you.

CONAL. Cross and bold he said you were.

SEUMAS. That no one should wed with you without he'd be as deaf as a beetle.

CONAL. That he wouldn't give the point of a rush for you.

ELLIE (*drawing back*). Troth, I'm greatly obliged to the two of you.

CONAL. Come on now with myself as you made your promise.

ELLIE. At that time I had not understanding.

SEUMAS. No, but come south with myself.

ELLIE. I have my mind made up to go foreign.

CONAL. It is you will wed with some stranger across the ocean?

ELLIE. Anyone would sooner wed with a stranger than with a man she would know. If God promised me a man I'll get a man in any part of the world.

SEUMAS. To America is it.

ELLIE. I am not without friends in that place, throwing money here and over. When I'll be known there will be no fear of me.

CONAL. The waves will rise like mountains the time there'll be a stir in the sea.

ELLIE. Let them rise. (*Sings*)

> There'll be passengers from Limerick and passengers from
> Nenagh

And passengers from Kerry and all quarters of the nation.

SEUMAS. It is given out they are great slaves out there.

ELLIE (*sings*)

> There are jaunting cars and carriages going to and fro like
> blazes
> And the buses back and forward for very little payment.

CONAL. A woman's foolishness. It's the hills far off that are green.

ELLIE (*as she turns to go, sings*)

> ... Confectioners with sugarsticks and dainties
> The lozenges and oranges the lemonade and raisins
> With gingerbread and spices to accommodate the ladies
> And the sporting Wheel of Fortune with four and twenty
> quarters.

SEUMAS. Heaven help your poor head.

ELLIE.

> There's half a million people there of all denominations—
> The Catholic, the Protestant and Jew and Presbyterian—
> There is yet no animosity no matter what persuasion
> but failte and prosperity inducing fresh acquaintance.

(*Goes off.*)

SEUMAS (*passing his hand over his eyes*). If I knew yesterday what I know to-day I would never have journeyed through half of the night time.

CONAL. Women are queer and change like the changes of the moon. It is not worth while we to fall out of friendship.

SEUMAS. That is so. Jealousy is a temptation from the Big Man.

CONAL. The bell didn't ring yet. There's a bank at the side of the field we can stretch over and stretch our bones.

SEUMAS (*taking up his fork, sings*).

> One evening last week I walked down by yon bush,
> I heard two birds singing, a blackbird and thrush—
> I asked them the reason they sang in such glee
> And the answer they gave—they were single and free.

(*They go off singing over again*)

> I asked them the reason they sang in such glee
> And the reason they gave—they were single and free.

THE DISPENSARY

THE DISPENSARY

PERSONS
 MARGY. *A servant.*
 PETER HESSION. *A farmer.*
 BRIDE LYDON. *A young girl.*

A bare looking room. A deal table, with desk and two or three medicine bottles, two or three chairs and a bench.

MARGY *is sweeping, and humming an air. Hearing someone at the open door she goes to it.*

VOICE AT DOOR. Is the new Doctor within, Margy?

MARGY (*going to door*). He is not. He was here a while ago but he went out. Look now at Peter Hession coming up the street with himself only. That's a comfortable man. (*She returns to her sweeping and hums*)

> When I was a bachelor airy and young
> I followed the bachelor's trade.

(*Looks out again.*) Is it to this door he is coming. (*Puts down brush and unties apron—a middle aged man in frieze coat comes in.*)

HESSION. Evening, Margy. Is the new doctor within?

MARGY. He is not, Mr. Hession, but gone to the Boardroom to make acquaintance with the guardians. It's there you will find him.

HESSION. Bad luck to him—this should be his Dispensary day. (*comes farther in.*) I'd sooner stop here till he'll come. Wanting a liniment I am for that old cross cat of a housekeeper.

MARGY. And is that old warrior with you yet?

HESSION. She is, and little comfort to me. Grumble and growl, grumble and growl. No use in the world to me but maybe she might wash a shirt. I'll have her tongue going if I fail to do her commands.

MARGY. It's some nice mannerly girl you have a right to bring into the house, Mr. Hession, and you with such a good way of living. But it's what the neighbours are saying, the world couldn't please you in a wife.

HESSION. One woman's tongue in the house is enough, and too much.

MARGY. Ah, wait till the right one comes down the chimney!

HESSION. I'm best as I am. I would never give in to put another chain around my neck . . . . When will he be coming in? It's often I wonder is there any use in any doctor at all.

MARGY. Indeed there's many of them that the world would know they aren't any good. But as to the man we have lost, if he had a long life, it was not one day too long for the poor.

HESSION. I'd nearly wonder you can be so lively and chatty and all the pains and aches and torments that are brought within these four walls.

A VOICE AT THE DOOR. Do you want any duck eggs, ma'am?

MARGY. I declare I was near forgetting the market that will be over without me. I must go make a little foraging—a bit of spring cabbage should be in it. Look now, Sir, maybe you will be stopping for a short while. The door is open for the doctor. It's likely you'll see him within five minutes of time. (*She puts shawl over her head and goes out.*)

HESSION (*takes a newspaper from his pocket, sits down at table, fumbles in his pockets*). My specs not here—just at the time they would serve me. It's a contrary day at the start whatever it may be at the finish. (*He sings*)

> 'Twas early, early, all in the Spring
> The pretty young birds began to sing—
> They sang so sweet and joyously—
> And the tune they played was sweet liberty.

(*He goes on humming the air. A knock at the door. A girl, BRIDE LYDON, comes to the door, poorly dressed, shawl over head, a basket in her hand.*)

BRIDE. Can I come in, Sir?

HESSION. Come on, come on.

BRIDE. The Lord be praised! To find this door closed would have gone across my heart!

HESSION. Is it from some far place you are come?

BRIDE. From the village is beside the bog that is beyond the big hill. (*She sits down at the table, tired. Puts the basket on the floor.*)

HESSION. That is a long road to travel. Maybe you got a lift?

BRIDE. I did not, sir. I chanced no one coming along the road. But I'm not so far in age for that to be a check to me when I heard the door of the dispensary was thrown open again.

HESSION. Aye. Everyone must pay the tenth of his span in sickness. I often heard that.

BRIDE. You should know, sir. You should know. It is many are the griefs and pains and aches and torments that have their story brought into this place.

HESSION. I see no appearance on you that you are in need of any cure.

BRIDE. Wait a while, sir. (*She takes a couple of small bottles from her bag, places them on table. Also takes a ragged handkerchief with knots on it—loosens a knot.*)

HESSION. Any person that is sickly will get heavy and his head weigh heavy with him. But what would you know about that?

BRIDE. It is I myself know plenty, and I do know it.

HESSION. I'd nearly say any lawyer would be satisfied to put your life in a lease.

BRIDE (*busy with knots and bottles*). I'll tell it all out now, sir. To have the appetite lost——

HESSION. And a fine appearance upon her yet.

BRIDE. To get very worn within a year, waking night till morning.

HESSION. And to be looking so lively and so sound.

BRIDE (*taking out another bottle and undoing another knot*). To get a fall into a sandpit—in the month of March it was. Every bit of the body went with the pain that burst out of the side.

HESSION. The Lord save us!

BRIDE. The weight of flesh that went away——

HESSION. It is easy to see that.

BRIDE. To get very heavy sometimes, and the heart to get heavy within.

HESSION. So it would, so it would.

BRIDE (*untying another knot*). To be able to use but little food— it's like as if angels are keeping up the strength. Where's the use of a bit of meat, or a chicken itself, when it's to toss it off the plate with a fork you should.

HESSION. No use indeed in the world.

BRIDE. There is nothing keeping life in the body only angels.

HESSION. I would nearly believe it is something outside the world should be keeping her so straight and in her bloom.

BRIDE (*putting bottles on the table and standing up*). Tell me now, sir, what can you give me to bring ease and relief for all this string of misery. Wait a minute. (*Takes up a bottle and puts hand to ear.*) I was near forgetting—is there any cure to bring back the hearing when you'd be as deaf as a beetle?

HESSION. And do you think is there any doctor in the wide world could do away with that string of troubles with the one cure?

BRIDE. You're out, sir! You're out. It is a separate cure I am asking for every one of these scourges and sicknesses I have told out. Look at all the little bottles I brought in my shawl and not one of them broke.

HESSION (*standing up*). Is it that you are in your right senses at all?

BRIDE (*indignantly*). There is no one in our village gone wild or mad since the time of the Clare election.

HESSION. All that string of sicknesses you are making a claim to have on you.

BRIDE. Listen, sir! Listen!

HESSION. I wouldn't believe it from the Bishop—— And you so lively and so young. (*Is taking up hat and going towards door.*)

BRIDE (*sinking on the chair and wiping her eyes*). If there was never misfortune upon me it has come upon me now.

HESSION. It is lies or of the nature of lies what you are saying. There is no one would believe a word of it!

BRIDE. My grief. I wish I could be killed on the minute. You to put me down as a liar—— And maybe I am that in the heel! (*Weeps and rocks herself.*)

HESSION. What at all is on you to go cry.

BRIDE. I that wouldn't tell a lie for the most thing in the mighty world.

HESSION (*pulling out his handkerchief tries to wipe her face*). Stop fretting now—and I'll promise to believe all. (*She sobs.*) The fret will put you in your grave.

BRIDE. The old doctor to rise up would tell you I ever and always spoke the truth as if the Pope was standing there!

HESSION. Do not be going on the way you are, crying tears down.

BRIDE. The old doctor knew that the world wouldn't make me tell lies.

HESSION (*dabbing his handkerchief on her face*). Have done with your fretting and I'll promise to believe all.

BRIDE. This is the crossest day that ever went over me! It is the curse of misfortune is cutting me down.

> (*She sobs.* HESSION *putting his arm round her clumsily tries to wipe her tears.*)
> (MARGY *bangs door open, comes in with apron full of cabbage —drops it on the floor.*)

MARGY. What at all happened my poor little girleen.

HESSION. I don't know in the earthly world. I'm in dread she will faint and fall.

MARGY. Be quiet now astore—the fret will put you in your grave. It's the terriblest thing known.

HESSION. She is in a bad way she was telling me. Every sort of pain running through her in the day and in the night time.

MARGY. Not a fear of her. She's as sound as a silver bell.

HESSION. The hearing lost——

MARGY. She'd hear the grass growing.

BRIDE. Oh Margy, Margy! make him believe it is not telling lies I was, if they looked to be of the nature of lies.

MARGY. You that would not tell a lie for all the world's gold.

BRIDE. He thinks it was to lie I did. He has no more respect for me than if I was an old drowned dog.

HESSION. I have every respect for you if it is not that my own wits are wandering.

BRIDE. Oh, Ma'am, will you tell out my case before my heart breaks entirely.

MARGY. Listen now, Peter Hession. It is the way it is, the village so far across hill and bog and the journey long, it fails the old people and the sick people to lag along as far as the town.

BRIDE. It would be too hard on them! They would faint and fall by the side of the road.

MARGY. And this little girl that is a God-loving girl, and as honest as the priest at the altar, got a habit of coming over bog and mountain to the old Doctor when he'd be here every second Wednesday of the month. To put the case before him of everyone that was sick or sorry she did, till he'd mix a bottle or give her a plaster that would bring ease. He had no need to hear a string of names or pedigrees, but used to bid her sort out their case and their need according to the knots on her string, and she bringing relief through frost and through snow to many a poor scalded man or woman. It is many a poor creature rose out of his complaint and his pain through what these two hands brought safe and through the mercy of God.

HESSION (*wiping his eyes*). Is that the way of it?

MARGY. So taking you to be the new Doctor——

BRIDE (*with a cry*). And is he not the Doctor? And I giving out every case so free. Oh, let me go, let me go. I was never rightly ashamed till now. (*Sinks down and covers her face and sobs.*)

MARGY (*to* HESSION). Now what do you say?

HESSION. I say no one in the mighty world ever did a grander deed or a better deed than that.

MARGY. And her mother good before her. It goes by nature in this one! It do run in the blood.

BRIDE. It's best for me go back to the village. This day has put me astray and out of my road.

HESSION. It is I myself will bring you safe. The mare and the cart are without.

BRIDE. But the real Doctor never came. It failed me to get the cures.

HESSION. I will call to your house and bring you to him whatever day he will be here. (*He leads her out of the door.*)

MARGY. You will. And if signs are signs it's not far off till you'll bring her to the priest. (*She picks up her cabbages singing*)

"Oh, Kitty will you marry me, or Kitty I will die!
Oh, Kitty you'll be fretting for your loving little boy!
Oh, Kitty can't you tell me will you marry me at all
Or else I'll surely go to sleep within the churchyard wall!"

Curtain.

THE SHOELACE

THE SHOELACE

PERSONS
> TAIG. *A wandering poet.*
> ART. *A Court poet.*
> THE KING OF MAYO.

SCENE. *Steps of a large house. A curtain at back.*
> (TAIG, *coming to right of steps looks about him cautiously. He wears ragged clothes and has rags bound around his bare feet.*)

TAIG. It has the appearance of a grand house—It might be some lady would be listening at the window—(sings—*Air, I wish I had the shepherd's lamb.*)

> I wish I had a silver string, a silver string, a silver string.
> I wish I had a silver string like Orpheus in the story;
> And all my songs I'd give to you, give to you, give to you—
> And my heart's service bring to you, and tell out all your glory.

> (*Goes nearer door.*) Ah! it's hard giving out fancy songs and you fasting—(*Sniffs.*) There's a good kitchen not far off—(*Sings.*)

> I wish I'd seven sorts of meat, sorts of meat, sorts of meat—
> Pork beef and venison all complete—
> And partridges on platters—
> Rum and Canary in a can, in a can, in a can—
> A jug of punch would rise a man—
> From all his rags and tatters!

> (*Goes nearer.*)

> I wish I had a well of wine, a well of wine, a well of wine—

ART (*coming on to upper step, looks at him scornfully*). What brings you here, rising your screeching and your noise? Beggar or vagabone or whatever you are?

TAIG (*shutting his eyes and groping as if blind*). What brought me here? Following the roads of Ireland I came. It is the crooked roads brought me to this door.

ART. Begging and questing is likely you are.

TAIG. Not at all. Giving out a ballad I am, might earn me a bit to put in my mouth.

ART. There is no person wanting these country songs in this place. It is I myself am well able to give out poems of ancient wars and genealogy.

TAIG. Perished I am through the night time—the snow in my face and frozen before it comes to the ground, and I sheltering abroad under a bush.

ART. You would easy have found a lodging fitting for the sort you are, and you seeking it.

TAIG. It failed me to find any shelter as far as I came. Not a shoe or a stocking with me, and a night of frost on the road.

ART. It's best for you to go farther. There is no welcome here for you or the likes of you.

TAIG. To travel the five provinces I did, under rain, under snow, under flood. It is what I am thinking. I never would be tired sitting still.

ART. Let you make off now and go to some common lodging. Will nothing serve you but to nail yourself to this door?

TAIG. There's a bad gale of a shower coming. It's a wild sort of a day. There is a good appearance on this house.

ART. If there is it is not for the likes of you it was furnished. Your face all caked with splashes and with dirt.

TAIG. My nourishment the bramble bush,—stones in my broken shoes. Give me shelter now for a couple of hours and a bit of meat. I think I never would be tired sitting still.

ART. Let you be off I say. Will nothing suit you without coming to the King of Mayo's door?

TAIG (*getting up*). The King's house is it! That should be a good harbour.

ART. If it is, it's not for the likes of you it is furnished.

TAIG. That's the way is it. A poor man will share a broken potato with you, but as to the rich, some are charitable and some begrudging you your means. As to myself, all my wealth is in the voice that can sound out a song.

ART. The King has no need of any person to rise a song for him only myself. It is given in to me that I'm the first singer of a song in all Ireland.

TAIG. Maybe so. But I heard the old people saying it's the blinded bard that sings best.

ART. Is it that you're letting on to be blind?

TAIG. Letting on is it. Amn't I well blinded with the snow?

ART. I'll engage you are very covetous to be humbugging poor farmers when you'll rattle the plate in a country house—

TAIG. Ah bad luck to your tongue that is as sharp as any scissors.

ART. If it is it's yourself I'd be well pleased to cut down with it.

TAIG. Yourself and your gaudy clothes and your ugly mug.

ART. I knew well you were only letting on.

TAIG. Why wouldn't I? If the people of a house think me to be blind they will not suspect me to be carrying newses of what I see. It's likely it was the one way with Homer of the Greeks. If he had the sight lost, what way could he tell out the beauty of Helen that hanged herself the first time she saw a grey hair in her head?

ART. Ah, let you make an end of your gab.

TAIG. Is it that this is an empty house having a niggard for an owner, the same as a roadside house I was in yesterday where all I got was a little white dab a canat would leave after him. That was no food for the poor of God.

ART. Let me tell you there is bullocks and sheep roasted whole here every day of the year. And wine flowing into every silver and every golden vessel for the feasts. I am not without one myself on odd day.

TAIG. The hollow of my hand is my silver cup, and I wish it was full this minute.

ART (*has gone for a moment behind curtain and brings out a plate and jug*). Here now is a bit to stop your gab. (*Gives plate and jug.*)

TAIG. A welcome word. (*He eats and drinks.*) It is what I would wish, to set a clock, and to feed every hour the time it strikes the bell.

ART. I give you my word I'd nearly be well pleased to change with you and to travel the roads for a while, the way I'd get enjoyment out of my meal, the way you are knocking satisfaction out of it.

TAIG. What way could you get satisfaction without you would pass a day, or two days, having no nourishment but the berries of the bush? Closed up here, and fed the same as a fighting cock in his pen.

ART. It is long ago I walked by a stream and saw the sun rising over the yellow bog.

TAIG. It is best for our trade not be wakened in the morning with the ringing of a golden bell, but with maybe the crowing of a little cock that would near take the roof off the house. It is the night time I make my songs.

ART (*crossly*). Ah that's well enough for night walkers and singers on the roads. Ye that are like the ancient Jews a scattered race.

TAIG. It's happy the roads are free to our questing the same as the sea to fishermen—Beggars, travelling men, friars. One shoal is caught by preaching and one by asking an alms.

ART. By sweet or sour. I wouldn't doubt you to change your song as quick as you'd put a worm on the hook.

TAIG. So I would too. And my path. For to go by the straight road always you'd come to the bitter sea.

ART. To look at the rags of you I wonder any decent man at all would let you into his kitchen.

TAIG. I am better pleased to be heard than to be looked at. I'd sooner have the friendship of the country's ears than its eyes. I'm the boy is well able to put fancy lies in a verse as easy as you'd put a bit of broken tin can on a hook (*rather drunk*). Praises in the same way, for many a big man has no call on them. It is not for love of lies I do it, but for the love of what they will bring me. (*Drinks.*)

ART (*who has also been drinking*). You'll find it hard to make a new praise for the King of this house. Sure he heard nothing else through the three score and ten years of his lifetime. I have the whole of the language wore out, warp and woof, stringing the names of the generations from Milesius down. I declare I'd near envy you walking the road according to your wish, and not to be bidden make a song of merriment maybe the time you are racked out with a rotten tooth. Or to string a song of praises for some schemer you wouldn't hardly trust with the lend of a coal to kindle his pipe.

TAIG. Well, you have no fault to find with your nourishment and your lodging.

ART. I declare on my oath I'd nearly sooner be like yourself going through roads and rocks and making your call to the little cabins where they will be content with some old Lillibulero, or to put curses on some parish is near at hand.

TAIG (*wiping his mouth*). I to make a praise at this minute it would be of freedom from winter cold and snow, and a sleep would last till the sprouting of the corn.

ART. The freedom I would wish would be from spies and traitors and the jealousy of covetous men.

TAIG. A roasted bullock at my call to be cutting me enough from, and I lying on a flowery bed, would be my choice thing.

ART. Not to have to put a grin on your face every time the King, or the King's big men come in the door or make some ugly joke.

TAIG. It is on my own face the grin would be fixed through the years and I getting warmth and nourishment at my desire. (*He continues picking bits off dish.*)

ART. To be saying out what is in my mind, without spies and illwishers putting a crooked twist on any word will come out of my mouth.

TAIG. To be in no dread of a cross dog rushing out to make his assault on your bare shins.

ART. Or of the lies schemers do be framing at the back of the King's chair to put him against every whole one.

TAIG. To have a safe harbour when the darkness comes around and the clouds gather from the western sea.

ART. To be free like the wind and the whirlwind. It's little would make me go follow my own thoughts wherever they might lead me.

TAIG (*drinking what is left in the cup—wiping mouth with hand*). Well I have ate enough. To put another bite into my mouth would be to choke and to spoil my melody and to put it astray.

ART (*changing mood*). Who now is asking a song of you?

TAIG. Is it that I would have the King's dinner ate and pay nothing? I never left a debt after me in any sort of a way.

ART. I tell you there's no one asking for a song.

TAIG. They need not be asking. Very liberal I am to pay with my voice for whatever I have put into my mouth. (*He stands up and hums the air. As he begins the song the curtain at back opens and the King is seen listening.*)

TAIG. To make a praise of Mayo's King
  I'll call the ancient Grecians
  The man that made the rushes sing
  The pick of the Phoenicians—
  The seven champions out from Greece,
  Great Ajax in his battles—
  The King of Mayo'd break their peace—
  And sweep their goods and chattels!

  Achilles that blind Homer praised,
  The time Troy was surrounded,
  And Hector who the Greeks amazed,
  When Priam's trumpet sounded—

Caesar that bent the world to Rome
And taxed it as his debtor
The King of Mayo here at home
Is seven times Seven better.

(*The King comes forward clapping his hands. Clapping and applause is heard from behind the curtain.*)
ART (*to* TAIG). Stand back out of this. It is the King.
TAIG. My hundred welcomes to him. That he may never be worse than I wish him. (*Sings.*)

Cuchulain coming from the North
To fight Queen Maeve for cattle
Or Angus breaking from his forth
To turn the tide of battle
They got their song that lasted long
But my song will last longer
For if those heroes were so strong
The King of Mayo's stronger.

(*The King, delighted, beats time to the singing. Claps hands.*)
ART (*going between* TAIG *and the* KING.) Oh sir, he is but a rambler from the roads. He strayed in unknown to me. He had a right to have stopped outside of the gate in his rags and his dirt the way he is.
KING (*pushing* ART *away, to* TAIG). Oh, this is the crown of all singers! Where now did you learn your trade?
TAIG. From the lark in the meadow, the screeching of the wild geese in the air, the talk of the blackbird and the thrush.
KING. I often heard tell of the birds of the Wood of Wisdom. They are masters of music sure enough.
TAIG. Why wouldn't they? Going into the high heavens the way they do. I'm a good warrant to put words to the music they do be sounding up in the clouds— Listen now and I'll give you out another verse—
ART. Oh, King, let you not heed his impudence. He never learned manners in a school.
KING. Leave meddling. It is music we want from our musicians and not to be mimicking manners. . . . Did you hear what he said about Ajax and the Phoenicians.
(*Sings again.*)

The King of Mayo'd break their peace
And sweep their goods and chattels! so I would too.

ART (*sulkily*). He is nothing but a cracked fool.

KING. It is a man is light-minded I want. I have had my fill of dull advisers.

ART (*pushing* TAIG). Go out now while there's a good word for you—and I'll promise you'll get a good luckpenny.

KING. Leave him alone. It is not your place to handle him and to give out orders. I give you my word this man has more melody and matter and mastery in his song than you yourself gave out in the whole of your lifetime.

ART. I was only saying—

KING. Running him down and he well able to hunt you around the five provinces and into the wide wilderness of the sea. I must get that song off my heart.

(*Sings.*)

They got their song that lasted long
But this song will last longer
For if their hero were so strong
It's I myself am stronger.

ART (*turning his back*). That's praise I never got for years. All that is new is beautiful.

KING (*to* ART). Strip off your coat and your cloak and your shoes and let this man put them on him and wear them from this out. For he is from this day the chief poet in this house. You that through all the years never saw into me the way this man does. If you drink from a silver cup he will have a golden cup. Give him the poet's dress I say. Make no delay. (*He goes out and is heard calling for the Queen.*)

ART (*weeping*). Did ever such a thing happen in all the years gone by. Or such a disgrace.

TAIG. Sure I did nothing against you. I never asked it.

ART. Bad cess to you. You left no praise for any other one to tell out, so covetous as you are.

TAIG. Didn't I tell you I was good at stringing lies? (*Takes off rags.*)

ART (*taking off cloak*). If you didn't mouth it you looked it. Your eyes stuck into the King like a calf taking a grip of the udder.

TAIG (*trying on cloak*). Well, who would refuse luck when luck comes to him?

ART (*weeping*). I that was on the height am in the hollow. You that are as wiry as the wall and as hard to be sheltered among high company, and I myself sent out astray in the provinces.

TAIG. Sure there must be a turn in everything the same as the turn of the tide.

ART. That the same tide may wash you under the billows of the great sea.

TAIG. Slap me out the coat now.

ART. And is it that I am to get into your old heap of tatters!

TAIG. It's roomy. And that is what your own coat is not. (*Fumbles with fastenings.*) Bad cess to it, itself and its hooks and its buttons.

KING (*putting in his head*). Hurry, hurry, get on your clothes. I'll get right respect from the queen now. She will give in to know the sort of man I am. (*Goes.*)

ART. Will he leave me with nothing on me but my nakedness. For I give my word I will never put on my back this greasy old body coat of your own.

TAIG. The stockings now. (*Art pulls them off.*) Striped the same as a cameleopard. (*Sits down and puts them on.*) Its myself will be proud stepping out through the streets of the town.

KING (*puts in his head*). Greece. Did you say Greece. It has near gone out of my memory that I ever went fighting in Greece. (TAIG *nods.*) (*Sings.*)

> The seven Champions out from Greece—Great Ajax in his battles—
> It's I myself that broke their peace
> And swept their goods and chattels!

I had it nearly forgot with the weight of this kingdom that is upon me. (*Goes.*)

TAIG. What way now will I tie on the garters?

ART (*impatiently trying one on for him*). If it wasn't for dread of the King in his passion I'd be well pleased to choke your throat with them. (*Flings them down, having kicked off his shoes.*)

TAIG. Would you say now those shoes would be my fit?

ART. The like of them were never made for you or the like of you.

TAIG (*pulls them on, gets up, walks a step or two*); They're middling easy—middling—(*they flop.*) What way now will I keep them that they will not be falling off my feet?

ART. The same way every other one keeps them on—with a shoelace—

TAIG (*as he throws laces to him*). With that bit of a string? (*Ties it round his shoes.*)

ART. That's not the way to be tying it the same as a rag round a sore heel.

TAIG. Can't you stop your scolding. Haven't I enough to do getting myself into this fancy suit without you picking at me?

ART. What you have to do is to put it in and out of every one of these little holes.

TAIG. Is that now what those small little holes are for? I thought seeing them they were maybe to let the wet run out the time I might be walking in the rain—

ART. You're done with walking around in the rain. You are under a roof from this out. Put the lace back and forward—criss cross—to and fro—

TAIG (*clumsily trying*). I think I am getting anear it—

ART. You are not. You have the one side entirely too lengthy. It will fail you to tie it as a bow.

TAIG. To tie it?

ART. In one hole and across to the hole that faces it. The way the knot will not come undone.

TAIG. I'd sooner it to come undone. I'd sooner it never to be done at all.

ART. You are talking like what you are, a fool.

TAIG. I'd have no comfort of sleep with them through the night time.

ART. Is it that you think you'd be wearing them through the hours of the night?

TAIG. Is it that I would be put to these straits night and morning? Fiddling with little strings the same as a fiddler. Taking aim at the holes the same as a fowler at a bird's eye.

ART. All right so. Let the shoes go falling off your feet before the King's face for the want of a string—and a rope'll be likely tightened around your neck. (*Music heard or trumpet.*)

TAIG (*gets up, kicking off shoes*). I give you my word I'd sooner be hung from a tree than to go myself into this bondage. (*Sings as he throws off coat and takes off stockings and garters.*)

> I'll not stop in a palace
> With jealousy and malice
> And lies to tell—I told them well
> For any golden chalice!
> The road that does be winding—
> The friends that I'll be finding

The larks that sing upon the wing
Are better worth the minding!

ART. What now will the King say to you!

TAIG. Let him say. And let him roar and cry and bawl and curse and damn and raise a row with me and fall upon his knees begging me to tie and torment and hamper and crush the poor innocent ten toes of my feet.

ART. It's what he'll do, he'll be apt to hang you from a tree.

TAIG. He has to catch me first. Well goodbye to you— That you may live happy—yourself and your ten toes! There is no one can call me a grabber or say I took any man's place.

(*Sound of a trumpet, the curtain opens the King appears. Sound of trampling and voices.*)

THE KING. Where now is he? Where is the Singer?

ART. It is my belief he was dreamed to us. Sure such a fool as that has never been in this world at all.

If my poor coat's in tatters
Sure not a pin it matters
My little path beside the rath
All melancholy scatters—
Blackberries on the bushes
The talk of jays and thrushes
The west wind's sigh, the curlew's cry
The breeze that stirs the rushes.
The tumbling of the river
That sees the heron shiver
The pike and eel, the crab and seal
That travel it forever.
The clamour and commotion
When Salmon take a notion
To go explore the rushy shore
And leave the salty ocean.
(*His voice dies away.*)

Curtain.

THE LIGHTED WINDOW

THE LIGHTED WINDOW

PERSONS
    MARTIN
    MICHAEL
    A SOLDIER

Two ragged men, MARTIN *and* MICHAEL, *come groping, one supporting the other. They are near the doorstep of a house. There is one lighted window. They wear tattered remnants of a uniform.*

MICHAEL (*low*). There must be some living person within, and the room having a light in it.

MARTIN. I can go no farther. Let me sink upon the doorstep, whether friend or enemy is in it.

MICHAEL. Take care you make any sound. It might be the English are within. Or the Dutch. (*He helps* MARTIN *to lie down, his back resting against the steps.*)

MARTIN. It was a terrible long road to drag from Aughrim here.

MICHAEL. And you so weak with the loss of blood. And myself nearly in the same case. (*Listens at window.*) There's people in it.

MARTIN. Whoever is in it let us ask a charity in the name of God.

MICHAEL (*listening, puts up his hand. Stoops to* MARTIN). It is the chance of a speedy death we are apt to get if King William's men are in it. I heard the rattle of a sword falling on the floor. (*Sits down beside him.*)

MARTIN. That was the worst Monday ever came upon the world.

MICHAEL. Many and many a one besides ourselves was left under a dark cloak of sorrow, without speaking of all that died.

MARTIN. When we could not banish the foreign devils from us it would be nearly better to have been killed in Aughrim. O'Kelly will have good manuring for his land with all that were left stretched in ridges.

MICHAEL. Indeed and indeed there was many a heart broken.

MARTIN. If I was as wise then as I am now I never would have quitted my own little patch of land.

MICHAEL. You are well enough that you were not killed out and out.

MARTIN. The knee preying on me, and the pain that is bursting out of my side (*moans.*)

MICHAEL. A great wonder the two of us to be living at all with such a welter and such a killing as was in it. Dutch and English and outsoldiers. One worse again than the other. They have the whole world killed.

MARTIN. Ah. (*Moans.*) The wet in the grass is enough to perish anyone. It is getting to be very cloudy. I'd be glad to be in any place without being here.

MICHAEL. To be lying under the sky everything that is lonesome would be coming down on you. If we had but a little tent, the same as a tinker, you'd come out of it in the morning as supple as a hare would come out of his nest.

MARTIN. It's more likely I'll die like a starved rabbit perished with the hunger. It is best chance giving a knock at the door.

MICHAEL. They would likely be questioning us. You couldn't say anything you'd think with the way the world is of late. This war has played on us entirely. The people are all out of tune.

MARTIN. If we could but meet with some of Sarsfield's men.

MICHAEL. Ah! it's he had the world of prayers down on him. My heart leaps up at his very name. He that is a whole gentleman through his whole lifetime.

MARTIN. Devil a better friend in Ireland. That Frenchman getting command over him lost the battle. If he lost his own life in it, and his head, there is no person will cry him. Sarsfield has no beat. He to be driven back is the breaking of my heart to me.

MICHAEL. King James to run from the Boyne the way he did, and many a poor mother's son dying for his sake! Any person that has anything at all wouldn't like to be knocked for the sake of another.

MARTIN. If I could but get back to my own little village (*moans.*)

MICHAEL. Try can you move at all and make a start. (*Puts his arm round him. MARTIN groans.*)

MARTIN. I can go no farther. The walk is gone from me, I'm perished with the length of the road. When I am in trouble there's no way at all in me.

MICHAEL. If you could but drag as far as our own parish—every one with his arms open for us—

MARTIN. It's likely if we got there we'd find they had burned mansion and hovel. . . . If we could but know on what side are the people within that door!

MICHAEL (*who has been groping in the grass comes back and whispers*). Look at this bottle that was lying on the grass.

MARTIN. My grief that it is empty, it has a good smell on it.

MICHAEL. I saw the like of it with a big Hollander at the commencement of the battle—a man that looked as black as the devil —with that length of teeth—(*holds up his finger.*)

MARTIN. It's as good die so, on the grass as we are. It's a crack on the head we'd be getting, you to knock at the door. It might be a Hession would open it, or a Sassanach pointing a gun at your heart.

MICHAEL. If you could but rise up, we might reach to some harbour.

MARTIN (*falling back with a groan*). It fails me to rise my foot. I cannot do it. Let you go on and leave me.

MICHAEL. I can not do that. (*Throws off jacket and cap.*) To rise a verse of a song they might take me in the half dark to be but a ballad singer and throw us out a charity.

MARTIN. Take care what song would you give out or we'll be in ten times a worse case than before, and a crack on your head for a reward. I am certain there is a noise again of the rattling of swords.

MICHAEL. Oh! If I was in my own village singing Lillibulero and every door open to me.

MARTIN. Sing it out here if you are craving a crack on the skull. Have sense and give out some ballad that is no party tune. The Colleen Rue now would be harmless.

MICHAEL (*going near to window, sings*).

As I roved out on a summer's morning a speculating most
    curiously,
To my surprise I soon espied a charming fair one approaching
    me.
I stood awhile in deep meditation contemplating what I should
    do.
Till at length recruiting all my sensations, I thus accosted the
    fair Colleen Rue.

"Are you Aurora or the goddess Flora, Artemidora or Venus
    bright?
Or Helen fair beyond compare, whom Paris stole from the
    Grecian sight?
O fairest creature you have enslaved me; I'm intoxicated in
    Cupid's clue,

Your golden sayings are infatuations that have ensnared me, a
 Colleen Rue!"

"Kind Sir be easy and do not tease me with your false praises
 most jestingly.
Your dissimulation and invocation are vaunting praises allur-
 ing me.
I'm not Aurora or the goddess Flora, but a rural female to all
 men's views
That's here condoling my situation; my appellation is the
 Colleen Rue."

"Oh were I Hector that noble victor who died a victim to
 Grecian skill,
Or were I Paris whose deeds are various, an arbitrator on Ida's
 hill,
I'd range through Asia, likewise Arabia, Pennsylvania seeking
 for you
The burning regions like sage Orpheus to see your face my
 sweet Colleen Rue!"

MARTIN. I think I heard like something against the window
pane ...
MICHAEL. There is no sign of anyone to stretch out a hand
anyway.
MARTIN. Sound out some verse would be more lively—Some-
thing with a skin on it.
MICHAEL. Faith, it is no way lively I feel myself, and I see no
lively appearance on yourself.
MARTIN. Hurry on. The weakness is going through me. Give out
Brennan on the Moor.
MICHAEL (*sings*).

It's of a fearless highwayman a story I will tell.
His name was Willy Brennan, in Ireland he did dwell.
It was on the Livart Mountains he commenced his wild career,
And many a wealthy gentleman before him shook with fear.
A brace of loaded pistols he carried both night and day,
He never robbed a poor man upon the King's highway.
But what he'd take from the rich like Turpin and Black Bess,
He always divided it with the widow and orphan in distress.

. . . Is there anyone at all giving an ear to me I wonder?

MARTIN. Rise it louder can't you.

MICHAEL.

"One night he robbed a packman the name of Peter Brown
They travelled on together till the day began to dawn,
The pedlar seeing his money gone likewise a watch and chain.
All at once encountered Brennan and robbed him back again."

A FOREIGN VOICE FROM THE WINDOW. Go away from this place if you wish not to be fired upon as a spy. Quick—quick, go on! Vagabonds—

MICHAEL (*low*). Vagabone yourself, coming to our country and no person wanting you.

MARTIN (*faintly*). Have care—have a care!

MICHAEL. Little I care if they make an end of myself—not giving you that are near quenched in the grip of death so much as leave to die like a dog at their door, and I after singing a song should delight them. Thieves and highway robbers themselves.

MARTIN (*faintly*). Maybe if you would give them some British song—

MICHAEL. I will not give in to Foreigners or Dutchmen. I'd sooner swing! Let them make a riddle of me with holes through my entire body. God is stronger than the Cromwellians! I'll sing for Ireland and Sarsfield if it is my last song. Let them do their worst. (*Goes nearer the door and sings.*)

O never fear for Ireland for she has soldiers still
For Reny's boys are in the wood and Rory's on the hill!
And never had poor Ireland more loyal hearts than these—
May God be kind and good to them, the faithful Rapparees!
        The fearless Rapparees.
The jewel were ye Rory with your Irish Rapparees!

O black's your heart Clan Oliver and colder than the clay
Oh high's your head Clan Sassenach since Sarsfield's gone
        away!
It's little love you bear to us for sake of long ago
But hold your hand for Ireland still can strike a deadly blow!
        Can strike a mortal blow!
Ach, dar-a-Chriost! it's she that still could strike the deadly
        blow!

249

(The door bursts open, the light shines out—A man in armour stands at the door with glass in hand. A great cheer within. Men bring out food and bottles.)

OFFICER *(in French accent)*. Come in! Come in! friends come in!

MICHAEL Oh! you are no Sassenach! No Dutchmen!

OFFICER. We are bringing our troop, French and Irish, to Sarsfield's aid! There is full and plenty in the house for his friends.
(ALL SING.)

Oh Sassenach and Cromweller, take heed of what I say!
Keep down your black and angry looks that scorn us night
  and day!
For there's a just and wrathful Judge that every action sees
And he'll make strong to right our wrong the faithful Rap-
  parees!
        The fearless Rapparees!
The men that fought at Sarsfield's side, the changeless Rap-
  parees!

(All cheer, as glasses are filled.)

Curtain.

NOTES AND MUSIC

NOTES AND MUSIC

"Twenty Five" "A Losing Game"

Before I belonged to the Irish National Theatre Society I sent in a little play, "Twenty-five," and it was refused, one of the grounds being that some of the members "did not approve of money being won at cards." Things have marched since then, and "Twenty Five" has been acted, and it was especially liked in England "because it is so sentimental." I have myself a leaning towards sentimentality, and to cover it have written a parody on the old play, letting loose the *Jackdaw* to croak upon its grave.

Spreading the News

The idea of this play first came to me as a tragedy. I kept seeing as in a picture people sitting by the roadside, and a girl passing to the market, gay and fearless. And then I saw her passing by the same place at evening, her head hanging, the heads of others turned from her, because of some sudden story that had risen out of a chance word, and had snatched away her good name.

But comedy and not tragedy was wanted at our theatre to put beside the high poetic work, *The King's Threshold, The Shadowy Waters, On Baile's Strand, The Well of the Saints*; and I let laughter have its way with the little play. I was delayed in beginning it for a while, because I could only think of Bartley Fallon as dull-witted or silly or ignorant, and the handcuffs seemed too harsh a punishment. But one day by the sea at Duras a melancholy man who was telling me of the crosses he had gone through at home said—"But I'm thinking if I went to America, its long ago to-day I'd be dead. And it's a great expense for a poor man to be buried in America." Bartley was born at that moment, and, far from harshness, I felt I was providing him with a happy old age in giving him the lasting glory of that great and crowning day of misfortune.

It has been acted very often by other companies as well as our own, and the Boers have done me the honour of translating and pirating it.

Spreading the News.

I thought, my first love, there'd be but one house be-tween you and me, And I thought I would find your - self. coax - ing my child on your knee. O - ver the tide I would leap with the leap of a swan, Till I came to the side of the wife of the red - haired man.

THE RED-HAIRED MAN'S WIFE

A Note on Spreading the News (from *The Arrow*, Vol. I, No. 1, October 20, 1906)

Some time ago at a debate in Dublin a speaker complained that the Irish peasantry were slandered in *Spreading the News*, because nowhere in Ireland would so improbable a story grow out of so little; and in the same speech he said our Theatre was not worthy of support, because we "had given our first performance at the Castle." Another speaker pointed to this fiction as a very Spreading of the News. Since that day it has been said of us that we never play but in Irish, that our Theatre is "something done for the Roman Catholics," that it has been "got up by the Irish Parliamentary Party with Mr. Healy at the head of them," that we have a special fee of fifty pounds a performance for anybody from Trinity College who wishes to hire the Theatre, that our "attitude to the Irish peasant arises out of class prejudice which keeps us from seeing anything that is good in him," that we encourage agrarian outrage by the performance of "Cathleen ni Houlihan," that through fear of offending the English we will not play anything founded upon events that happened since their arrival under Strongbow, that we are neglecting Dublin for England, that we are "a Fenian lot," and that we give ourselves airs. Some at least of these accusations must be founded on evidence as airy as that given in the case of the murder of Jack Smith.

Hyacinth Halvey

I was pointed out one evening a well-brushed, well-dressed man in the stalls, and was told gossip about him, perhaps not all true, which made me wonder if that appearance and behaviour as of extreme respectability might not now and again be felt a burden.

After a while he translated himself in my mind into Hyacinth; and as one must set one's original a little way off to get a translation rather than a tracing, he found himself in Cloon, where, as in other parts of our country, "character" is built up or destroyed by a password or an emotion, rather than by experience and deliberation.

The idea was more of a universal one than I knew at the first, and I have had but uneasy appreciation from some apparently blameless friends.

The "Irish Peasant" on Hyacinth Halvey

The "Irish Peasant," in a long article signed "Pat," on the first production of Hyacinth, describes that play as "a realistic comedy of current life on a background of implicit criticism." It considered that the play is an exposure of the lack of any genuine public opinion in Ireland, where "popularity" is "the only standard of human worth," which results in "all sorts of despicable characters being set upon stilts for standards;" and it winds up with "Did Lady Gregory intend the sermon? I think not. The thorough success of her play as a play indicates that she was concerned with the dramatic interest of her theme and nothing else, deriving her motive from the determining features of the life around her as every dramatist has a right to do." In the performance "nothing is ever overdone, there is never the least appeal to the gallery; the faults are never of the fixed kind that limit progress, and there is never an attempt to magnify a part at the expense of the artistic symmetry of the whole. Accordingly the audiences most worth having in Dublin, from an artistic point of view, are to be met at the Abbey Theatre, whatever their numbers."

The Rising of the Moon

When I was a child and came with my elders to Galway for their salmon fishing in the river that rushes past the gaol, I used to look

The Rising of the Moon.

As through the hills I walked to view the hills and sham-rock plain, I stood a-while where na-ture smiles to view the rocks and streams, On a ma-tron fair I fixed my eyes be-neath a fer-tile vale, As she sang her song — it was on the wrong of poor old Gran-u-aile.

Her head was bare, her hands and feet with i-ron bands were bound, Her pen-sive strain and plain-tive wail ming-les with the eve-ning gale, And the song she sang with mourn-ful air, I am old Gran-u-aile, Her lips so sweet that mon-archs kissed—

GRANUAILE

with awe at the window where men were hung, and the dark, closed gate. I used to wonder if ever a prisoner might by some means climb the high, buttressed wall and slip away in the darkness by the canal to the quays and find friends to hide him under a load of kelp in a fishing boat, as happens to my ballad-singing man. The play was considered offensive to some extreme Nationalists before it was acted, because it showed the police in too favourable a light, and a Unionist paper attacked it after it was acted because the policeman was represented "as a coward and a traitor"; but after the Belfast police strike that same paper praised its "insight into Irish character." After all these ups and downs it passes unchallenged on both sides of the Irish Sea.

The Rising of the Moon.

There was a rich far-mer's daugh-ter lived

near the town of Ross; She court-ed a' High-land

sol - dier, His name was John-ny Hart; Says the

moth-er to her daugh-ter, "I'll go dis-tract-ed

mad If you mar - ry that High - land

sol - dier dressed up in his High-land · plaid."

JOHNNY HART

The Jackdaw

The first play I wrote was called "Twenty-five." It was played by our company in Dublin and London, and was adapted and translated into Irish and played in America. It was about "A boy of Kilbecanty that saved his old sweetheart from being evicted. It was playing Twenty-five he did it; played with the husband he did, letting him win up to £50."

O, then, tell me, Shawn O' Far-rell, where the
gath'ring is to be. In the old spot by the
ri-ver, Right well known to you and me.
One word more, for sig-nal to-ken whis-tle
up the march-ing tune, With your pike up-on your
should-er at the ris-ing of the moon.

THE RISING OF THE MOON

It was rather sentimental and weak in construction, and for a
long time it was an overflowing storehouse of examples of "the
faults of my dramatic method." I have at last laid its ghost in "The
Jackdaw," and I have not been accused of sentimentality since the
appearance of this.

The Workhouse Ward

I heard of an old man in the workhouse who had been disabled
many years before by, I think, a knife thrown at him by his wife in
some passionate quarrel.

One day I heard the wife had been brought in there, poor and sick. I wondered how they would meet, and if the old quarrel was still alive, or if they who knew the worst of each other would be better pleased with one another's company than with that of strangers.

I wrote a scenario of the play, Dr. Douglas Hyde getting in plot what he gave back in dialogue, for at that time we thought a dramatic movement in Irish would be helpful to our own as well as to the Gaelic League. Later I tried to rearrange it for our own theatre, and for three players only, but in doing this I found it necessary to write entirely new dialogue, the two old men in the original play obviously talking at an audience in the wards, which is no longer there.

I sometimes think the two scolding paupers are a symbol of ourselves in Ireland—

—"it is better to be quarrelling than to be lonesome."
The Rajputs, that great fighting race, when they were told they had been brought under the Pax Britannica and must give up war, gave themselves to opium in its place, but Connacht has not yet planted its poppy gardens.

The Bogie Men

A message sent to America from Dublin that our Theatre had been "driven out with hisses"; an answering message from New York that the *Playboy*, the cause of battle, was now "as dead as a doornail," set me musing with renewed delight on our incorrigible genius for myth-making, the faculty that makes our traditional history a perpetual jjoy, because it is, like the Sidhe, an eternal Shape-changer.

At Philadelphia, the city of trees, where in spite of a day in the police court and before a judge, and the arrest of our players at the suit not of a Puritan but a publican, and the throwing of currant cake with intent to injure, I received very great personal kindness, a story of his childhood told by my host gave me a fable on which to hang my musings; and the Dublin enthusiast and the American enthusiast who interchanged so many compliments and made so brave a show to one another, became Dermot and Timothy, "two

Air of "All round my hat I wore a green ribbon!"

harmless drifty lads," the *Bogie Men* of my little play. They were
to have been vagrants, tatterdemalions, but I needed some dress the
change of which would change their whole appearance in a moment,
and there came to mind the chimney sweepers of my childhood.

They used to come trotting the five miles from Loughrea, little
fellows with blue eyes shining out from soot-black faces, wearing
little soot-coloured smocks. Our old doctor told us he had gone to
see one of them who was sick, and had found him lying in a box,
with soot up to his chin as bedding and blanket.

Not many years ago a decent looking man came to my door, with
I forget what request. He told me he had heard of ghosts and fairies,
but had never met with anything worse than himself, but that he
had had one great fright in his lifetime. Its cause had been the
squealing and outcry made by two rats caught in one trap, that had
come clattering down a flight of steps one time when he was a little
lad, and had come sweeping chimneys to Roxborough.

Coats

I find some bald little notes I made before writing *Coats*. "Hazel
is astonished Mineog can take such a thing to heart, but it is quite
different when he himself is offended." "The Quarrel is so violent
you think it can never be healed, but the ordinary circumstances of
life force reconciliation. They are the most powerful force of all."
And then a quotation from Nietzsche, "A good war justifies every
cause."

Damer's Gold

In a lecture I gave last year on playwriting I said I had been
forced to write comedy because it was wanted for our theatre, to
put on at the end of the verse plays, but that I think tragedy is
easier. For, I said, tragedy shows humanity in the grip of circum-

stance, of fate, of what our people call "the thing will happen," "the Woman in the Stars that does all." There is a woman in the stars they say, who is always hurting herself in one way or other, and according to what she is doing at the hour of your birth, so will it happen to you in your lifetime, whether she is hanging herself or drowning herself or burning herself in the fire. "And," said an old man who was telling me this, "I am thinking she was doing a great deal of acting at the time I myself made my start in the world." Well, you put your actor in the grip of this woman, in the claws of the cat. Once in that grip you know what the end must be. You may let your hero kick or struggle, but he is in the claws all the time, it is a mere question as to how nearly you will let him escape, and when you will allow the pounce. Fate itself is the protagonist, your actor cannot carry much character, it is out of place. You do not want to know the character of a wrestler you see trying his strength at a show.

In writing a little tragedy, *The Gaol Gate*, I made the scenario in three lines, "He is an informer; he is dead; he is hanged." I wrote that play very quickly. My two poor women were in the clutch of the Woman in the Stars. . . . I knew what I was going to do and I was able to keep within those three lines. But in comedy it is different. Character comes in, and why it is so I cannot explain, but as soon as one creates a character, he begins to put out little feet of his own and take his own way.

I had been meditating for a long time past on the mass of advice that is given one by friends and well-wishers and relations, advice that would be excellent if the giver were not ignorant so often of the one essential in the case, the one thing that matters. But there is usually something out of sight, of which the adviser is unaware, it may be something half mischievously hidden from him, it may be that "secret of the heart with God" that is called religion. In the whole course of our work at the theatre we have been I may say drenched with advice by friendly people who for years gave us the reasons why we did not succeed. . . . All their advice, or at least some of it, might have been good if we had wanted to make money, to make a common place of amusement. Our advisers did not see that what we wanted was to create for Ireland a theatre with a base of realism, with an apex of beauty. Well, last summer I made a fable for this meditation, this emotion, at the back of my mind to drive.

I pictured to myself, for I usually first see a play as a picture, a young man, a mere lad, very sleepy in the day time. He was surrounded by people kind and wise, who lamented over his rags and idleness and assured him that if he didn't get up early and do his work in the daytime he would never know the feel of money in his hand. He listens to all their advice, but he does not take it, because he knows what they do not know, that it is in the night time precisely he is filling his pocket, in the night when, as I think, we receive gifts from the unseen. I placed him in the house of a miser, an old man who had saved a store of gold. I called the old man Damer, from a folk-story of a chandler who had bought for a song the kegs of gold the Danes had covered with tallow as a disguise when they were driven out of Ireland, and who had been rich and a miser ever after. I did not mean this old man, Damer, to appear at all. He was to be as invisible as that Heaven of which we are told the violent take it by force. My intention at first was that he should be robbed, but then I saw robbery would take too much sympathy from my young lad, and I decided the money should be won by the lesser sin of cardplaying, but still behind the scenes. Then I thought it would have a good stage effect if old Damer could just walk once across the stage in the background. His relations might have come into the house to try and make themselves agreeable to him, and he would appear and they would vanish. . . . Damer comes in, and contrary to my intention, he begins to find a tongue of his own. He has made his start in the world, and has more than a word to say. How that play will work out I cannot be sure, or if it will ever be finished at all. But if ever it is I am quite sure it will go as Damer wants, not as I want.

That is what I said last winter, and now in harvest time the play is all but out of my hands. But as I foretold, Damer has taken possession of it, turning it to be as simple as a folk-tale, where the innocent of the world confound the wisdom of the wise. The idea with which I set out has not indeed quite vanished, but is as if "extinct and pale; not darkness, but light that has become dead."

As to Damer's changes of mood, it happened a little time ago, when the play was roughly written, but on its present lines, that I took up a volume of Montaigne, and found in it his justification by high examples: "Verilie it is not want but rather plentie that causeth avarice. I will speake of mine owne experience concerning this subject. I have lived in three kinds of condition since I came out of my infancie. The first time, which continued well nigh twentie yeares, I have past it over as one who had no other means but casual without any certaine maintenance or regular prescription. My expenses were so much the more carelessly laid out and lavishly employed, by how much more they wholly depended on fortunes rashnesse and exhibition. I never lived so well at ease. ... My second manner of life hath been to have monie: which when I had once fingred, according to my condition I sought to hoorde up some against a rainy day ... My minde was ever on my halfe-penny; my thoughts ever that way. Of commoditie I had little or nothing. ... And after you are once accustomed, and have fixed your thoughts upon a heape of monie, it is no longer at your service; you dare not diminish it; it is a building which if you touch or take any part from it, you will think it will all fall. And I should sooner pawne my clothes or sell a horse, with lesse care and compulsion than make a breach into that beloved purse which I kept in store. ... I was some yeares of the same humour: I wot not what good Demon did most profitably remove me from it, like to the Siracusan, and made me to neglect my sparing. ... I live from hand to mouth, from day to day, and have I but to supplie my present and ordinarie needs I am satisfied ... And I singularly gratifie myself this correction came upon me in an age naturally inclined to covetousnesse, and that I am free from that folly so common and peculiar to old men, and the most ridiculous of all humane follies. Feraulez who had passed through both fortunes and found that encrease of goods was no encrease of appetite to eat, to sleepe or to embrace his wife; and who on the other side felt heavily on his shoulders the importunitie of ordering and directing his Oeconomicall affairs as it doth on mine, determined with himselfe to content a poore young man, his faithfull friend, greedily gaping after riches, and frankly made him a present donation of all his great and excessive riches, always provided hee should undertake to entertaine and find him, honestly and in good sort, as his guest and friend. In which estate they lived afterwards most happily and mutually content with the change of their condition."

And so I hope it may come to pass with the remaining year of Simon and of Damer.

Hanrahan's Oath

I think it was seeing a performance of "The Dumb Wife" in New York, and having a memory of Mollère's Lucinde, that made me wonder how it would fare with a man forced to be silent in the same way. I do not count Jonson's Epicoene, for he had been with much labour trained for the part. So Hanrahan, poet and talker, borrowed from Mr. Yeats' "Celtic Twilight," took the sudden plunge into silence.

I have looked back into an old copybook where I began the writing, and I see that Mary Gillis was at the first given more of the argument, and told him that "To speak lets the bad blood out of you, the same as to vomit, and leaves the soul clean"; and "it is worse to have bad thoughts than bad words, and to be cursing and damning in the mind." And I see also I had written for my own guidance that "it is after reaching the height of sanctity the fall is greatest"; and "how far the carrying out comes short of the imagining!" And this last I found true in the writing of the play, as Hanrahan did in the keeping of his vow. It was written in 1915.

The Wrens

I wrote this what seems a long time ago, before the war, and in looking at it now I find it hard to get into the mood in which I wrote it. I had been reading the history of the passing of the Bill for the Union between Great Britain and Ireland, that now, in this year 1921, seems likely to be undone. This is how its story is told in folk lore: — "As to the Union, it was bought with titles. Look at the Binghams and the rest, they went to bed nothing, and rose up lords in the morning. The day it was passed, Lady Castlereagh was in the House of Parliament, and she turned three colours, and she said to her husband, "You have passed your treaty, but you have sold your country." He went and cut his throat after that. And it is said by the old people, there was no priest in Ireland but voted for it, the way they would get better rights, for it was only among poor persons they were going at that time. And it was but at the time of the Parliament leaving College Green they began to wear the Soutane that they wear now."

Book History tells us that the Bill was passed on its first reading, on January 22, 1799, by only one vote; and my little play imagines the losing of a vote that would have at least made the numbers equal, through so slight a cause as a quarrel between two strolling vagabonds, that disturbs the attention of a servant from watching the moment to call his master, who would have cast his vote against the Bill.

I see in some notes made before the writing that I had planned "a human comedy, the changing of sides of man and wife," and that if she helps to a victory for the over-Government "to bring away the Parliament out of Ireland" it is against her own conviction, and but to save her husband from drunkenness and gain a home for herself, and that in so doing it is likely she would be praised by moralists, but the common people would put their curse upon her and him as they have put it on the even less responsible Wrens that lost Ireland a victory through awakening the Danish sentinels by pecking at the crumbs upon their drums.

Sometimes in making a plan for a play I set the scene in some other country that I may be sure the emotion displayed is not bounded by any neighbourhood but is a universal one. And I see upon a forgotten stray page that the persons of the play in my mind were at one time an Athenian who is for the victory of his city and quarrels with his wife who belongs to Sparta. But he is too fond of the wine cup to be of much use to the one or the other side, and hearing that the Spartans are at the very gates of Athens he is persuaded to abstain from the juice of grape or barley until their victory is declared, and this he is assured, will be before nightfall. Then the wife turns round and is all for Athens in order that his pledge may be forever kept, and so "they work against each other and upset each others plans and the plans of others, and she is said to be 'A good woman for her husband,' but others said she was a bad woman for the country."

The Wrens was written in 1914.

On the Racecourse

This is a rewriting of my first play, that was called *Twenty-Five*, and was about a country boy who saved his old sweet-heart from being evicted by losing "up to fifty pounds" to her husband at cards. It was given by our Irish players in Dublin and London and was liked, but it was rather sentimental and weak in construction and I did not publish it with my other plays. I thought I had laid its ghost in *The Jackdaw*, where a brother saves his sister from bankruptcy but without romance or sentiment. But a ghost will not always be obedient, and I hope this appearance of a *revenant* may be forgiven.

The airs to which the songs are sung may be found : —
The Wild Birds' Nest (The Verdant Braes of Skreen) in Irish Country Songs; ed. Herbert Hughes; pub. Boosey & Co.
The Poor Irish Harper (The Bard of Armagh), arranged by Dr. Larchet; pub. Pigott, Grafton Street, Dublin.
Irish Molly O!; No. 403 in the Joyce Collection of 842 Irish Songs; pub. Longmans, Green & Co.
Righ Shamus (The Irish Rapparees); Irish Song Book; pub. Fisher Unwin & Sons.

Michelin
The tune used for the song is "The Swaggering Jig" to be found in Graves' "Irish Song Book" (page 72).

The Meadow Gate
"Single and Free" appears in Joyce's "Old Irish Folk Music and Songs" as no. 213 (page 104).

The Dispensary
The air sung at the end of the play is to be found in Joyce, no. 69 (page 37).

The Shoelace
The first song is sung to the tune of "I wish I had the shepherd's lamb", Joyce no. 426 (page 238).

The Lighted Window
The first song is "The Colleen Rue", to be found in Joyce no. 394 (page 202). The song on page 248 is "Brennan on the Moor", no. 379 in Joyce (page 186). "The Irish Rapparees" is to be found in the Irish Song Book, edited by A. P. Graves (page 84).

FIRST PERFORMANCES AT THE ABBEY
THEATRE AND THEIR CASTS

FIRST PERFORMANCES AT THE ABBEY
THEATRE AND THEIR CASTS

The following plays in this Volume have been performed at the Abbey Theatre and the casts and the date of the first productions are given below:

Twenty Five

14th March 1903

Michael Ford (a middle-aged farmer) . . . W. G. Fay
Kate Ford (his young wife) . . . Maire Nic Shiubhlaigh
Christie Henderson . . . . . . P. J. Kelly
A Neighbour . . . . Dora Hackett
Another Neighbour . . . . . P. MacShiubhlaigh

Spreading The News

27th December 1904

Bartley Fallon . . . . W. G. Fay
Mrs. Fallon . . . . Sara Allgood
Mrs. Tully . . . . Emma Vernon
Mrs. Tarpey . . . . . Maire Ni Gharbhaigh
Shawn Early . . . . J. H. Dunne
Tim Casey . . . . George Roberts
James Ryan . . . . . . Arthur Sinclair
Jack Smith . . . . . . P. MacShlibhlaigh
A Policeman . . . . R. S. Nash
A Removable Magistrate . . . . . F. J. Fay

Hyacinth Halvey

19th February 1906

Hyacinth Halvey . . . . F. J. Fay
James Quirke, a butcher . . . . . W. G. Fay
Fardy Farrell, a telegraph boy . . . . Arthur Sinclair
Sergeant Carden . . . . . . Walter Magee

Mrs. Delane, Postmistress at Cloon . . .	Sara Allgood
Miss Joyce, the Priest's housekeeper . .	Brigit O'Dempsey

The Rising of the Moon

9th March 1907

Sergeant	. Arthur Sinclair
Policeman X	. J. A. O'Rourke
Policeman B	. J. M. Kerrigan
A Ragged Man	. W. G. Fay

In the programme of the first performance the *Sergeant* is described as *Policeman Z* and *A Ragged Man* as *Ballad Singer*.

The Jackdaw

23rd February 1907

Joseph Nestor	. F. J. Fay
Michael Cooney	. W. G. Fay
Mrs. Broderick	. Sara Allgood
Tommy Nally	. Arthur Sinclair
Sibby Fahy	Brigit O'Dempsey
Timothy Ward	. J. M. Kerrigan

The Workhouse Ward

20th April 1908

Mike McInerney	. Arthur Sinclair
Michael Miskell	Fred O'Donovan
Mrs. Donohue	. Maire O'Neill

The Bogie Men

8th July 1912

Taig O'Harragha	. J. M. Kerrigan
Darby Melody	. J. A. O'Rourke

Coats

1st December 1910

Mineog	. Arthur Sinclair
Hazel	. J. M. Kerrigan
John	. J. A. O'Rourke

Damer's Gold

21st November 1912

Delia Hessian	Sara Allgood
Staffy Kirwan	Sidney Morgan
Ralph Hessian	J. M. Kerrigan
Damer	Arthur Sinclair
Simon Niland	A. Wright

Hanrahan's Oath

29th January 1918

Mary Gillis	Mary Delany
Margaret Rooney	May Craig
Owen Hanrahan	Fred O'Donovan
Coey	Arthur Shields
Mrs. Coey	Christine Hayden
Michael Feeney	Peter Nolan

Appendices

APPENDIX I
A LOSING GAME

A LOSING GAME

PERSONS

MICHAEL FORD. *A middle-aged farmer.*
KATE FORD. *His young wife.*
CHRISTIE HENDERSON.
FIRST NEIGHBOUR.
SECOND NEIGHBOUR.
OLD WOMAN.
A BOY.
A FIDDLER.
OTHER NEIGHBOURS.

SCENE. *A kitchen in a farmer's cottage, neat, well-furnished, and set out for company.* MICHAEL *rummaging in a chest.*

MICHAEL. All the clothes will fit in this chest, Kate, and a share of the blankets. The rest can go in a bundle. There's some small things here, no good to keep or sell, you could give them among the neighbours. There's something here, I don't know what it is. A little glass picture in a frame. Who is it I wonder?

KATE. It's nothing. Give it here to me.

MICHAEL (*holding up candle*). Wait till I see. It's none of my family, anyway. Some young chap that looks well pleased with himself. Maybe it was some friend of yours in Kilcolgan?

KATE. You are always thinking I have friends among the boys, Michael, and its not right for you to think it. If you have any fault to find with me, say it out.

MICHAEL. Well, I don't say I have, but when there's a young wife in the house, Jack the Journeyman is apt to come slipping round the corner. Give me my specs till I see the picture better.

KATE. It's no one you ever saw or ever will see. Give it here to me. It's time for you to go tell the Brennans to come over for the spree, you sent them no word yesterday. We have all ready now.

MICHAEL (*giving her the picture*). Well, don't be cross the last night we can call this house our own. I'll go over and call to the Brennans before the rest of the neighbours come. (*He goes out.*)

KATE (*looking at the picture*). Poor Christie, it's long since I

279

looked at that before. I forgot it was in the chest I put it. It's well Michael asked no more about him. I think he's jealous of the birds on the tree sometimes if I listen to their song, thinking it might be Kilcolgan they came from. (*A knock at the door.*) Who is that? I didn't think the neighbours would be here yet awhile. (*She opens the door. A young man comes in. He wears dark clothes and a round hat. He takes her hands and comes into the light.*)

KATE. Christie Henderson!

CHRISTIE. It is a great surprise to you to see me, Katy?

KATE. I never thought you would come back from America.

CHRISTIE. Didn't I say I would come back to you Kate? But you did not wait for me.

KATE. O Christie, how did you know where to find me?

CHRISTIE. Two days ago I landed, and last night I got to Kilcolgan, and I went up the road by the chapel thinking to surprise you. And when I came in sight of the little house near the bridge, and the twisted thornbush beside it, I went up to the door, and my hands stretched out like this. And what did I see but strangers there before me.

KATE. We left the place a year ago, after my father dying.

CHRISTIE. The neighbours told me that. The herd is dead, they said, and the widow woman is gone to Ballindereen, and Kate is married to a man of the Fords in Kilbecanty.

KATE. I am married indeed.

CHRISTIE. When I heard that the life seemed to go out from me, and my wits to go astray. I thought we would have the one house between us, and you coaxing my child on your knee, and to find you as far from me as the red man's wife herself. Take care would you hear me screeching for you yet at the day of judgment.

KATE. You always had that wild sort of talk. Sometimes I thought you might be making fun of me.

CHRISTIE. Why weren't you content to wait for me, Kate? Hadn't I your promise?

KATE. You had it indeed, Christie, but what could I do? My father died and another man got the herding, and I couldn't go with my mother to be a burden on Bridget in Ballindereen. I thought you had forgotten me.

CHRISTIE. I had not forgotten you, I was working night and day for you. If I didn't write often I was never any great hand at writing, and the thoughts I had of you were enough to go round the world of themselves.

KATE. Michael Ford used to be coming to fairs at Kilcolgan, and he asked would I marry him, and the priest and all the neighbours pressed me to do it.

CHRISTIE. Did you never tell Michael about your promise to me?

KATE. I did not. I was shy to speak of it at first, and I was afraid after. He is someway jealous, he is middling old. I wouldn't like him to see you here Christie when he comes in. Isn't it a strange thing he is just after seeing your picture (*takes it from the table*) and asking who was it, and I gave him no answer.

CHRISTIE. Well four years in the States didn't leave me much of the face I had when that was done. Tell me, Kate, do you like Michael? Do you like him better than you liked me?

KATE. I must like him. Amn't I married to him?

CHRISTIE. Does he treat you well?

KATE. He does indeed, he is kind enough most times. He takes a little drop sometimes when he's in trouble, but there's many do that.

CHRISTIE (*looking round*). It's a good house you have here. Ah you are better pleased to have a house like this than to be coming across the sea along with me, and leaving that grand dresser after you.

KATE. Indeed, Christie, the better the house is, the worse for me, for I won't be in it long.

CHRISTIE. How is that?

KATE. There have great misfortunes come on Michael Ford since I married him a year ago, and we are to auction the holding to-morrow and to go then to Manchester, he has a brother there who will find work for him.

CHRISTIE. That is bad. What brought him to that?

KATE. He lost a good deal of his stock last year with a blood murrain that came on them, and the rent was in arrears, and he owes twenty pounds to the bank in Gort, and five pounds to the shops for seeds and manures. And his sister got married and left the house at the time I came to it, and she's asking for the fortune her father left her ever since, and it must be paid, forty pounds it is. We cannot wrestle with our bad luck any longer, we must give in. (*She sits down and* CHRISTIE *sits down beside her.*)

CHRISTIE. Manchester is no good place for you to go to, and you used to country ways.

KATE. It will be death to me to be there, and it will be death to Michael, too. But what can I do? I am fretting often that I brought no fortune with me. I often think Michael must be sorry he took me at all.

CHRISTIE. He could never be that. O Katy if you had but waited!

I settled down better than you thought. I have good employment near Boston on a railroad, they are keeping my place for me when I go back. I can make no long delay here, see, there's my return ticket (shows it to her). I thought to have bought another ticket and to have brought you with me so soon as we could be married. There's no use fretting, but it's worse to me to be leaving you in trouble than to have lost you myself.

KATE. Well, it can't be helped. We must go wandering. The poor know all the troubles of the world.

CHRISTIE. It might be helped. Would a hundred pounds clear you, Katy?

KATE. It would surely; but we have no way to get it but to sell the holding.

CHRISTIE. It is I myself will help you, Katy. Look what I have here in this bag. (*Takes it from his pocket.*) A hundred pounds in gold and notes. That is what I have saved up in the last four years. It was for you I saved it, and when I landed here yesterday I got it all changed into sovereigns and notes, the way we could be looking at it and counting it together. Take it now and welcome.

KATE. O Christie, I can do no such thing! I can't take your money.

CHRISTIE. It is yours it is, I would never have worked without the thought of you. Don't refuse me.

KATE. I can't take it indeed.

CHRISTIE (*pouring out the money*). There it is. Take the gold in your hand and see how weighty it is. I never had a sovereign in my hand till yesterday, but the one I had with me when I set out for America, and that I kept in this little handkerchief always. To buy the wedding ring I kept it. Well, that's done with now. Here, put away the money.

KATE. O Christie, God bless you for thinking of it, and I not deserving it, but there's no use talking. If I would take it myself, Michael wouldn't let me.

CHRISTIE. Sure you could say you found it in a field under a bush, or that some uncle you had in America sent it to you, I'll say I brought it from him.

KATE. I have no uncle in America. (*Putting the money back into the bag.*) It's no use, I couldn't take it, Christie.

CHRISTIE. You will take it. I have my mind made up. I'll leave it in the corner of the cowshed outside, you can let on to find it in the morning. (*He goes towards the door.*)

KATE (*rushes to the door and puts her back against it*). You will not leave it there or anywhere, Christie. There, now you can't go out, I hear Michael coming, and some of the neighbours with him. O Christie don't tell him I knew you before, he might be questioning me.

CHRISTIE. Never fear, I won't tell him, but I'll get my way yet (*puts the bag in his pocket*). If you don't take it one way you'll have to take it another way. (*He steps aside.* MICHAEL FORD *and three or four neighbours come in.*)

CHRISTIE (*to* MICHAEL). Can you tell me the road to Gort? I think I missed it turning up the road awhile ago.

MICHAEL. You did, indeed. You must go down to the highroad again and turn to the left. You are a stranger here, I suppose?

CHRISTIE. I landed at Queenstown yesterday, I was never in this part before.

MICHAEL. Well, sit down awhile now till you rest yourself. There's a few of the neighbours coming in to spend the evening with us.

FIRST NEIGHBOUR. Indeed, Michael, I'm sorry to think what brought us here, to say good-bye to you before you quit the house.

MICHAEL. Well, we'd best not be thinking about that, but to try and forget it for this night. Here are some of the neighbours coming. (*Three or four elderly men and women come in. He pours a little whisky in glasses and hands it to each and offers a glass to* CHRISTIE.)

CHRISTIE. I don't take any drink, thank you all the same, but I wish health and prosperity to the woman of the house without it. (*Sits down.*) It's a long time since I sat beside a turf fire before.

MICHAEL. What was it brought you to County Galway?

CHRISTIE. Looking for a treasure I had a dream about.

SECOND NEIGHBOUR. Where did you dream it was?

CHRISTIE. Near a twisted thornbush it was, beside a little white house near a bridge. I found the place easy enough.

MICHAEL. And did you find the treasure?

CHRISTIE. I did not. Some other man went there before me and brought it away. I dreamed about it often enough, but whatever happened I didn't dream right. I suppose it was a morning dream and they go by contrarys.

OLD WOMAN. They do so. And if you will tell a morning dream to the trees, fasting, they will all wither.

CHRISTIE. Faith it's well I didn't meet many trees on the road yesterday, they'd be withered up now the same as Raftery's bush. Woman of the house do you ever have good dreams?

KATE. I don't think much about dreams. It's best not to mind them, but to be working in the daytime.

CHRISTIE. That's true, indeed. It's a pity the master didn't teach me that, and I a little chap going to school.

OLD WOMAN. Maybe the poor man that got the treasure wanted it more than you.

CHRISTIE. That might be so. I didn't think of that.

MICHAEL. Well, stop the evening with us and welcome. We'll be having a dance by and bye when the fiddler comes and the youngsters. (*He takes a pack of cards from the dresser and lays them on the table.*)

CHRISTIE (*getting up and coming to the table*). That's what will suit me better than dancing. I didn't play a game of cards this long time.

MICHAEL (*sitting down*). Well we'll start with a game. (*Looking round.*) Who's for Twenty-Five?

CHRISTIE. I'd sooner play with yourself only in the beginning, till I get into it again.

FIRST NEIGHBOUR. Go on, go on. Here, Andy, put a coal in the pipe. (*They light pipe and hand it round.* KATE *looks doubtfully at the players.*)

OLD WOMAN. And what will you do with all the things on the dresser, Mrs. Ford? Is it auction them you will? You can't bring them with you. (*She goes to the dresser with* KATE *and they consult, taking down cups and jugs.*)

CHRISTIE. You shuffle the cards and I'll cut. Here, I'll put down gold for luck. (*Puts down a sovereign. The neighbours stare and whisper.*)

FIRST NEIGHBOUR (*comes over from the hearth, takes up sovereign, bites it, nods three times*). That's good gold wherever it came from.

MICHAEL. I can't put down so much as that.

CHRISTIE. Well, I have no change anyway, nothing but gold in my pocket. Put what you can against it, and we'll settle all fair after.

MICHAEL. Stop, maybe I can make it up. (*Puts money down and deals.*)

FIRST NEIGHBOUR (*watching the play*). The five of spades is trumps. Nine of diamonds takes that. Ha, three of spades—he has the master of it.

MICHAEL. Twenty-five. That's mine.

CHRISTIE. Here now, double the stakes. I've turned up the ace— that's five to me and I rob. Now I bet you five to one I'll beat you.

MICHAEL. Well I'll take you. Come play on that (*puts down a card*), and that (*puts down another*), here's the ace of diamonds to you (*puts down*). Come now (*puts down*). Here again (*puts down*). That game's mine.

FIRST NEIGHBOUR. That was bad play, and he having the ace all the time.

CHRISTIE. I told you I was out of the way of it, I'll get into it presently. I know well what I'm doing. (*He puts down gold and notes on the table.* KATE *turns from dresser, comes over and touches money on the table.*)

KATE. Stop playing now, Michael.

MICHAEL. Well, maybe we'd best stop. You have too much lost for one night.

CHRISTIE. Do you call that much! It's nothing at all to what I lost yesterday.

SECOND NEIGHBOUR (*from the hearth*). Where was that?

CHRISTIE. At Kilcolgan.

MICHAEL. Kilcolgan! Who were you with there?

KATE (*hurriedly*). I hear the fiddler coming. Open the door, Michael. (*He opens it and fiddler comes in playing.*) Now, Michael, we must clear the house.

SECOND NEIGHBOUR. The youngsters aren't come in yet ma'am. Let them play their game out.

CHRISTIE. Here now, shuffle the cards. I have a right to my revenge. Win or lose, I'll have my game.

OLD WOMAN. I never saw one come back from America with that much money. Maybe you found the treasure under the bush after all.

CHRISTIE. Well I didn't. I didn't find it in that place, but I found it in another place, and I know where to find more of it. You'd be surprised to see the way the spade was throwing it up, and I digging.

OLD WOMAN. I dare say you're the richest man in the house now?

CHRISTIE. I am that. I suppose I'm the richest man in Ireland to-night.

FIRST NEIGHBOUR. Are you, indeed?

CHRISTIE. Wouldn't you call a man rich when gold and bank notes are no more to him than tintacks and wisps of straw and withered leaves? Here, come on again.

KATE. Don't play with him, Michael. He ought not to be losing his money.

MICHAEL. Well, maybe we'd best stop.

CHRISTIE. I give you my word if I lost all that's on the table I'd think it little enough to pay for one pleasant evening. You wouldn't begrudge a lonely man one pleasant evening?

KATE. Give him back your winnings, Michael, and stop the game.

CHRISTIE. Well, it's a pity for women to be in the house when there's card playing going on. Keep quiet ma'am and don't have so much to say. I'm not a child on the floor that's making for the pot of scalding water, or a pig turning down every wrong road, or a Connemara sheep making for the wall, to be dragged and shoved and screeched at this way, and not to be let sit quiet with the man of the house. What's the good of all my riches if I'm not let use them. It would be as good for me to throw them all in the fire.

KATE (*taking up the money and putting it in his hand*). Throw it in the fire if you like, but you won't play here with it.

CHRISTIE (*getting up*). Very well, ma'am, take your own way, and I'll do as you bid me. (*He goes to the fire and takes the tongs from* OLD MAN.) Give me a coal here, the woman of the house isn't satisfied to let me sit down to a game. She wants to be warming herself beside a fire of bank notes, she's tired of looking at turf so long. (*Holds note to coal.*)

SECOND NEIGHBOUR. He's not going to burn it!

FIRST NEIGHBOUR. Not at all, I never knew a man do that.

CHRISTIE. There it goes (*note blazes up*). Here's another.

FIRST NEIGHBOUR (*seizing his arm*). O he's burning it! O isn't it the pity and the sin to see good money turned into ashes!

OLD WOMAN. Indeed it's a shame of you, Mrs. Ford, to interfere with the men.

SECOND NEIGHBOUR. You'd best leave them alone, Mrs. Ford. Here are the youngsters coming in.(KATE *turns to them.* CHRISTIE *and* MICHAEL *sit down at the table. The* NEIGHBOURS *gather round.*)

CHRISTIE. I'll let no one be looking over my hand this time. It brings me no good luck. (*He pushes back his chair to the wall, so that no one can stand behind him.*)

MICHAEL. My deal now.

CHRISTIE. Put down what you like now, and I'll put five to one against it.

MICHAEL. Well—— (*puts down some money*).

SECOND NEIGHBOUR. Open your hand, Michael, give it out. (MICHAEL *puts down more.*)

FIRST NEIGHBOUR. Bad turn up, two of diamonds, the worst card in the pack. (CHRISTIE *plays*.) O he's played the three of spades, Michael has it with the deuce. Now, Michael. (MICHAEL *plays again*.) The five fingers by the hokey! O it's drawn a good trump, isn't that lucky? (MICHAEL *plays again*.) Ace of heart! Wasn't he strong! Ha, that takes the trump from him. Now, Michael, play a good one! (MICHAEL *plays*.) Ah, nine of clubs, he's beaten on that. The Butt's in. Come on again. (*They shuffle cards*.)

FIRST NEIGHBOUR. O that's a grand game, the Butt's in. Michael hasn't it yet. Wasn't it lucky he had the draw that time with the five fingers! (CHRISTIE *deals*.)

FIRST NEIGHBOUR. The three of diamonds. A poor turn up. (MICHAEL *lays down a card*.)

SECOND NEIGHBOUR (*excitedly*). O but it's done the business as bad as it is! What a bad hand he has to have only the six! That's yours Michael.

CHRISTIE (*takes up the pack hurriedly and mixes his own cards through them; takes bag from his pocket and empties it on the table. His return ticket falls on the floor*). Now I'll tell you what I'll do, I'll put this much against what you have there.

FIRST NEIGHBOUR. O that wouldn't be fair. He has more than you now.

MICHAEL. Well, now it's not out and out fair, but as you're a losing man I'll tell you what I'll do, I'll put this much against you, hit or miss.

KATE (*comes over and takes* MICHAEL'S *arm*). Give up playing, Michael. It is too long you have played and too much money you have won. (*To* CHRISTIE) I know well it wasn't real play, it's only humbugging you were. Take back your money.

CHRISTIE. Be quiet now, ma'am, this is the last hand.

KATE. Take back your money.

CHRISTIE. There are some things no man can take back, and they once gone from him.

KATE. You will take this back, anyway.

OLD WOMAN. Don't be quarrelling with your luck, Mrs. Ford. Who knows what was it that sent this luck into the house.

KATE. Michael, give back that money. It's not rightly won. If you won't do it of yourself I can make you do it with what I'm going to say. Before you came in to-night——

CHRISTIE (*standing up hurriedly and looking at the* NEIGHBOURS). Wouldn't anyone say I was her old sweetheart come back, and she taking my side against her own man?

287

(KATE *shrinks back and sits down, her face in her hands. She sobs from time to time.* CHRISTIE *goes on playing quickly, standing up.* NEIGHBOURS *watch in silence.*)

MICHAEL (*with a deep sigh of relief*). Twenty-Five! That's mine. (*He counts money and looks up.*). It's a hundred pounds all but five!

SECOND NEIGHBOUR. A hundred pounds! There was never such a game played in this parish. Faith, Michael Ford, you won't quit Kilbecanty this time!

CHRISTIE. Well, I must learn to play a better game before I come this way again. I'm no match for the people of Kilbecanty!

OLD WOMAN. It must be a grand thing to be rich!

CHRISTIE. It's grand, indeed. It's a grand thing to be free in the world, and not to be tied to your little bit of ground, in dread of the drought in the spring-time and the rain in harvest. It's a grand thing not to be shut up in a narrow little house, keeping a watch on the little store you have hid under the hearthstone and the wife you have may be begrudging you the use of it in your lifetime. It's a grand thing to be able to take up your money in your hand and to think no more of it when it slips away than you would of a trout that would slip back into the stream! Didn't I tell you I was a rich man!

A BOY (*who has picked up ticket from the floor and been examining it*). Here's a return ticket to America, third class it is. (*To* CHRISTIE) Is it you it belongs to?

OLD WOMAN. Not at all. It wasn't in the steerage he came. I tell you sovereigns are as plenty with him as pebbles you'd be playing jackstones with.

CHRISTIE (*looking at ticket*). That ticket I suppose it dropped from the bag. Who owns it? I think it belonged to some poor man who was in the ship with me. Coming home he was to look for his wife.

MICHAEL. And what happened him? Did he die?

CHRISTIE. He died—or some one died—or something happened. Give it here to me. I want it for a labouring man I know, that has to quit Ireland tomorrow. (*Puts ticket in his hatband and hat on his head.*) Well I must be going now. This was a grand evening we had!

MICHAEL (*feebly*). Maybe you'll come back some other time to take your revenge?

CHRISTIE. Who knows? I might get my revenge yet. But I don't think I'll be pasing this way again. It's time for the dance to begin. Woman of the house, will you take a turn with me before I go?

KATE. I won't dance to-night.

CHRISTIE. You wouldn't refuse the greatest stranger in the house? Give me a dance now, and I'll be thinking of you some time when I'm dancing with some high-up lady having golden shoes, in a marble court by the sea. Here Fiddler, here's gold for you, and give us a reel. (*He throws the little handkerchief to the fiddler who strikes up.* CHRISTIE *takes* KATE'S *hands, dances for a minute, stops, kisses her and flings over to the door. Turns round and waves his hat.*)

CHRISTIE. Good-bye, neighbours!! That was a grand evening we had! (*Goes out and is heard singing*)

> But before the break of morn
> I'll leave them all forlorn,
> For I'm off to Philadelphia in the morning.

Curtain.

APPENDIX II
THE BOGIE MEN

THE BOGIE MEN

The text given below is that part of *The Bogie Men* which was replaced by new dialogue in Lady Gregory's revised version.

DARBY (*almost crying*). You are a mean savage to go keeping from me my tin can and my rag!

TAIG. Go wash yourself at the pump can't you?

DARBY. That we may never be within the same four walls again, or come under the lintel of the one door! (*He goes out.*)

TAIG (*calling after him while he takes a suit of clothes from his bag*). I'm not like yourself! I have good clothes to put on me, what you haven't got! A body-coat my mother made out—she lost up to three shillings on it,—and a hat—and a speckled blue cravat. (*He hastily throws off his sweep's smock and cap, and puts on clothes. As he does he sings*).

> All round my hat I wore a green ribbon,
> All round my hat for a year and a day;
> And if any one asks me the reason I wore it
> I'll say that my true love went over the sea!
>
> All in my hat I will stick a blue feather
> The same as the birds do be up in the tree;
> And if you would ask me the reason I do it
> I'll tell you my true love is come back to me!

(*He washes his face and wipes it, looking at himself in the tin can. He catches sight of a straw hat passing window.*) Who is that? A gentleman? (*He draws back.*)

(DARBY *comes in. He has changed his clothes and wears a straw hat and light coat and trousers. He is looking for a necktie which he had dropped and picks up. His back is turned to* TAIG *who is standing at the other door.*)

TAIG (*awed*). It cannot be that you are Dermot Melody?

DARBY. My father's name was Melody sure enough, till he lost his life in the year of the black potatoes.

TAIG. It is yourself I am come here purposely to meet with.

293

DARBY. You should be my mother's sister's son so, Timothy O'Harragha.

TAIG (*sheepishly*). I am that. I am sorry indeed it failed me to be out before you in the street.

DARBY. Oh, I wouldn't be looking for that much from you. (*They are trying to keep their backs to each other, and to rub their faces cleaner.*)

HAIG. I wouldn't wish to be anyway troublesome to you. I am badly worthy of you.

DARBY. It is in dread I am of being troublesome to yourself.

TAIG. Oh, it would be hard for *you* to be that. Nothing you could put on me would be any hardship at all, if it was to walk steel thistles.

DARBY. You have a willing heart surely.

TAIG. Any little job at all I could do for you——

DARBY. All I would ask of you is to give me my nourishment and my bite.

TAIG. I will do that. I will be your serving man.

DARBY. Ah, you are going too far in that.

TAIG. It's my born duty to do that much. I'll bring your dinner before you, if I can be anyway pleasing to you; you that is used to wealthy people.

DARBY. Indeed I was often in a house having up to twenty chimneys.

TAIG. You are a rare good man, nothing short of it, and you going as you did so high in the world.

DARBY. Any person would go high before he would put his hand out through the top of a chimney.

TAIG. Having full and plenty of every good thing.

DARBY. I saw nothing so plentiful as soot. There is not the equal of it nourishing a garden. It would turn every crop blue, being so good.

TAIG (*weeping*). It is a very unkind thing to go drawing chimneys down on me and soot, and you having all that ever was!

DARBY. Little enough I have or ever had.

TAIG. To be casting up my trade against me, I being poor and hungry, and you having coins and tokens from all the goldpits of the world.

DARBY. I wish I ever handled a coin of gold in my lifetime.

TAIG. To speak despisingly, not pitiful. And I thinking the chimney sweeping would be forgot and not reproached to me, if you handled the fooleries and watches of the world, that you don't know the end of your riches!

DARBY. I am maybe getting your meaning wrong, your tongue being a little hard and sharp because you are Englified, but I am without new learnments and so I speak flat.

TAIG. You to have the millions of King Solomon, you have no right to be putting reflections on me! I would never behave that way, and housefuls to fall into my hand.

DARBY. You are striving to put ridicule on me and to make a fool of me. That is a very unseemly thing to do! I that did not ask to go hide the bag or the brush.

TAIG. There you are going on again. Is it to the customers in your shops you will be giving out that it was my lot to go through the world as a sweep?

DARBY. Customers and shops! Will you stop your funning? Let you quit mocking and making a sport of me! That is very bad acting behaviour.

TAIG. Striving to blacken my face again at the time I had it washed pure white. You surely have a heart of marble.

DARBY. What way at all can you be putting such a rascally say out of your mouth? I'll take no more talk from you, I to be twenty-two degrees lower than the Hottentots!

TAIG. If you are my full cousin Dermot Melody I'll make you quit talking of soot!

DARBY. I'll take no more talk from yourself!

TAIG. Have a care now!

DARBY. Have a care yourself!

(*Each gives the other a push. They stumble and fall, sitting facing one another.* DARBY'S *hat falls off.*)

TAIG. Is it *you* it is?

DARBY. Who else would it be?

TAIG. What call had you letting on to be Dermot Melody?

DARBY. What letting on? Dermot is my full name, but Darby is the name I am called.

TAIG. Are you a man owning riches and shops and merchandise?

DARBY. I am not, or anything of the sort.

TAIG. Have you teems of money in the bank?

DARBY. If I had would I be sitting on this floor?

TAIG. You thief you!

DARBY. Thief yourself! Turn around now till I will measure your features and your face. *Yourself* is it! Is it personating my cousin Timothy you are?

TAIG. I am personating no one but myself.

DARBY. You letting on to be an estated magistrate and my own cousin and such a great generation of a man. And you not owning so much as a rood of ridges!

TAIG. Covering yourself with choice clothing for to deceive me and to lead me astray!

DARBY. Putting on your head a fine glossy hat and I thinking you to have come with the spring-tide, the way you had luck through your life!

TAIG. Letting on to be Dermot Melody! You that are but the cull and the weakling of a race! It is a queer game you played on me and a crooked game. I never would have brought my legs so far to meet with the sooty likes of you!

DARBY. Letting on to be my poor Timothy O'Harragha!

TAIG. I never was called but Taig. Timothy was a sort of a Holy day name.

DARBY. Where now are our two cousins? Or is it that the both of us are cracked?

APPENDIX III
THE WORKED-OUT WARD
A Sinn Féin Allegory

THE WORKED-OUT WARD

PERSONS
JOHN DILLONELL   ⎫
STEPHEN GWYNERNEY ⎬ *Political paupers.*
MRS. HOULIHAN. *A countrywoman.*

SCENE. *A Political Ward in an Irish city. The two old politicians should be in bed.*

JOHN DILLONELL. Isn't it a hard case, Stephen Gwynerney, myself and yourself to be left out in the cold, and it the Peace Day of St. Woodrow, and the elected Sinn Feiners attending on the Peace Conference?

STEPHEN GWYNERNEY. Is it sitting at the Conference you are wishful to be, John Dillonell, and you with cold feet and heckled speeches? Let you raise up the Party, if you're able to do it, not like myself that has Unionism, the same as tin-tacks within in my inside.

JOHN DILLONELL. If you have Unionism within in your inside, there is no one can see it or know of it to be any different from my own Provincialism that is propped up with rameis, and the Party that is twisted in its ideas the same as an old cabbage stalk. It's easy to be talking of nationality and independence, and they maybe not to be in the Party at all.

STEPHEN GWYNERNEY. To open me and to analyse me you would know what sort of a Unionist and West Briton I am in my heart and in my mind. But I'm not one like yourself to be orating and boasting and bluffing the time Conscription was at hand, thinking to get a bigger share than myself of the popularity and the votes.

JOHN DILLONELL. That's the way you do be picking at me and faulting me. I was an Irishman, and a good Irishman in my early time, and it's well you know that, and both of us reared in Constitutionalism.

STEPHEN GWYNERNEY. You may say that, indeed. We are both of us reared in Constitutionalism. Little wonder you to have good

299

nourishment the time we were both rising, and you to have been brought up away from Trinity, the time I was floundering there.

JOHN DILLONELL. And you didn't get away from Trinity, I suppose, and get my principles from the Party, letting on they to be your own? For you were always a cheater and a schemer, grabbing every political stunt for your own profit.

STEPHEN GWYNERNEY. And you were no grabber yourself, I suppose, till your Party and all your votes wore away from you!

JOHN DILLONELL. If I lost it itself, it was through the crosses I met with and I going through the war. I never was a Trinitarian West Briton like yourself, Stephen Gwynerney, that ran from all nationalism and turned Imperialist unknown to your Chief.

STEPHEN GWYNERNEY. Imperialist, is it? And if I was, was it you yourself led me on to it, or some other one? It is in my own college I would be to-day and in the face of the Gwynerney family, but for the misfortune I had to be joined to a bad Party that was yourself. What way did my credit go from me? Spending on fencing, spending on votes, making up lies, putting up sham fights, that would keep your followers from coming through desperation on to the Sinn Fein side, and every intelligent man in Ireland from seeing through your game.

JOHN DILLONELL. O, to listen to you! And I striving to please you and to be kind to you, and to close my ears to the abuse you would be calling down upon the Party. To ruin your credit, is it? It's little credit there was for my poor beasts to ask of the country. My God Almighty! What were you but a Trinity shoneen?

STEPHEN GWYNERNEY. And what do you say to my recruiting campaign, that your henchmen destroyed on me, the time that Lynch was stumped and the Sinn Feiners making gaps in his speeches.

JOHN DILLONELL. Ah, there does be a great deal of gaps knocked in a distracted party. Why wouldn't they be knocked by the Diehards, the same as were knocked in the Liberals by Lloyd George?

STEPHEN GWYNERNEY. It was the Diehards, I suppose so, that gave up the Home Rule Bill? And compromised on recruiting, and petitioned President Wilson himself from the Mansion House, after denying Ireland to be an international question?

JOHN DILLONELL. And what happened myself the day I tried to run a pro-Irish policy? Two brazened dogs that rushed round making recruiting speeches against me. I never was the better of it, or of the start I got, but wasting from then till now!

STEPHEN GWYNERNEY. Thinking you were a pro-German Sinn

Feiner they did, that had made his escape out of Frongoch. Sure any Britisher with life in him at all would be roused and stirred seeing the like of you going Sinn Feining.

JOHN DILLONELL. I did well taking a line against you that time. It is a great wonder you not to have gone over to Flanders, but the laws of England is queer. Isn't it a bad story for me to be wearing out my days beside you the same as a spancelled goat. Chained I am and tethered I am to a man that is ransacking his mind for pro-Ally lies!

STEPHEN GWYNERNEY. If it is a bad story for you, John Dillonell, it is a worse story again for myself. A semi-neutral to be next and near to me through the whole four years of the war. I never heard there to be any great name on the Dillonells as there was on my own race and name.

JOHN DILLONELL. You didn't, is it? Well, you would hear it, if you had but ears to hear it. Go across to Ballaghadereen, and down to Tipperary, and you'll hear of Dillonell.

STEPHEN GWYNERNEY. What signifies Ballaghadereen and Tipperary? Look at all my own generation buried in Trinity College. And what do you say to St. Columba's College and Brasenose, Oxford? Aren't they apt to have knowledge of a superior race? Was a Dillonell ever Regius Professor of Divinity, or chaplain of T.C.D.?

JOHN DILLONELL. It is a pity you are not in any of those places this minute, that you might be quitting your brag and your chat, your unionism and your imperial ways; for there is no one under the rising sun in Ireland could stand you. I tell you you are not behaving as in the presence of an Irish nation!

STEPHEN GWYNERNEY. Is it wishful for my resignation you are? Let it come and meet me now and welcome, so long as it will part me from yourself! And I say, and I would kiss the book on it, I have one request only to be granted, and I leaving it in my will, it is what I would request, nine furrows of the House of Commons, nine ridges of political molehills, nine waves of the *Irish Times* to be put between your Party and mine, the time we are elected again.

(MRS. HOULIHAN *comes in with a parcel. She is a country-woman with orange, white and green shawl. She stands still a minute. The two old politicians compose themselves.*)

MRS. HOULIHAN. I never was in this place at all. I don't know am I right. Which, now, of the two of ye is a Nationalist?

JOHN DILLONELL. Who is it is calling my Party name?

MRS. HOULIHAN. Sure amn't I your mistress, Molly Hibernian Maguire that was, that is now Kathleen ni Houlihan.

JOHN DILLONELL. I didn't know you till you pushed anear me. It is time indeed for you to come and see me, and I in politics these thirty years or more. Thinking me to be no credit to you, I suppose, among the tribe of Parliamentarians. I wonder at Sinn Fein to give you leave to come ask am I living yet or dead?

MRS. HOULIHAN. Ah, sure, I buried generations of great Parliamentarians. Parnell himself was the last to go. Sure we must go through our crosses. And he got a wonderful lever on the English; it would delight you to hear his like in Westminster again. My poor Charles Parnell! A nice clean man, you couldn't but admire him. Very severe on the English, and he wouldn't touch a compromise.

JOHN DILLONELL. And is it in Ireland you are living yet?

MRS. HOULIHAN. It is so. A wide lovely house I have, four beautiful provinces, and harbours, and industries, and minerals. It is what I'm thinking yourself might come and look after me. It is no credit to me now, you to be going to Westminster at all.

JOHN DILLONELL. What luck could there be in a place and a statesman not to be in it? Is that a new national programme you have brought with you?

MRS. HOULIHAN. It is so, the way you'll be tasty coming back to the people of your own country. Sure you could be keeping the fire of nationality in, and stirring the nation to a sense of its own dignity, and dealing yourself with the problems of the day, developing our industries, fostering our culture, and maybe leading the country to prosperous independence. For when Parnell died, Westminsterism died.

JOHN DILLONELL. Let me out of this! (*He spreads out the national programme and tries to grasp it.*) That now is a good idea ... if I could only adopt it.

STEPHEN GWYNERNEY (*alarmed*). And is it going to abstain from Westminster you are, John Dillonell?

JOHN DILLONELL. Don't you hear I am. Going to work, I am, in the only place where I can get every good thing for Ireland.

STEPHEN GWYNERNEY. Ah, John, is it truth you are saying, you to go from Westminster, and to leave the nice people, the English people, and people from the best universities, and they having a great liking for us. You'll be craving the talk. Not to be lying at Westminster would be the abomination of misery!

JOHN DILLONELL. Look now, Kathleen ... It is what I often heard said, two Irish Parties at Westminster to be better than one.

If you had an old programme full of holes, wouldn't you put another under it that might be as tattered as itself, and the two parties together would make some sort of a decent show.

MRS. HOULIHAN. Ah, what are you saying? There is no holes in the policy I brought you now, but sound it is as the day I spun it.

JOHN DILLONELL. It is what I'm thinking, Kathleen . . . I do be weak an odd time. Any point I would carry, it preys upon my mind. Maybe it is a hard thing for a man that has spluttered on the floor of the House for thirty years to go changing from place to place.

MRS. HOULIHAN. Well, take your luck or leave it. All I asked was to save you from the harm of the year. Give me back my fine programme so (*gathers up the parcel*) till I'll go look for men of my own! Yourself and your Party, that never left fighting and scolding and attacking one another! Sparring at the English like young pups, and then coming docile to the heel of your masters. It's mad I was to be thinking any good could be got of you, and you the slave of habits, and the admirer of Imperial England. It's queer in the head you've grown from asking questions in Parliament; your heart's not with your own people.

STEPHEN GWYNERNEY. Let her go so, as she is so pro-German and disloyal, and look for men of her own—God help them! We could not go with her at all.

MRS. HOULIHAN. It is too much time I lost with you, and dark days waiting to overtake me on the road to freedom. Let you stop together, and the back of my hand to you. It is I will leave you the same as God left the Jews!

(*She goes out. The old politicians are silent for a moment.*)

STEPHEN GWYNERNEY. Maybe the house is not as wide as she says.

JOHN DILLONELL. Why wouldn't it be wide? What would you know about Ireland? Whatever sort of a house you had in it, was too narrow for the growth of your brains.

STEPHEN GWYNERNEY. Stop your impudence and your chat, or it will be the worse for you. I'd bear with the mere Irish as long as any man would, but if they'd vex me, I would conscript and coerce them as soon as an Englishman!

JOHN DILLONELL. That Sinn Fein may chew you from skin to marrow bone! (*Seizes the "Freeman's Journal."*)

STEPHEN GWYNERNEY (*seizing the "Irish Times"*). By cripes, I'll pull out your pin-feathers.

JOHN DILLONELL. You factionist! You sorehead! You West Briton, you!

STEPHEN GWYNERNEY (*hurling phrases from the "Irish Times"*). Take this so, you defeatist, you Bolshevik, you flaunter of Ireland's shame.

> (*They throw the "Irish Times," "Freeman's Journal," and all the abusive words in their respective political vocabularies at one another.*)

Curtain.